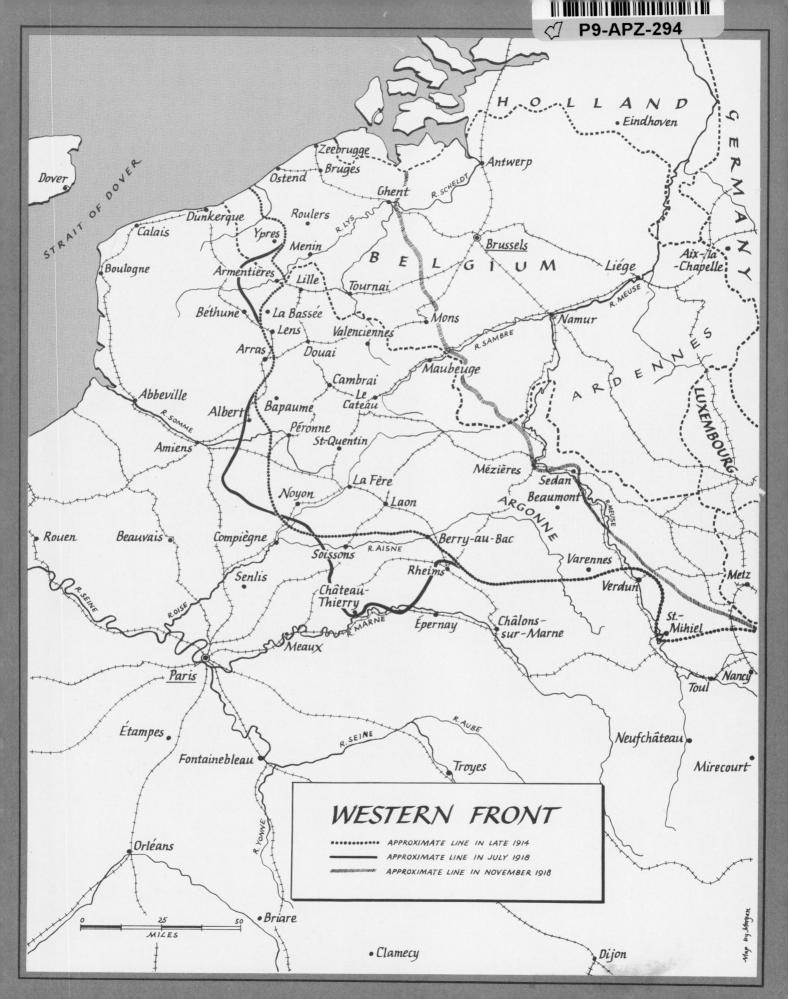

WESTERN FRONT

•••••••••• APPROXIMATE LINE IN LATE 1914
▬▬▬▬▬ APPROXIMATE LINE IN JULY 1918
▨▨▨▨▨ APPROXIMATE LINE IN NOVEMBER 1918

THE GREAT WAR : 1914-1918

THE GREAT WAR
1914-1918

A PICTORIAL HISTORY

by John Terraine

THE MACMILLAN COMPANY, NEW YORK

Acknowledgment is gratefully made to the following publishers for permission to reprint copyrighted material:

Charles Scribner's Sons, for the quotation from *The World Crisis,* One Volume Edition, by Sir Winston Churchill. Copyright 1933 by Charles Scribner's Sons. The Viking Press, Inc., for four lines from "The General" from *Collected Poems* by Siegfried Sassoon, Copyright 1918 by E. P. Dutton & Co., Copyright 1946 by Siegfried Sassoon; and for four lines from "Memorial Tablet" from *Collected Poems* by Siegfried Sassoon, Copyright 1920 by E. P. Dutton & Co., 1948 by Siegfried Sassoon, both selections reprinted by permission of The Viking Press, Inc.

Author and publisher wish to extend their thanks to the following sources for permission to reproduce the illustrations in this volume: Imperial War Museum, London; The Mansell Collection; Hulton Picture Library; Photo E. C. Armées; London Electrotype Agency, Ltd.; Central News Limited; R. Perkins, Esquire; Alfieri Picture Service; Syndicat de la Propriété Artistique; and Shuttleworth Trust.

IMPERIAL WAR MUSEUM, *pages:* 15, 24–25, 29, 40, 54–55, 68, 84–85, 86, 90, 97, 100, 103, 105, 108, 112, 118, 119, 125, 127, 128, 130, 134, 135, 136, 138, 144–145, 147, 149, 150, 150–151, 157, 158–159, 162, 165, 168–169, 173, 182, 190, 191, 196–197, 199, 201, 218, 224, 226, 230, 232, 233, 236, 239, 240–241, 242, 245, 247, 248–249, 250, 251, 252, 253, 254, 255, 256–257, 258, 259, 260, 261, 262–263, 268, 272, 273, 274, 275, 278, 279, 280, 290, 291, 293, 295, 300, 302–303, 304, 305, 307, 309, 310, 311, 312, 313, 315, 317, 319, 320, 325, 329, 330–331, 332, 333, 334, 338, 339, 341, 342, 344, 345, 346–347, 348, 355, 357, 358, 360, 363, 364, 365, 367, 368, 370–371, 376, 377, 378–379, 382–383.

THE MANSELL COLLECTION, *pages:* Frontispiece, 7, 10, 13, 16–17, 18–19, 26–27, 28, 35, 36–37, 38; 39, 41, 42–43, 45, 49, 50, 51, 52, 57, 60–61, 69, 71, 72, 76–77, 80–81, 82–83, 84, 88, 89, 94–95, 96, 100, 106–107, 108, 111, 115, 122–123, 172, 174–175, 176, 178, 183, 186–187, 190–191, 198, 272.

HULTON PICTURE LIBRARY, *pages:* 2, 4, 5, 6, 8–9, 32–33, 70, 74–75, 110, 125, 127, 140–141, 170, 181, 184–185, 188, 192–193, 204, 216–217, 219, 229, 242, 247, 265, 266, 270–271, 280, 282, 298, 337, 343, 350–351, 372–373, 374–375, 380.

PHOTO E. C. ARMÉES, *pages:* 23, 199, 214, 344.

LONDON ELECTROTYPE AGENCY, LTD., *page* 143.

CENTRAL NEWS LIMITED, *page* 222.

R. PERKINS, ESQUIRE, *pages* 230–231.

ALFIERI PICTURE SERVICE, *pages* 286–287.

SYNDICAT DE LA PROPRIÉTÉ ARTISTIQUE, *pages:* 210–211, 220–221.

SHUTTLEWORTH TRUST, *pages* 278–279.

CONTENTS

PREFACE

"... the great British War Minister of 1906 to 1911 ..." Lord Haldane walking from Whitehall to the House of Lords, July 1914.

"The German militarism, which is *the* crime of the last fifty years, has been working for this for twenty-five years. It is the logical result of their spirit and enterprise and doctrine. It *had* to come."

"It *had* to come": this considered verdict of the United States Ambassador in London, Walter Hines Page, in August 1914, has stood the

"The base of modern war is technology . . ." Krupp factories at Essen in 1912.

test of time. The slowly woven unity of the German people was warlike from the first; it could scarcely fail to continue so, framed by three military empires, Russia, Austria-Hungary, and France under a second Bonaparte. Indeed, for Germany the problem of existence was always primarily strategic, whether it sought its solution through diplomatic arrangements or through war plans. Under Bismarck, war was very much an instrument of policy, and diplomacy remained vigorous and decisive. After Bismarck, diplomacy languished; war plans, down to their very details, became the deciding factor. Lord Haldane, the great British War Minister of 1906 to 1911, who understood Germany better than any other British statesman of his time, carried Walter Hines Page's thought one step further when he wrote:

"The reason why the war came appears to have been that at some period in the year 1913 the German Government finally laid the reins on the necks of men whom up to then it had held in restraint. The decision appears to have been allowed at this point to pass from civilians to soldiers. . . . It is not their business to have the last word in deciding between peace and war."

A second German war within twenty-five years has supplied an illumination which was lacking to the writers of the '20s and '30s; it is now evident that 1939 was closely linked to 1918, that the interval was a breathing space in a continuous action, and that that action was the burgeoning of the German state and people, their striving toward world supremacy through their traditional instruments—the armed forces. Germany, then, is the starting point of the great European conflict of the first half of the twentieth century; Germany must be the starting point of understanding it.

The base of modern war is technology, disseminating itself through industry. Without technological advances, without industrial expansion, neither German diplomacy nor German war preparation could have carried the weight they did. In the period between 1871 and 1914 both

". . . a war lord, identified with the military party." Kaiser Wilhelm II (1859–1941), with the King of Greece at German Army maneuvers. The Kaiser (arm outstretched) is pointing something out to the Greek King (who also wears German uniform, as a compliment, though an officer in Greek uniform is visible at the right of the picture). On the Kaiser's right, behind the map table, stands an officer in the uniform of the Uhlans (German Lancers), and to his right an officer of Hussars, possibly the famous "Death's Head" Hussars to which the Crown Prince belonged.

made huge progress: "the country which had been poor became suddenly rich."[1] A primarily agricultural, rural nation became an urban one. Coal production, which until the advent of atomic power was, with steel, the very foundation of a modern state, went up from 30 million tons in 1871 to 190 million tons in 1913. In the decade of the 1880s, the German Empire doubled its output of steel and almost doubled that of iron. Sweeping educational reforms, with particular stress upon higher and technical education, bore swift fruit in Germany's quickly won leadership in the new chemical and electrical industries. Her shipping expanded, and with it her overseas trade. As with every other industrial revolution, the population itself also increased rapidly in numbers—by 11 millions between 1880 and 1900, and by rather more than that figure between 1900 and 1914.

All this added up in the minds of a professional military hierarchy, not only to a further proof, if any were needed, that Germany was marching from strength to strength, but to the assurance of a solid material base from which operations of war could be launched. From the moment when, in 1890, the young Kaiser Wilhelm II dismissed the Iron Chancellor, Bismarck, the military hierarchy, organized in the General Staff, steadily acquired greater and more dangerous influence. The Kaiser, mystically dedicated to the concepts of the supremacy of Germany and of the monarchy within Germany—industrious, intelligent, pious, ardent, but also vain and impulsive and at times hysterical—gradually ceased to be a presiding head of state, and turned himself instead into a war lord, identified with the military party. Only when it was too late did he realize to what an extent, in surrendering his arbitrating authority, he had become the prisoner of his own might. The army itself had become the prisoner of an idea.

The essence of the German military problem—the "German problem" —was simple and deadly: war on two fronts. A secret alliance with Austria signed in 1879 ruled out any likelihood of further danger from that quarter—and at the same time linked together the aspirations and policies of the two Germanic empires. There remained Russia and France. When these unlikely partners—the most autocratic imperialism in Europe and the young Third Republic—came together in 1888, the year of the Kaiser's accession, war on two fronts became inevitable. All General Staff thinking would have to be based on this fact.

The famous Schlieffen Plan which, in a modified form, shaped German movement in 1914 contained two cardinal elements: a holding operation

[1]H. A. L. Fisher: *A History of Europe*, 1936.

on the Russian front, in co-operation with Austria, and a lightning offensive against France with the mass of the German Army, aiming at a second Sedan. In the ebullient mood of pre-1914 Germany, this solution seemed well within her powers. That General Graf Alfred von Schlieffen,[2] whose name is associated with no personal victory in the field at any time, played as significant a part in shaping the nature of war as Napoleon, Lee, Grant, or von Moltke—to name four of the outstanding soldiers of his century—is astounding. It is also an indication of the special nature of the German Army, in which "the Staff Officer . . . possessed an authority probably unknown in other armies."[3] Single-minded, humorless, as mystical as the Kaiser in his attitude to the army, von Schlieffen displayed in the development of his plan on the one hand the immense intellectual and professional grasp which one might expect from a man of this stamp, and on the other hand the fatal limitation of this very professionalism when not restrained by a wider view.

For the plan contained two grave faults: first, it required from the German Army an effort beyond its strength, as von Schlieffen himself apprehended before he died; secondly, it presupposed infringements of neutrality which would forfeit all Germany's moral rights and multiply her enemies. This, at least, could have been prevented by statesmanship—but the German statesmen had laid down the reins.

[2]Chief of General Staff, 1891–1906.

[3]*Times History of the War.*

THE GREAT WAR : 1914-1918

THE LAMPS GO OUT

It did not need a Fort Sumter cannonade to set the world in flames in 1914, only the pistol shots of an assassin. The Archduke Franz Ferdinand, heir to the Austrian throne, was visiting Sarajevo, capital of the recently annexed province of Bosnia. It was a state visit, planned to include a ceremonial drive through the town by the Archduke, accompanied by his morganatic wife, Sophie, and escorted by the civic dignitaries, with inspections of troops, and finally an official address of welcome at the town hall.

Matters quickly went awry: on the way to the town hall a bomb was thrown; it missed the Archduke, but wounded one of his aides in a following motorcar, as well as several bystanders. This effectively blighted the official welcome; ceremonies were cut short, and soon the royal procession was making its way back to the railway station with, it would seem, an amazing lack of precaution, considering what had already occurred. Among those watching the departure was a Slav schoolboy, Gavrilo Princip, one of thousands who considered Austrian rule an intolerable affront to the upsurge of their own nationalism. He, too, was armed with a bomb. He threw it, but it did not explode. At once he pulled out a revolver, and fired three shots. They hit the Archduke and his wife, who threw herself in front of her husband to shield him; both died almost at once. Princip and his confederates were arrested immediately.

The Austrian Government's reactions were prompt; it laid the blame at the door of the neighboring Kingdom of Serbia, behind whose frontier, it alleged, killers like Princip and other dissidents found shelter and support. Austria determined upon drastic retribution; within five weeks her unappeasable anger had drawn the nations of Europe into a war which would spread across the world, and, before it ended, would sweep away the Habsburg Empire and much else besides.

At first, however, the event, although it shocked men everywhere, was not recognized as the portent that it was. In the stormy climate of Balkan politics, even the assassination of an heir apparent could be regarded as something of a commonplace. Franz Ferdinand was killed on June 28th; not until July 21st did so responsible a newspaper as the

"... a war which ... would sweep away the Habsburg Empire ..." The Emperor Franz Joseph, 1818–1916, inaugurator of the Dual Monarchy of Austria-Hungary.

"Princip and his confederates were arrested immediately." The arrest of Gavrilo Princip after the assassination of the Archduke Franz Ferdinand and his wife at Sarajevo, June 28, 1914.

London *Times* bring the consequences into its main news page. By then, war was only fourteen days away from England. Summer holidays, the cricket season, boating, picnics, going to the seaside—these were the preoccupations of the people. For some of these holiday makers there was pageantry, too, to be marveled at, though its significance was not fully appreciated: on July 18th, at Spithead, outside the great naval base of Portsmouth, King George V paid an "informal" visit to the Royal Navy. Forty miles of ships, 260 vessels, including 24 of the new "Dreadnought" battleships and 35 older battleships, were drawn up for the King's inspection. To one spectator, they gave "the feeling of being in a vast town of iron castles, each standing alone and independent of each other." After the display, the fleet put to sea for tactical exercises lasting several days. The sailors did not know it, but in effect they were already at war. These squadrons were not dispersed; they passed straight to their war stations.

The days that followed the Spithead Review saw a frightening acceleration of the tempo of events. Austria's threatening posture toward Serbia aroused instant reactions in Russia; sentiment on behalf of fellow Slavs and political apprehensions over the possibility of Austrian aggrandizement in the Balkans, a well-recognized Russian sphere of

2

influence, made it unthinkable that the Czar's empire could stand aside from this quarrel. In turn, faced with Russian support for Serbia, Austria invoked her ally, Germany; more than any other factor, it was German assurances of full backing for whatever action Austria might feel impelled to take that brought about a world conflagration. For Russia, meeting the menace of war with the two German empires, looked instantly to her own ally, France, whose President, Raymond Poincaré, and Prime Minister René Viviani, were actually visiting St. Petersburg. The French response had been foreseen in Germany; it formed the very basis of the war plan. Had the French been far more reluctant than they were to join their Russian allies, the Germans would have been obliged to force France into the war in order to put their plan into effect and reinsure themselves by her overthrow. There were only two doubtful factors. Could the Central Powers, Germany and Austria, depend upon their third partner, Italy? Could France depend upon her latest, recent, and decidedly reticent ally, England?

It was in England that recognition of the serious turn of affairs came last and most haltingly, for reasons which were not all connected with the summer sunshine. British politicians in July 1914 had their own preoccupations, quite apart from those of the man in the street. Not for almost a hundred years had England been nearer to civil war than she came between March and July 1914. The cause of the danger was Ireland: the insistent demand of the Catholic southern Irish for Home Rule, and the bitter refusal of the Protestant North to allow itself to be governed from Dublin. Already, at the mere possibility of having to coerce the Ulster Protestants, there had been a mutiny of British Army officers. The army had been split from top to bottom; the Secretary of State for War and the Chief of the Imperial General Staff had resigned, and the King himself had called a conference at Buckingham Palace to try to find a solution. It was upon the deliberations of statesmen engaged with the details of partition, tracing Irish parish boundaries on large-scale maps, that the European crisis intruded itself abruptly.

On July 30th King George V wrote in his diary: "Foreign telegrams coming in all day, we are doing all we can for peace and to prevent a European War but things look very black. . . . The debate in the House of Commons on Irish question today has been postponed on account of gravity of European situation." Where would England stand? This was the question that was being asked in all the European capitals, but in none more anxiously than in Paris; during the next few days the urgings and remonstrances of the French Ambassador in London became in-

JULY 30

3

"Russia . . . looked instantly to her own ally, France . . ." President Poincaré driving with Czar Nicholas II to the Imperial Palace of Peterhof, St. Petersburg, July 1914.

creasingly heated. The sense of being taken by surprise was acute in Britain; its effect continued long after the opening stages of the war.

Yet nothing could be further from the truth than to say that Britain was unprepared for war in 1914. Despite the powerful pacifist feeling that ran through the ruling Liberal Party, no period in British history can match the first fourteen years of the twentieth century for reappraisal and drastic reorganization of military resources. At that time Britain was the world's leading naval power, her Empire, spaced across the globe, held together and supported by the Royal Navy. Alarmed and provoked by the Kaiser's fleet building, the British Admiralty, inspired by the demonic energy of Admiral Sir John (Jacky) Fisher and the vigor of Winston Churchill, had embarked upon a vast program of reequipment and construction. The Spithead Review provided a glimpse of its results. Under Lord Haldane, at the War Office, a General Staff had come into being for the first time. The army's functions had been reexamined and

"'. . . a vast town of iron castles . . .'" The royal review of the British fleet at Spithead, July 1914; H.M.S. Africa in foreground.

redefined; the result was an organized Expeditionary Force. The expansion of the army in wartime had been considered; the result was a second-line Territorial Army. The heterogeneous forces of the Empire were modernized and reshaped; new weapons and new drill were created and adopted. At the discussions of the Committee of Imperial Defence the large questions of strategy were gone into; they received attention from the best brains in the country. If the results were not what they might have been, it was not for want of thought; it was because neither in Britain nor anywhere else was the full nature of the twentieth century revolution of warfare yet understood.

The final expression of British preparation was the famous War Book, which laid down, stage by stage, the entire process of entry into war for every department of public life. The man most responsible for this remarkable work was Lord Hankey, Secretary of the Committee of Imperial Defence, at that time a relatively junior and unknown officer of Marines. Summing it up, he has written: "Every detail had been thought out and every possible safeguard provided for ensuring that, once decided on, these arrangements should be put in operation rapidly and without a hitch. . . . From the King to the printer, everyone knew what he had to do." The War Book was completed and approved on July 14th; only fourteen days later, when Austria declared war on Serbia, the precautionary stage laid down in it was already being put into effect.

Nevertheless, the question remained whether Britain would go beyond precautionary stages. If she did not, the possibility of a short war, albeit disastrous to her allies and her interests, would remain strong; if she did, if she entered the struggle, nothing could prevent it from spreading across the world, and for those with eyes to see there arose the extreme likelihood of a long-drawn-out conflict. The decision was fateful, and for Mr. Asquith's Liberal Ministry it proved particularly hard to make. Despite all the activities of the Committee of Imperial Defence, despite the work of Haldane and Churchill—presided over, it must be added, by Asquith himself—neither the nature of the crisis nor the extent of Britain's involvement in it were recognized. Something

"The decision was fateful. . . ." The British Prime Minister, the Honorable Herbert Henry Asquith, on the steps of the War Office.

(opposite) " . . . Russia mobilized fully on the 31st." Crowds on the Nevsky Prospect in St. Petersburg, July 29, 1914, during the period of partial mobilization.

(pages 8 and 9) "On August 1st France . . . mobilized . . ." French reservists leaving a railway station on their way to report at the depots, August 1914.

more would be needed to draw Britain out of an isolationism as real if not as total as that of the United States. Germany, now entirely the slave of the General Staff's plan, was not slow in providing the extra something.

Declarations and ultimatums were flying thick and fast by now. On July 28th Austria declared war on Serbia; the British First Fleet moved to its North Sea bases facing Germany. On the 29th Germany asked for a guarantee of British neutrality in the event of a European war; this was rejected by the British Foreign Secretary, Sir Edward Grey, on the following day. On that day, too, Russia ordered partial mobilization, whereupon Germany threatened to mobilize unless the Russians ceased; a stream of German propaganda about "frontier incidents," later admitted to be false, so alarmed the French government that it ordered all its forces to retire to a line about six miles inside the common frontier. Belgrade was bombarded. Austria and Russia mobilized fully on the 31st. Turkey, an unknown factor so far, did the same. Britain asked both France and Germany for assurances that they would respect Belgian neutrality; France agreed at once, but Germany could give only an evasive answer for reasons that would quickly become apparent.

JULY 28
JULY 29

JULY 30

JULY 31

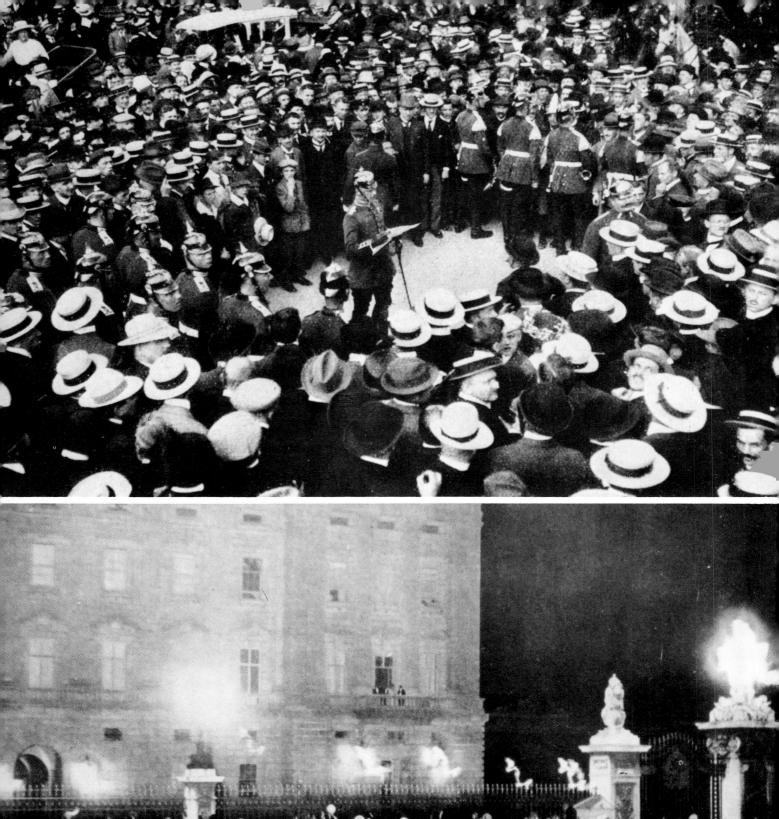

On August 1st France, Germany, and Belgium mobilized; Germany declared war on Russia. On the 2nd the British government still felt unable to offer more to France than a promise to prevent the German fleet from passing through the North Sea to attack French ports. But it was on this day that Germany demanded unrestricted passage of her armies through Belgium; German troops entered Poland, Luxembourg, and France. France and Germany declared war on each other on the 3rd; Sir Edward Grey addressed the House of Commons; no formal vote was taken, but the mood of the House was perceptibly favorable to the government's policy. On August 4th Germany declared war on Belgium and immediately crossed her frontier; Britain ordered mobilization—three days after her French ally—and issued an ultimatum to Germany that unless guarantees of Belgian neutrality were given within twelve hours the two powers would be at war. German Chancellor von Bethmann-Hollweg commented bitterly to the British Ambassador in Berlin: "Just for a scrap of paper Great Britain is going to make war on a kindred nation." And so it was; the ultimatum expired at midnight. Standing in a Foreign Office window with a friend, watching the lamps being lit around St. James's Park, Sir Edward Grey commented with prescient sadness: "The lamps are going out all over Europe; we shall not see them lit again in our lifetime."

But the crowds along the Mall and outside Buckingham Palace were singing "God Save the King" with cheerful vigor. Now tension was released; all were keyed up to a great endeavor. There were few who understood what it might cost.

Germany, Austria, Russia, Serbia, France, Belgium, and now Britain —all were at war. Yet the European roll call was still incomplete; there would be others to follow. Italy had declared neutrality, but how long would it last? Already a sardonic Frenchman had defined Italian policy as it would be shaped in two wars: ". . . awaiting an opportunity to rush to the aid of the victors." Turkey's posture pointed to the dilemma of the Balkan States; each would sooner or later have to choose sides, an unenviable decision which neither idealism nor materialism seemed able to assist. For all Europe, the tragic hour had come.

(above) "**Britain . . . issued an ultimatum to Germany. . . .**" A German officer reads a proclamation announcing England's declaration of war against Germany on August 4, 1914.

(below) "**. . . singing 'God Save the King' with cheerful vigor.**" Crowds gathered outside Buckingham Palace on the night of August 4th.

2 BALANCE OF POWER

If war could be fought and won on paper, as simply as a mathematical calculation, obvious and massive advantages lay with the Entente Powers in 1914, as they had lain with the North against the Confederacy in 1861. Yet in each case a four-year struggle, ferocious, costly, and frequently uncertain, would be needed to bring the thing to an issue. The reasons for this were of the same nature in each case: the American Civil War provides the first example of a great modern war, based upon the products and mechanics of the Industrial Revolution, which created situations and problems hitherto undreamed of, above all in the matter of scale; the First World War, fifty years later, carried the process several stages further, tapping even vaster reservoirs of power, and complicated by the ever-accelerating speed of technical and industrial growth.

The balance of apparent military strength at the outbreak of the war was unequal: 136 German and Austrian infantry divisions, with 22 cavalry divisions, against 199 Allied infantry divisions, with 50 cavalry divisions. But such arithmetic is deceptive. All through the war amateur strategists would fall into the temptation of making such simple comparisons, and be baffled when events belied their calculations. The Central Powers possessed in the German Army, which provided 87 of their infantry divisions and half their cavalry, a priceless asset; for if this force attained excellence only in particular 'and limited parts, its general standard was nevertheless extremely high. This fact, in the early days at least, more than offset the weaknesses of the polyglot array of Austria-Hungary. The military quality, the productive capacity, the practical homogeneity, and the central position of the Germanic empires equalized their numerical inferiority.

The "driving-wheel" of the German Army was its General Staff, which, as well as providing the central plan and organization upon which all formations would act, supplied also the corpus of highly trained and efficient staff officers within those formations that was necessary for the easy running of the great machine. Thorough, unified training and

"The 'driving-wheel' of the German Army was its General Staff. . . ." The Kaiser with General-oberst Helmuth von Moltke, German Chief of Staff (in effect, Commander in Chief), and General Staff officers in 1914.

doctrine counted as weapons in themselves: "The higher commanders were accustomed to deal with large bodies, were trained to disregard loss of life, and to believe in resolute and united action; and vigorous subordinate initiative was taught as the leading principle of all command."[1] Yet within this very citadel of martial virtue there lay a weakness: the Chief of the General Staff was Generaloberst Helmuth von Moltke, nephew of the great von Moltke of the Franco-Prussian War. He had not inherited the talents of his namesake; irresolute and oversensitive, he lacked the grip and determination of his famous uncle. The most formidable mass army in the world would enter the war under a direction all too prone to vacillation and compromise.

Drawing upon a reserve of 4,300,000 trained men, the active German Army was organized in 25 army corps, each of two divisions. Alongside the active army, ready to take part with it immediately in action, stood 32 reserve divisions, whose capabilities proved to be one of the first major surprises of the War. Hardiness, endurance, and often great bravery were the characteristics that ran through this whole great mass of infantry. The cavalry, on the other hand, despite the Kaiser's personal interest in it, proved to be a disappointment; Dragoons, Cuirassiers, Hussars, even the Uhlans (Lancers) whose name had become a byword, all seemed to lack the dash and thrust that had been expected of them. The German cavalry divisions had been diluted with light infantry to give them firepower; the effect of this was a sapping of the true cavalry spirit that put them at a disadvantage on all fronts.

The German field artillery was ill equipped; its standard 77-mm. (3-inch) gun, though light and easy to handle, was an adaptation of an out-of-date model, inferior to that of any other great European power. But Germany had a second surprise in store for her enemies, one that placed its brand immediately on the nature of the War and kept it firmly there. This was the provision of large numbers of heavy guns for use in the field, particularly the 5.9-inch howitzer, which was to emerge as the outstanding artillery piece of the War. It was, in fact, to be an artillery war, largely a heavy-gun war, and Germany obtained an important advantage by foreseeing this and preparing accordingly. The German machine gun, too, was an efficient weapon, of which she possessed ample reserve stocks. The actual proportion of machine guns to infantry in 1914 was no larger than in the British Army, but Germany enjoyed greater numbers and the ability to replace them. All in all, her army was a mighty instrument of war. For over four years it endured

[1] *Times History of the War.*

unbelievable hammerings, put forth prodigious exertions; this was the pillar of German ambition, which would have to be pulled down before she could be beaten.

The Austro-Hungarian Army, in any sustained endeavor, could only prove to be a liability. A bare 25 percent of the men in it were of German stock, 23 percent were Magyar; and the remainder—more than half of the whole—were Slavs, Czechs, and Italians: that is to say, belonging to races fundamentally opposed to the Habsburg Dual Monarchy, people who increasingly saw their true champions among the ranks of their ostensible enemies. The spectacular Austrian collapses which inevitably followed were largely attributable to this cause. On the other hand this army displayed some fine qualities: under heavy defeat the Austrian soldiery showed remarkable patience; their cavalry, fired by Magyar élan, did some good work; their very heavy artillery, the huge Skoda siege howitzers, made a most valuable contribution to German plans. The Chief of the Austrian General Staff, General Field Marshal Conrad von Hötzendorf, has been doubtfully described as "probably the best strategist of the war";[2] his grandiose schemes were often far beyond the abilities of his forces, but generally they were re-

[2] Sir James Edmonds, *A Short History of World War I*.

". . . the outstanding artillery piece of the war." German 5.9-inch howitzers.

"... the Austrian soldiery showed remarkable patience." Austrian infantry on the march.

stricted by his status as "second fiddle" to the German High Command.

The vast bulk of outward Allied strength was supplied by Russia: 114 infantry and 36 cavalry divisions. This was the "Russian steamroller," slow in movement but seemingly sure in purpose, which was confidently expected, once it had gained momentum, to beat down all opposition and lumber into Berlin. Much had been done to improve the Russian Army since its humiliating defeat by Japan in 1905; it remained,

however, a clumsy giant. Its mobilization was slow; there were grave
material deficiencies, with reserves of ammunition, even rifles, in short
supply. The army suffered seriously from a lack of educated leadership
in the lower formations; at the top there were corruption and inefficiency on the grand scale. Ignorance, fraud, and prejudice found their
personification in the Minister of War, General Vladimir Sukhomlinov;
against this, and strong German influence at the Czar's court, the more

17

(pages 18 and 19) ". . . millions of
brave, devoted, ill-equipped, usually illiterate soldiers." Russian infantry in extended order.

able Russian soldiers struggled in vain. Theirs was to be a tragic fate, fully shared by their millions of brave, devoted, ill-equipped, usually illiterate soldiers. Yet this army would also have its victories, in which the endurance of the infantry would be matched by the skill of the artillery, as long as it had shells to fire, and the savage dash of the Cossacks across the wide plains of eastern Europe.

The hard military core of the Alliance was the French Army. By prodigious efforts—at times, indeed, overzealous—the French had dragged their army out of the utter ruin of 1871 and turned it into a force that frightened their conquerors. It was this amazing revival which dictated German war plans, which made the immediate crushing of France a necessity before which all else must bow. The discrepancy of population made it impossible for France to match German numbers in the field, but by extending the period of compulsory service and by drawing on colonial manpower, the French were able to field 62 infantry and 10 cavalry divisions. This was a formidable body of troops which, in conjunction with a powerful fortress system, offered at least a promising chance of holding and damaging any German attack until Russia's intervention made itself felt. Active, intelligent, adaptable, the French soldiers were rare stuff out of which to build an army. Parts of it were excellent: efficient staffs; some resolute, able commanders; many officers whose only fault was an excess of dedicated courage; and a famous quick-firing field gun, the 75 mm. ("soixante-quinze"). On the other hand, the French Army was the prisoner of a doctrine whose ill effects seeped down from broad strategic conceptions into the spheres of tactics, organization, and equipment.

The material reconstruction of the French Army after 1871 would have been pointless without intellectual and psychological accompaniments. A recipe for victory, or at the very least for avoiding further catastrophes like Sedan, had to be discovered. This was sought in the example and teachings of France's greatest soldier, Napoleon I. One element of the Napoleonic method was diagnosed as the decisive war winner—a vigorous, all-out offensive carried straight to the enemy. This provided the strategic foundation of French thinking; the spirit of the offensive had therefore to be implanted in every part of the army, to create the emotional drive, the self-confidence without which such a concept would be meaningless. At all levels French soldiers were taught the virtues of headlong attack. This made for tactical rigidity; it led to over-reliance on field artillery, ignoring the value of heavy guns; it even, in the name of tradition's inspiration, kept the French infantry in conspicuous red trousers and heavy dark-blue coats, while the cavalry still wore the cuirasses and helmets of the First Empire, or the flowing cloaks of desert warfare in North Africa. Trained exclusively as a shock weapon, the French cavalry carried, besides the saber or lance, only a small carbine; its attempts to fight on foot would have been ludicrous had their results not been so disastrous.

At the head of this misguided, but potentially splendid force stood its Chief of Staff and Commander in Chief designate in war, General Joseph-Jacques-Césaire Joffre, an officer of Engineers whose solid authority had been thrown behind the teachings of the offensive school but who, when their plans collapsed in chaos, revealed an unshakable nerve, a steadfast courage, and a quite unexpected flexibility of mind to pluck victory out of defeat.

The smaller Continental Allies both had their contributions to make. The Serbs fielded eleven infantry divisions and one cavalry division; experienced and encouraged by their successful part in the Balkan Wars of 1912–1913, they were a force to be reckoned with. They were among the best natural fighters in Europe, whose indomitable ardor proved to

"This was the Russian 'steam-roller' . . ." Mass formations of Russian infantry deploying through a harvesting countryside. Photograph probably taken from a village church spire, to take in the vast expanse of flat landscape beyond.

be out of all proportion to their numbers. Belgium, with only 6 infantry divisions and 1 of cavalry, was more or less disregarded in the strategic thinking of the great powers; this turned out to be an unfair assessment. If the famous phrase "gallant little Belgium" finally owed more to sentiment and propaganda than to actual military achievement, and if it was more fully expressed in the dauntless dignity of King Albert than in the performance of his troops, the unprepared Belgian Army did, nevertheless, illustrate a brave attitude with some brave deeds.

There remained the British, masters of the oceans, armed with the most powerful fleet in the world. But what would they be able to offer to the warfare of these vast hosts? The British Army was wholly different in kind from all that we have described. It was a Regular Army, fundamentally designed for the protection of the British Empire, for imperial garrisons, of which the most important by far was India. At its fullest stretch this army could be organized into 11 infantry divisions—the same as Serbia—and 3 cavalry divisions; the Expeditionary Force available in August 1914 could not amount to more than 6 divisions of infantry and 1½ of cavalry. But they were Regulars, "British Volunteers" to their admirers, who proudly asserted that each was "worth twenty pressed men"; "an army of mercenaries" to those with a different viewpoint. Setting sentiment aside, the raw material of this force was not the most promising. Except in times of agricultural depression (in Ireland that meant any time) the main recruiting areas were the great industrial cities of Britain. As physical specimens the throw-outs of modern urban society were not impressive; tall Scottish Highlanders, a few upstanding Guards regiments, and brawny Irish countrymen created an image which was not really typical. But these were long-service soldiers—seven years with the colors, five with the reserve—and it was amazing what regular food, hard physical exercise, an open-air life, early to bed and early to rise could do, even for the stunted children of the slums. The diversity of conditions under which they might have to fight on the fringes of the Empire gave them experience and adaptability. "They were adepts in musketry, night operations, and habits of concealment, matters about which the other belligerents had scarcely troubled."[3] The cavalry had had a useful mounted-infantry training. The artillery, remembering the Boer War, took a proportion of heavy guns into the field, as well as a first-rate 18-pounder field gun. The transport and administration of the Expeditionary Force were far above general European standards. Like

[3] *British Official History.*

22

"... a quick-firing gun ... which achieved eminence ..." French 75-mm. (3-inch) field gun with caisson. Note the extreme simplicity and sturdiness of the gun, requiring only three men to fire it.

the United States Regulars among the northern volunteers at Bull Run, this highly trained body of men was to set a tone in the early days of the War that few could match.

But weakness in numbers brings other drawbacks with it. There were few officers who had ever commanded more than a small group of men at one time; the strains and hazards of mass command were not appreciated. The Commander in Chief, Field Marshal Sir John French, distinguished as a cavalry general in South Africa, was neither intellectually nor psychologically endowed to meet those strains.

Whatever it might achieve in the opening battles, a force of this size could not continue indefinitely unsupported. It was an essential part of Lord Haldane's Army Reforms to create a second-line army, the Territorials, behind the Regulars. This was a "part-time" citizen army, also volunteers; it comprised 14 infantry divisions and 14 cavalry brigades trained by Regular officers. Its weakness, of course, was that it would take a long time to prepare itself for the field. For this and other

". . . stamped this war as part of the twentieth century . . ." General Sir Horace Smith-Dorrien taking the salute at the first Air Review in May 1913. The contrast between the glittering uniforms of past wars and the surprisingly "modern"-looking airplane is most striking.

25

"Colonial contingents from all over the world . . ." West African infantry at Freetown (Sierra Leone), on their way to the campaign in the Cameroons.

reasons, there were many who doubted its worth, and we shall see how unfortunately these doubts affected the course of events.

There was also the Empire itself. Only India possessed Regular forces at sufficient readiness to make any immediate contribution; not many

Indian soldiers went to France, but in the end India put out a larger effort than any other part of the British Empire, with no less than four separate expeditionary forces in the field. The much smaller English-speaking Dominions were faced with all the problems of raising troops and improvising war machinery. It would be some time before their help could match their eagerness, but finally Canada sent four divisions, Australia five infantry divisions, with a Mounted Division in Palestine, and New Zealand one infantry division—all of rare quality. South Africa played a great part in campaigns against the German colonies, as well as sending a brigade to France. Colonial contingents from all over the world assisted according to their means. All this was made possible by sea power; this imperial gathering was something that Germany had not taken into consideration.

Infantry, cavalry, artillery, these were the classic subdivisions of armies, familiar in all civilized states. Classic weapons were also still in use: lances with fluttering pennants, swords (the young officer who was

". . . a fleet of 30 airships . . . inspired great alarm." A Zeppelin passes over shipping in the Kiel Canal. 40-50 m.p.h. was the average speed of the earliest types, rising later to a maximum of 74 m.p.h. (L. 70). Lengths varied from 453 feet (L. 7) to 754 feet (L. 57). L. 61 could carry 6,270 pounds of bombs to a height of 22,000 feet.

to become Field Marshal Viscount Montgomery of Alamein obeyed the instruction "that all officers' swords were to go to the armourers' shop on the third day of mobilisation to be sharpened. It was not clear to me why, since I had never used my sword except for saluting. But . . . my sword was made sharp for war . . ."), bayonets, which Federals and Confederates alike in an earlier firepower war had found useful for fishing and cooking, but not often for much else. There were, of course, modern innovations: quick-firers, machine guns, field telephones, range finders, field cookers, motor transport. But one novelty above all stamped this

28

war as part of the twentieth century: for the first time men would be fighting in a third dimension, the air.

In August 1914 Germany possessed 384 military airplanes and a fleet of 30 airships. The latter—popularly named after the ingenious old ex-cavalryman who had done more than anyone to promote their development, Count Zeppelin—inspired great alarm. Their huge size (they grew to over 700 feet in length), their much superior range to that of any airplane, their weight-carrying capacity, their climbing and hovering abilities, all combined to make up a fearsome image. If, in the end, they proved a disappointment, it must yet be remembered that they played a

"... Germany possessed 384 military airplanes..." German aircraft in 1914. Note the three different types of biplane, one with steeply "swept" wings; the seven monoplanes are all "Taubes."

"... so many famous names, like Blériot ..." A Blériot XI monoplane, with 50 h.p. Gnome engine; French Gnome engines performed invaluable service during the war.

definite part in the War. With these Zeppelins and her airplane complement, Germany enjoyed a distinct advantage. The French, who had contributed so many famous names, like Blériot and Farman, to aviation pioneering, had 123 airplanes and 10 airships. Britain had 113 aircraft, of which 63 accompanied the Expeditionary Force. The simple sentence "The squadrons flew to France" spells the end of a British way of life and a mode of making war—of island security, in fact. The uncertain flight of these frail machines to their airfields in France was also a flight into a darker future.

THE PLAN UNFOLDS 3

We began to wonder by what sign we would really know when the Germans were there. . . . We imagined the endless columns of grey-clad men with spiked helmets, . . . flattening out poor little Belgium in their overwhelming advance. But what would it be like when the infantry whose movements we had been marking down inch by inch on maps as they crept forward, were actually upon us . . . ?

SPEARS, LIAISON 1914

With the mass armies of the twentieth century, the opening moves of war assumed a crucial significance; to complete one's deployment, to avoid being taken by surprise were major considerations. But equally, with such mass armies, deployment is a complex matter; it would be some time before the unfolding of major movements was perceived. In the moment of making war a great screen descends abruptly between the belligerent forces; silence falls; movement ceases across an invisible line, and the empty, peaceful landscape of yesterday fills with ominous shadows. At the front, in those early August days, there was uncertainty, with men straining their eyes to pierce the fog of war. Behind the armies, the air was filled with the rumble of troop trains; "thousands of drill sergeants were barking and bellowing all over Europe."[1] Only here and there was added the roar of guns.

Significantly, it was on the Western Front that the first clashes took place; speed was an essential factor of the German plan, which allowed forty days for the overthrow of France. This was to be accomplished by a great wheel of three of their seven western armies, a mass of 34 infantry and 5 cavalry divisions, through Belgium and northwestern France, passing to the west of Paris, and finally defeating the French armies with their backs to their own frontier defenses. It was a remarkable concept; one thing which it clearly needed was a practically unhindered march through Belgium. To ensure this, and to save time while their main bodies assembled along the frontier, a selected group of six brigades entered Belgium on August 4th, and on the 5th attempted to rush the commanding fortress of Liége.

Fortresses, in 1914, bore no resemblance to medieval castles and very little even to the scientific masterpieces in which the engineers of the eighteenth century excelled. Strictly speaking, they were fortified areas; a ring of twelve actual "forts" on both banks of the river Meuse, built of

[1] Cyril Falls, *The First World War*.

AUGUST 4, 1914

(pages 32 and 33) ". . . a great screen descends . . . silence falls . . ." Londoners in the Strand reading the first bulletin from the front—a very short document by comparison with the official notices beside it. Note at the left of the telegraph office window "Lord Kitchener's Appeal" for volunteers, and on the right the "Aliens Restriction" Order in Council, with the word "Penalty" prominent at the bottom. The Boy Scouts were probably acting as messengers for government departments, a service they immediately undertook.

reinforced concrete with steel cupolas for their heavy artillery, and containing 400 guns between them, constituted the Liége obstacle. Some of the forts were as much as three miles apart, and it required a field division of the Belgian Army to cover the gaps between them.

Instantly, when the German assault group attacked, some of the features which were to become dreadful characteristics of the whole War were seen. The Belgian commander, General Gérard Leman, displayed a firmness and courage which made him the War's first hero. Forts and infantry together threw back the German advance with sickening loss; in some units there was dire confusion. Only the presence of mind of the Deputy Chief of Staff of the German Second Army, Major-General Erich Ludendorff, prevented a serious defeat. Belgian machine-gun and rifle fire was mainly responsible for this result, and the Belgians themselves were appalled at the revelation of what these weapons could effect against dense formations of determined men. But no such losses as these would hinder the German High Command in the ferocious pursuit of its main purposes. On the night of the 5th, Ludendorff penetrated into the city of Liége, and on the 6th the Belgian field division was ordered out of the place.

AUGUST 5-6

The Germans were jubilant, and issued a prematurely proud communiqué. Six more days would pass before they were even able to bring into action the massive 420-mm. (17-inch) Krupp siege howitzers which provided "the first tactical surprise of the World War."[2] Yet another four days would be needed for these terrible engines of destruction to smash the last of the forts into submission. The defense of Liége was Belgium's first contribution to the Allied cause; it is hard to state precisely just how much delay it caused to the Germans—in the case of their main masses, perhaps as little as one day. But it showed the world that even such a war machine as the German Army could be halted and damaged by staunch resistance. At the same time, by briefly checking the thrust of the German right wing, and thus postponing recognition of what its intentions were, the Liége defenders added one more element to the prevailing obscurity.

AUGUST 10

AUGUST 16

To the accompaniment of the Liége bombardment, the August days hastened by. There were disagreeable surprises for the Central Powers on the Eastern and Southern Fronts. The most immediate and apparently simple task for the Austrians was the overthrow of Serbia, the outward purpose for which they had gone to war. But the inefficient Russian Empire displayed a wholly unexpected, if misguided, burst of energy,

[2] Liddell Hart, *A History of the World War.*

34

"... the war's first hero." General Leman, commander of the Belgian garrison of Liége.

"... a bloody repulse ..." Abandoned guns and limbers in the Austrian retreat, following their first defeat in Serbia.

and in response to French appeals set two armies in motion against East Prussia without waiting to complete their assembly or equipment. The nine divisions of the German Eighth Army under Lieutenant General von Prittwitz und Gaffron, which were all that the Schlieffen Plan allowed for the eastern holding operation, were at once in trouble. The ripples would spread far, but their first effect was to disrupt Austrian plans, compelling a detachment of strength from the Serbian to the Russian front; the immediate result of this was a bloody repulse when the Austrian invasion of Serbia began on August 12th. Fighting with fanatical bravery and considerable skill on ground they knew well, the Serbs engaged and defeated, during the remainder of the year, almost half a million Austro-Hungarian troops, inflicting a loss of more than half that number. The astronomical casualty lists of the First World War were thus almost immediately presented, and remained a lasting attribute: the nations of the West were staggered and hypnotized by those that occurred on their own front, but on other fronts the percentages were at least as great and in some cases greater.

During the last ten days of the month the decisive maneuvers unfolded which the historian may now regard with an Olympian eye, but whose complex interrelation could not be perceived at the time. On the

"Their masses now on the move . . ." German Dragoons advancing through Belgium. They were fired on (or believed that they had been fired on) from the house on the right. The usual reprisals followed. The troops looking toward the right of the picture may have been studying the results of these.

17th, the day after the final submission of Liége, the Russians entered East Prussia, while the main body of their forces, four armies under General Ivanov, gathered along the frontier with Austria in Galicia.

In the east and in the west tides of savage energy were unleashed. Their masses now on the move, the Germans brushed aside the resistance of the Belgian field army, hitherto fairly successful in small skirmishes and combats with the German advance guards. At Haelen on the 12th the Belgians even won a small defensive victory, but now they had no option save to withdraw to Antwerp. General von Kluck's First Army, the loaded tip of the German flail, entered Brussels on the 20th, and on the 21st the Second Army opened its attack on the fortress of Namur. Ruthless brutality was the hallmark of the German advance. Making no allowance for the outraged sentiments of a ravished neutral (and bitterly remembering their grim experiences with the *francs-tireurs* of 1870–1871), asserting that their soldiers had been shot at by Belgian civilians, the Germans burned down villages as a matter of course, and executed civilian hostages all along their route. The pinnacles of atrocity were reached with the burning of Louvain, whose famous library contained a

"... brushed aside the resistance of the Belgian field army ..." These Belgian infantry, some still wearing their old-fashioned shakos, are said to be "on the way to the firing line." Their general appearance suggests they were coming back from it.

AUGUST 20
AUGUST 21

39

"General von Kluck's First Army ... entered Brussels ..." A German artillery column passing through the streets, part of the long defile to overawe the population.

unique collection of medieval manuscripts, and the destruction of Dinant, where 678 civilians were massacred, including a child three weeks old. Not since the Thirty Years' War had Europe known the meaning of such deliberate terror, equaled, if not surpassed, by Germans and Austrians alike in Poland and the Balkans. Roads were filled with refugees clutching their pathetic bundles, pushing perambulators, the more fortunate urging on a horse and cart, a few wealthy ones in motorcars, but all creating a serious impediment to military movement, and a sign of the savage nature of modern war.

Burning and destroying, the German right wing swung through Belgium, toward the encirclement of the French and their British allies. The French themselves were already on the move, in accordance with their offensive doctrine, and drawn by the magnet of their "lost provinces," Alsace and Lorraine. Marching to the program of their notorious Plan 17—"Whatever the circumstances, it is the C.-in-C.'s intention to advance with all forces united to the attack of the German Armies," ran the preamble of the plan—the French Command proposed to thrust four of its five armies in a Napoleonic "lozenge" across the frontier,

40

leaving only one to guard the left flank against the possibility of an attack through the Ardennes. Even this army was assigned an offensive role. Meanwhile, until all was ready for the great dash forward, a detachment entered Alsace, capturing Mulhouse with fanfares, losing it again, and then retaking it. By August 18th the main French offensive was set to open, spearheaded by De Castelnau's Second Army in the direction of Morhange. But developments on the left were already nullifying Plan 17, forcing Joffre to extend his flank up into Belgium, drawing his Fourth Army, which should have been his strategic reserve, into line to fill up the ensuing gap. Everywhere the fog of war was dense; cavalry proved useless in reconnaissance, and aircraft, without wireless, did not attain their full value.

Wrapped in a mystery and silence of particular opacity, the British Expeditionary Force, not without heart searchings, was moving to its positions of assembly around the old fortress of Maubeuge, on the extreme left of the French line. Never in British history has an army gone overseas with such smooth efficiency. Even so, there was some grit in the wheels. Britain's greatest serving soldier, Field Marshal Lord Kitchener

41

"Ruthless brutality was the hall-mark . . ." German transport passing through one of innumerable sacked, gutted, empty villages. The tension of men and horses suggests that they are still expecting trouble.

(pages 42 and 43) "Not since the Thirty Years' War had Europe known the meaning of such deliberate terror . . ." This is part of the Belgian town of Termonde. The sunlight, falling through the shells of houses, patterns their outlines and windows on the street. Just one Belgian town, out of many. . . .

of Khartoum, had been appointed Secretary of State for War on August 5th; coming fresh to the situation and problems of European war, Kitchener's military instinct at once conceived a deep distrust of the arrangements which had been agreed between the French and British staffs. He did not like the place of assembly; he thought it dangerously far advanced; nor did he feel able to leave Britain naked (as he saw it) to the threat of invasion by sending away all the available Regular troops at once. It was too late to change the timetables that would carry the army to Maubeuge, but—despite naval assurances—Kitchener insisted on holding back two divisions, so that Sir John French's force consisted of only four divisions and a large cavalry division, a tiny drop in the great tides of armed might that were now in full flow. Advance parties landed

AUGUST 7

in France on August 7th; by the 20th the concentration was completed; the Battles of the Frontiers were by now in full blast, and the British, as Kitchener had apprehended, would shortly find themselves in the sector which a dead German general had made decisive.

On four fronts the Central Powers faced the onslaught of their enemies. With the Austrians already retiring before the attack of the Serbs, on August 18th a new threat developed from General Ivanov's group of armies in Poland and Galicia, while simultaneously the grand French attack opened in Lorraine; on the 19th the leading Russian army

AUGUST 19

in East Prussia gained a victory at Gumbinnen. Everywhere, except in Serbia, the remedy adopted by the Germans and Austrians was a determined offensive of their own, even at the price of abandoning carefully laid plans. Von Prittwitz, despite his relatively small forces, was ordered to attack. Conrad von Hötzendorf had his own large schemes. In the west, a cardinal principle of the Schlieffen Plan, the strict defensive on the left flank, was given up. Casually, in a jocular conversation, the German High Command threw its subtlest design overboard.

It was Crown Prince Rupprecht of Bavaria, temporarily in command of the two German armies on the left, who put forward the idea of counterattacking the French instead of drawing them into the trap Schlieffen had prepared. On the telephone, von Moltke's deputy told Rupprecht's Chief of Staff:

"No, we won't oblige you by forbidding an attack. You must take the responsibility. Make your own decision as your conscience tells you."

The answer was: "It is already made. We attack."

Moltke's deputy merely replied: "Not really! Then strike, and God be with you."

AUGUST 20

Thus it came about, on the 20th, as the French First and Second

armies swept forward with incomparable élan, but also with a minimum of precaution, inspired by De Castelnau's order—"The enemy is retiring on our front. . . . He must be pursued with the utmost vigor and rapidity. . . ."—that they ran full-tilt into the forward movement of the German Sixth and Seventh armies. The dense, conspicuous French lines were swept by machine-gun fire, staggered by the weight of an artillery that no amount of dash could reach. The battles of Morhange and Sarrebourg were almost unrelieved French disasters. It was small wonder if, for a short time longer, the French Grand Quartier Général (GQG) fixed its stunned attention on this sector, not noticing that the German entry into Brussels had not stopped there, but was flowing forward westward and southward, while at Namur a new bombardment was beginning, with sinister implications. The anxieties of the commander of the French Fifth Army, facing the Belgian frontier, General Charles Lanrezac, were brushed aside. He was rapidly becoming unnerved by what he learned of

"... the German right wing swung through Belgium . . ." This regiment of Belgian cavalry is retiring through Louvain, not long afterward reduced to flames, while infantry make a rough and practically useless barricade across the road.

AUGUST 21

45

the enemy's movements in front of him and by the indifference of GQG. Nor did he extract much comfort from the arrival of the British; their numbers were small, their quality unknown, and he had not formed a very high opinion of the mental caliber of their leader, Sir John French.

But the Russians were still advancing; Königsberg, capital of East Prussia, was threatened. Germany now also experienced the painful exodus of refugees from frontier districts. Both the First (Rennenkampf) and Second (Samsonov) Russian armies were well on the move, though divided from each other by the barrier of the Masurian Lakes, and with the Second Army dangerously echeloned behind the First. Much would evidently depend on the efficiency of communication between Rennenkampf and Samsonov. The Germans were amazed and delighted when they found themselves able to listen in to uncoded Russian wireless messages, including orders to both generals from Jilinsky, in overall command of the Russian northern front. Later, in the south, Conrad found himself in the same happy position, and much mockery has been directed at the backward Russians for this crassness; deliberate treachery has even been suggested. Yet even as late as October, a British intelligence officer at Ypres had his work made easier by a German corps commander doing the very same thing, and wrote in his diary: "God bless him! I'll give him a drink if ever I see him when the war is over."[3] And no doubt the British and French were sometimes guilty themselves; this was a war in which both sides had everything to learn the hard way.

Whatever the faults of their organization and method, the Russians were producing an undoubted effect. Von Prittwitz gained the unenviable distinction of being the first of a long line of senior officers in all armies to fall by the wayside; his alarmist reports of Russian progress to von Moltke so disturbed the latter that, on the 21st, he began to consider shifting large forces from the Western to the Eastern Front, and on that day, too, he sent for Ludendorff, the victor of Liége, to be Chief of Staff to General Paul von Hindenburg, who came out of retirement at the age of sixty-eight and took over from von Prittwitz on August 22nd.

"The situation looks to me very grave, and I feel it my duty to tell you so," reported De Castelnau to Joffre on the 21st. The French First and Second armies were in retreat; there was even some question of abandoning the fortified area of Nancy, the gateway to eastern France. Joffre was called upon for the first of those large drafts of healing imperturbability which, during the next fortnight, made a greater contribution to ultimate Allied victory than any other factor except the echo they

[3] Brigadier General John Charteris, *At G.H.Q.*

aroused among the fighting troops. In the Second Army itself Joffre's unyielding spirit was matched by that of General Ferdinand Foch, commanding the crack XX Corps, which now became the backbone of the defense of the heights of Nancy. Neither the pleas of General Lanrezac, whose advanced units were driven from the line of the river Sambre, nor Air reports of endless German columns filling the roads south from Brussels, affected Joffre's equilibrium. The enemy could not, he assured himself, be strong *everywhere,* and he still had a shot in his locker. His Third and Fourth armies, facing the Ardennes—the central pivot of the German battle line—were now about to enter the fray. Might it not be that the obvious strength of the enemy on the left and right flanks spelled a weakness in the center? If so, a thrust by these two armies could ruin them.

But it was not so. French military thinking had attached too exclusive an importance to the virtues of fully trained men. The Germans produced their second major tactical surprise with the use they made, from the outset, of reserve formations, and it was these that provided them with sufficient strength everywhere, if not to fulfill the grand concept of the Schlieffen Plan, at least to balk Joffre. Pressing forward impetuously, like their comrades in Lorraine, into the steep, blind, wooded country of

"... incomparable élan, but ... a minimum of precaution ..." French infantry moving into the attack; red kepis and red trousers made their lines conspicuous, excellent targets for machine guns.

the Ardennes, the French Third (Ruffey) and Fourth (De Langle de Cary) armies at once met with a similar and equally damaging check. Their 75-mm. guns were almost helpless, lacking the high-angle fire that the terrain demanded; well-handled machine guns, in positions which the French scorned to waste time over reconnoitering, cut their infantry to pieces. Routs and panics occurred, which not even the superb gallantry of the officers could stop; ignorant of modern battle conditions as these officers frequently were—"many of them thought it chic to die in white gloves"—the lavish spending of their lives in these early days left a mark on the French Army for the remainder of the War. "Où sont mes officiers?" cried a French general in despair, watching his troops march past to the counteroffensive a few weeks later. The answer was that they were lying, wasted and irreplaceable, under the battlefields of Lorraine and the Ardennes. Ten percent of the Officer Corps of the French Army fell in August alone.

August 23rd was a climactic day, on which the roar of battle rose to crescendo at both ends of the Continent. The French armies were everywhere in retreat: De Castelnau disputing every inch of ground in Lorraine, Ruffey and De Langle de Cary trying to regroup their broken commands in the center, Lanrezac defeated at Charleroi. Carried forward by the last, outermost ripples of official French optimism, and unaware of the magnitude of the disaster which had befallen their allies, the British had made their last advance to the drab industrial center of Mons, just inside the Belgian frontier. There, on this day, they clashed with the inner columns of von Kluck's host. The Germans arrived piecemeal on the battlefield, and piecemeal they were "shot flat" by the rapid, aimed musketry fire of the almost invisible British Regular infantry. At Mons alone they experienced what they themselves had inflicted upon the French elsewhere. "The rushes became shorter, and finally the whole advance came to a stop. . . . With bloody losses the attack came gradually to an end."[4]

But the British success was illusory; well into the afternoon, under the influence of his passionately Francophile Deptuy Chief of Staff, Sir Henry Wilson (the man more responsible than any other for the full integration of British movements into French plans), Sir John French was contemplating a further British advance. Neither Intelligence reports, which were full and accurate, nor the experiences of his troops deterred him, until a message from Joffre revealed more of the true situation. A fresh German Army, the Third, under General von Hausen,

[4] German Official Account.

48

"The Russian advance . . . was continuing . . ." Cossacks entering a town in East Prussia.

". . . slow-moving, cautious Rennenkampf . . ."

"... Moltke ... ordered two corps to East Prussia." German reinforcements on their way to repel the Russian invasion.

had made its presence felt on Lanrezac's right flank, in the gap between him and de Cary, forcing the Fifth Army to retreat again. Worse than that, Joffre confirmed the weight of the German deployment opposite the British. Reluctantly, the BEF withdrew: "If the Cabinet had sent six divisions instead of four, this retreat would have been an advance and defeat would have been a victory," wrote Wilson in his diary. High hopes and radiant dreams died hard, even in the searing heat of war.

The Germans did well on the Western Front on August 23rd, but their achievement was less than it might have been, and was robbed of much reward by the uncertain grip of their Supreme Headquarters (OHL), far away from the scene of battle in Coblenz on the Rhine. In the east the story would be different. The Russian advance into East

Prussia was continuing; another small victory at Frankenau brought Rennenkampf's army into Insterburg, and added to the German tale of woe. But there were resolute men on the Eighth Army staff, and none more so than Lieutenant Colonel Max Hoffmann, in charge of Operations. He proposed the daring plan of leaving the slow-moving, cautious Rennenkampf almost unopposed, while concentrating all available force against Samsonov, some fifty miles away to the south. The unfortunate von Prittwitz had already approved this scheme, and permitted preliminary movements to be set in hand, when Hindenburg and Ludendorff arrived and relieved him. With commendable decision and open-mindedness, the new team accepted Hoffmann's plan. They were sustained by encouraging news from the south, where Conrad was now engaged in an encounter battle with the Russian Fourth and Fifth armies between Przemysl and Lublin. The Battle of Krasnik opened on the day of Mons, and ended three days later with a distinct Austrian success.

During these three days, swaying fortunes in the east, and the steady forward flow of the German line of battle in the west, disguised the significance of the events which were shaping themselves in the minds of commanders. For Hindenburg and Ludendorff, there were anxious hours as their troops, entrained or on foot, swung between one sector and another. For von Moltke, the anxiety was even greater, and was not relieved by fortitude such as theirs. It had already been in his mind to transfer as many as six army corps from the west to the east; his courage revived sufficiently to whittle this number down, but on the 25th he ordered two corps to East Prussia. They were taken from the right wing

"The Battle of Krasnik . . . a distinct Austrian success." Austrian infantry advancing.

of his western forces, from the decisive area. "I admit that this was a mistake," said von Moltke afterward, "and one that was fully paid for on the Marne." Taken in conjunction with the strong detachment covering Antwerp, with further detachments for the investment of fortresses (Namur fell on the 23rd, but almost at once the Germans came up against Maubeuge, which held out until September 8th), and with losses in battle, this diversion spelled the final ruin of the Schlieffen Plan.

On the Allied side, Jilinsky and Ivanov were floundering blindly, apprehensively conscious of grave weaknesses in their armies. Some French commanders had patently lost their nerve; General Ruffey was the first to be dismissed, but the most serious case was Lanrezac, in whom the last ember of offensive spirit had now expired, so that he was no longer capable of grasping tactical opportunities. Sir John French's volatile temperament, all optimism on the 23rd, now went to the other extreme, under the impression of having been "let down" by his allies, and a preoccupation with the extrication of his army, whatever the strategic circumstances, took hold of him. It was now that the character of Joffre asserted itself. Shaken but undaunted, he applied his mind to the new problem that had unfolded itself, and fastened his attention on

what he belatedly recognized as the point of greatest danger. Joffre's personal energy, physical and mental, during these August days, was remarkable for a heavily built man of sixty-two. Traveling ceaselessly up and down his long front, appraising, dismissing, exhorting, encouraging, day by day he gripped the battle more firmly. The process began with his perception, on the 25th, that the "decisive point" was on his extreme left, the very sector where, because it was held by the British Expeditionary Force, he could give no direct orders, but would have to depend on persuasion. Something, he realized, would have to be done about this. He took the decision, against the advice of some of his staff, to form a new French Army (Sixth) under General Michel-Joseph Maunoury on the left of the British. It was the existence of this army, which Joffre alone had the power to create, that made the Battle of the Marne possible.

AUGUST 25

Ironies, contradictions, and catastrophes mounted to another climax on the 26th. Conrad's advance in Poland carried him to Lublin, and a brilliant opportunity of encircling the Russian Fifth Army then presented itself. Conrad seized it eagerly; his left and center began a long-drawn-out battle at Komarow that at once produced excellent results for the

AUGUST 26

(opposite) ". . . Namur fell . . ." A smashed Namur fort, after bombardment by Krupp and Skoda siege artillery.

"Traveling ceaselessly up and down his long front . . ." General Joffre and his staff snatch a hasty breakfast in a farmyard.

(pages 54 and 55) "Sir John French's volatile temperament . . ." Field Marshal Sir John French, the first Commander in Chief of the British Expeditionary Force, leaving his headquarters. Every inch a cavalryman, French had won a great reputation for himself as such in the South African War.

53

Austrians. But Ivanov's "steamroller" was only just entering the fray, and signalized its presence with a brisk victory over Conrad's right center at Zlotchow. Thanks to the vigor of the Serbs, the Austrian right flank was weak and vulnerable; Conrad ignored this danger, boldly bidding for a decisive win on the left. This gamble looked all the more promising as the German Eighth Army completed its redeployment against Samsonov at Tannenberg. The Russians resisted firmly at first, and there was some wavering at Hindenburg's headquarters; it was the aggressive and determined General von François, commanding the German I Corps, who settled matters by a threat to the Russian flank.

AUGUST 27

On the 27th Samsonov began to fall back southward, opening up glittering prospects for the Central Powers if Conrad could maintain momentum in his northern sector. The whole center of the Russian line—three of their six armies—might then be bagged, with the probability that they would be forced out of the War. This was such "stuff as dreams are made on." Far away on the other side of Europe, where the German Supreme Headquarters resided, it was a dream of another kind, a foreboding of humiliating defeat in the east, rather than splendid victory, which caused the two army corps set free by the fall of Namur to be entrained for Russia on the 26th. By the time they arrived the critical moment would be gone; meanwhile, on the Western Front, their absence would have dire effects.

On that front, the flaws and weaknesses both in the concept and in the execution of the great German plan were being exposed. The friction of war was at work. Extraordinary pendulum swings between dejection and wild optimism seemed to rule von Moltke's mind; fearing defeat in the east when success was in sight, on the Western Front he persisted with enterprises which had now lost all their promise. Thus the Sixth and Seventh armies, which might have fed his weakening right, were ordered to press home their attacks against Nancy and in the Vosges, in the vain hope of producing a double envelopment of the French, a super-Cannae. The German center was making progress through the Trouée de l'Oise, the classic line of advance upon Paris from the north. But on the right there were vacillation and confusion. Von Kluck and von Bülow, commanding the First and Second armies, were ill-fitted by temperament to work in double harness. Von Bülow was slow and cautious, characteristics which deprived him of many advantages over his shaken opponent, Lanrezac; von Kluck was bold but opinionated, so that his maneuvers against the British frequently lacked reality. At Le Cateau, on the 26th, the British II Corps, isolated from I Corps by a wide gap, was forced to

AUGUST 26

"... the aggressive and determined General von François ..."

stand and fight through sheer fatigue. It should have fallen an easy prey, but thanks to General Smith-Dorrien's able handling, it inflicted severe losses on the Germans before withdrawing from the battlefield in full daylight and resuming its retreat.

Le Cateau was one of the finest British achievements of the whole War; yet it was one of those tactical victories which produce exactly opposite effects on the higher plane. The British II Corps was badly knocked about, as was inevitable, but sustained by the consciousness of having fought a superior enemy to a standstill. No such knowledge upheld the British General Headquarters (GHQ), where the belief grew that half the Expeditionary Force had been to all intents lost. Joffre, meeting Sir John French on that day, formed the gloomiest view of British prospects. "When I left British Headquarters in the early afternoon," he wrote, "I carried away with me a serious impression as to the fragility of our extreme left, and I anxiously asked myself if it could hold out long enough to enable me to effect the new grouping of our forces." This new grouping, the build-up of General Maunoury's Sixth Army, now became his main care; time became a matter of increasing importance, and space expendable. But he also considered that something more than a mere yielding of space would be required if the timetable of the German advance was to be seriously checked.

East and west, the decisions of August drew nearer, to the now continuous thunder of guns—the decisions that would shape the War. A great weariness was beginning to descend upon the soldiers of all armies, stumbling down the *pavé* roads of France and Belgium, or through the dust clouds of East Prussia and Galicia, under a blazing summer sun. It was calculated that in the British Expeditionary Force during the thirteen days of retreat the infantry averaged about four hours sleep in twenty-four, the cavalry only three. Men staggered along in a daze, losing all count of time, seeing strange mirages all about them.

"Le Cateau was one of the finest British achievements . . ." Officers of the 1st Cameronians on the lookout for the enemy at Le Cateau.

(pages 60 and 61) ". . . buoyed up by the knowledge that they were advancing . . ." German artillery on the way to Paris—and looking very smart.

One of the miracles was how they were kept supplied with food and drink; the western Allies, falling back on their supply depots, enjoyed an advantage here. Before it was all over, many Germans would know what hunger was, and whole divisions of cavalry would be immobilized for want of such a simple commodity as horseshoe nails. On the other hand, the Germans were buoyed up by the knowledge that they were advancing, while the British and French suffered the chagrin of having their backs to the enemy.

No one was more irked by this than General de Langle de Cary, commanding the French Fourth Army; despite his severe losses in the Ardennes, De Langle de Cary was constantly on the lookout for chances of turning on his foes. Joffre had to restrain him, in the light of what was happening elsewhere. By contrast, it seemed that nothing could mitigate the despondency of General Lanrezac, part of whose Fifth Army was by now little better than a mob. Yet it was Lanrezac who, reluctantly, fought the one successful French counteroffensive battle of the retreat, and thereby drew the Germans into the maneuver for which they paid so dearly on the Marne. Von Kluck, after Le Cateau, had lost all track of the British Army; he swung out in a wide loop toward Amiens, clashing with the slowly assembling forces of the French Sixth Army, putting them in peril of destruction before they were even deployed. But this swing drew the German First Army well away from the Second, and exposed its long flank to an attack by the British I Corps under General Haig and Lanrezac's Fifth Army. Haig was the first to perceive the opportunity, and proposed a joint blow to Lanrezac; then Sir John French, still in the grip of his dire misgivings, forbade Haig to move. Joffre, on the other hand, went personally to Lanrezac's headquarters to make sure that he did fight.

AUGUST 29

What followed was a remarkable feat of arms, for as the French Fifth Army moved to attack the columns of the German First Army passing down the river Oise, the German Second Army came into action on the right flank of the French. With great adroitness, in the full confusion of battle, Lanrezac swung his Army round, and defeated the Second Army at Guise. Von Bülow immediately uttered a loud cry for help, and it was this that caused von Kluck to turn his march inward from Amiens, leaving the French Sixth Army in relative peace and bringing the Germans across the face of the Paris defenses, instead of encircling them from the west as von Schlieffen had intended. None of this was clear at the time, but day by day the picture would clarify, until at last Joffre's invincible resolution found its reward.

It was as well that the promise of such an advantage unfolded in the west, for the news which reached him from his eastern allies was discouraging in the extreme. Von François' boldness had paid its dividends. The day of the Battle of Guise was also the day of fullest intensity at Tannenberg, where the Russians were now in full retreat and dire confusion. "It was like herding stock into a corral, and the head cowboy was François." [5] By the 30th, the Russian Second Army had disintegrated; 90,000 prisoners were taken by the Germans. General Samsonov, threatened with capture, shot himself in a wood. The northern pincer of the Central Powers' offensive had done brilliantly; could Conrad match this performance? He could not. Ivanov's southern armies, the Fifth (Russki) and Eighth (Brusilov), were now in full flood, sweeping away Conrad's right wing, pinning his center back against Lemberg. The armies which

[5] Cyril Falls, *op. cit.*

". . . Germany . . . found herself 'fettered to a corpse.'" Austrian wounded being treated at a field dressing station.

should have marched to meet their German allies in the destruction of the Russian center had to fall back with severe losses, and at the grave risk of being cut off as Samsonov had been. Conrad had been too bold; now, while Hindenburg turned on Rennenkampf, the Austrians were forced into a retreat that carried them back 200 miles and brought their total losses against the Russians to some 350,000 men. Added to the cost of their battles with the Serbs, such a figure spelled ruin for the Habsburg Empire. The damage done in these early days could have been repaired only by swift victory and peace; neither was obtained. From 1914 onward, Germany, in the blunt phrase of certain staff officers, found herself "fettered to a corpse." Yet it was amazing how long the "corpse" would be able to go on kicking.

September came with the Germans everywhere victorious; on the Allied side only Brusilov, one of the outstanding commanders of the war, and the Serbs were making progress. On the 2nd the French Government left Paris and established itself in Bordeaux. The retirement of the French Sixth Army had now brought it within the region of the Paris defenses, commanded by General Galliéni. Galliéni was one of France's most distinguished soldiers, the only possible rival in stature to Joffre; for that very reason, unfortunately, relations between the two men were always cool. But their minds now reached out, independently, toward the same solution. Joffre told the Minister of War on the 2nd that he would resume the offensive "in a very short time." On the 3rd he ordered Galliéni to threaten the flank of von Kluck's army, becoming daily more exposed, with the French Sixth Army; Galliéni had anticipated such an order by already commanding the Sixth Army to halt its retreat. The

next day brought considerable clarification of the position to both sides. Von Kluck was now in full progress across the front of the Paris garrison and the BEF—which he had rashly written off—with the French Sixth Army poised on his right rear, and his leading columns in action against the Fifth Army at Montmirail, fifty miles *east* of Paris. The German Second Army was a day's march to the north of him, and the Third echeloned behind that. One of von Kluck's officers described this stage of the advance: "The men stagger forward, their faces coated with dust, their uniform in rags, they look like living scarecrows. They march with their eyes closed, singing in chorus so that they shall not fall asleep on the march. The certainty of early victory and of triumphal entry into Paris keeps them going and acts as a spur to their enthusiasm. Without this certainty of victory they would fall exhausted." At German Supreme Headquarters the certainty was much diminished. "Victory means annihilation of the enemy's power of resistance. When armies of millions of men are opposed, the victor has prisoners. Where are ours?" von Moltke was asking. It was a fair question. The truth, exposed vividly by Allied Air reconnaissance, was that the whole of the German right wing was now thrusting itself into a huge sack formed by the French Sixth Army, the BEF, the French Fifth Army, a new Ninth Army under Foch, and the Fourth Army. "The situation was impressive," wrote Joffre.

The final dispositions which would reverse the movement of this whole retreating line, 150 miles long from the tip of Maunoury's left flank in the west to the pivot of Verdun in the east, were inevitably somewhat confused. The greatest uncertainty surrounded the role of the BEF, which once again found itself in a vital sector. At the lowest ebb of his spirits, Sir John French had informed the British Government of his intention "to begin my retirement tomorrow in the morning behind the Seine, in a southwesterly direction west of Paris. This means marching for some 8 days without fatiguing the troops at a considerable distance from the enemy. . . ." This astounding plan brought Lord Kitchener posthaste to France on September 1st, and in a stormy interview French was overruled and ordered to cooperate with his allies. Now, on the 4th, as Joffre prepared his orders for the great about-turn, two separate sets of French emissaries were concerting this cooperation with the British: General Galliéni was conferring with Sir Archibald Murray, French's Chief of Staff; General Franchet d'Esperey, who had taken over the Fifth Army from Lanrezac, was talking at the same time to Murray's deputy, Wilson. What was agreed at the two meetings was the same in broad intention, but different in significant detail. Galliéni, from his post in Paris, perceived that a great opportunity was presenting itself in his sector, and wished to grasp it as soon as possible, knowing that such chances are not often repeated in war. D'Esperey, who had taken command of a shaken, partly demoralized Army only twenty-four hours earlier, would have preferred to wait, but was willing to take part in a *general action.* "My Army can fight on the 6th," he told Joffre, "but its condition is far from brilliant." The plan which he put forward involved three armies besides his own, and it was this plan that Joffre adopted. The BEF, however, was acting on Galliéni's proposals. It is small wonder that such misunderstandings should occur in the existing circumstances. The result was a time lag between French and British movements on the 6th, when the great counteroffensive began.

It was Maunoury who started the ball rolling, on September 5th,

SEPTEMBER 4

65

(pages 66 and 67) ". . . within the region of the Paris defenses . . ." A street barricade constructed in Paris as the Germans came near.

SEPTEMBER 5

SEPTEMBER 6

striking at the rear of von Kluck's First Army along the river Ourcq. The distinguishing feature of the first part of the Battle of the Marne was the progressive diversion of corps after corps of the German First Army to face Maunoury; von Kluck's tired soldiers fought well, and the French Sixth Army was often hard put to it to hold its ground against their counterattacks; but it was this diversion which caused the fatal gap to open between the German First Army and the Second. The 6th of September was the Day—yet another of those swelling choruses of combat for which the first month of the War is known. Von Hindenburg was marching his forces to the north in a furious attempt to pin Rennenkampf against the Baltic shore. Ivanov was hammering the Austrians back toward Lemberg, driving in their center at Rawa Russka. Prince Rupprecht was unleasing a new, determined offensive by the German Sixth Army against De Castelnau's position along the chain of heights known as the Grand Couronné de Nancy. The stubborn French defense in this sector contributed as much to the victory of the Marne as any

68

(opposite) "It was Maunoury who started the ball rolling . . ." General Maunoury (left) with an A.D.C.

"Gallieni was one of France's most distinguished soldiers . . ."

other part of the Allied effort. To the remainder of his battle line, Joffre said:

"At the moment when the battle upon which hangs the fate of the country is about to begin, all must remember that the time for looking back is past; every effort must be concentrated on attacking and throwing the enemy back. . . . Under present conditions no weakness can be tolerated."

The Battle of the Marne was a confused, swaying struggle across open fields, over rivers, up and down wooded slopes, through old-fashioned, pretty villages. Fortunes were mixed. Maunoury was often forced back on the defensive, and at one stage had to be reinforced by a brigade rushed out from Paris in taxicabs—the first tactical use of motorized infantry in a War that was full of innovations. Foch fought a mainly defensive battle in characteristic style. But the key elements were the Fifth Army, urged on by the ruthless energy of Franchet d'Esperey, and the BEF, facing the growing gap between von Bülow and von Kluck. The British advance, despite the enthusiasm of all ranks, was not dashing; starting late, from too far back, it displayed great caution. "I thought our movements very slow today, in view of the fact that the enemy was on the run!" recorded General Haig on the 7th. Two days

". . . rushed out from Paris in taxicabs . . ." A survivor of the "taxis of the Marne."

later he was urging on a hesitant cavalry brigade: "I explained . . . that a little effort now might mean the conclusion of the War! The enemy was running back. It was the duty of each one of us to strain every effort to keep him on the run."

Slow as it was, the British advance was decisive. Their very reappearance was unnerving for an enemy who had dismissed them from his calculations; and this was a battle that was fought as much by the nerve of commanders as by the impact of troops. By the 8th, von Bülow's nerve was in a very poor condition. When von Moltke's liaison officer, Lieutenant Colonel Hentsch, visited him on that day, von Bülow stated that he thought retreat unavoidable; Hentsch went on to von Kluck's headquarters, where the atmosphere was somewhat different, but by then he knew that the British were actually behind the German First Army, and he knew, too, how von Bülow's mind was working. He used the powers of command that von Moltke had given him, and ordered the First Army to retreat toward Soissons. The whole German line progressively gave way as far east as Verdun, until by the 13th their right wing was back on the steep ridge that skirts the north bank of the river Aisne. This ridge, known as the Chemin des Dames (from the road made by Louis XV as a drive for the royal princesses), running for some

SEPTEMBER 8

"'The enemy was running back.'" German infantry, on the defensive, manning a street barricade.

"... ordered the First Army to retreat toward Soissons." Dead soldiers and civilians at a street corner in Soissons after a lightning raid by Germans in motorcars.

twenty miles between Soissons and Berry-au-Bac, with its superb observation northward across the valley of the river Ailette, and southward across that of the Aisne, with its many spurs jutting out like bastions from an ancient castle, forms one of the finest defensive positions in all France. Yet it was only by a remarkable chain of the accidents of war that the Germans did not lose it.

Two hours separated disaster from security for the Germans. The fortress of Maubeuge, invested on August 25th, had stoutly resisted until September 8th; its fall released the VII Reserve Corps, which was at once set in motion toward the Aisne. Meanwhile, the British had worked up some acceleration. On September 13th units of their I and II Corps briskly crossed the Aisne by bridges which the Germans had failed to destroy and by other means. A German witness has described the scene: "From the bushes bordering the river sprang up and advanced a second line of skirmishers, with at least ten paces interval from man to man.

Our artillery flashed and hit—naturally, at most, a single man. And the second line held on and pushed always nearer and nearer. Two hundred yards behind it came a third wave, a fourth wave. Our artillery fired like mad: all in vain, a fifth, a sixth line came on, all with good distance, and with clear intervals between the men. Splendid, we are all filled with admiration."

The British I Corps faced the thinnest sector of the German defense —the famous "gap" itself. General Sir Douglas Haig pushed his brigades forward up the spurs leading to the Chemin des Dames ridge, as one by one they completed their crossings; IInd Corps was well up on the left, the French Fifth Army apparently advancing successfully on the right. "The prospects of a break-through were never brighter." [6] At 1:00 P.M. the British 1st Division was ready to advance again. But the Germans had arrived. General von Zwehl had brought his VII Reserve Corps to the scene by a forced march of forty miles in twenty-four hours. Nearly a quarter of his infantry had fallen out along the way, but the rest were there. At 11:00 A.M. on the 13th they were on the crest of the Chemin des Dames, facing Haig's Corps. General von Bülow, anxious and alarmist as ever, ordered von Zwehl to continue his march eastward to assist the right flank of the Second Army; the fatigue of the VII Reserve Corps came to Germany's rescue. Von Zwehl ignored the order, and stayed where he was; the British advance was blocked.

SEPTEMBER 13

This was the turning point not only of the battle but also of the War. On the 14th Haig's Corps forced its way onto the crest of the main ridge at Cerny (where over 12,000 Frenchmen and Germans lie buried in a great double cemetery today). But von Zwehl's Corps was merely the advance guard of a new German Seventh Army which was being created between the Second and the First. The British reached the top, only to be attacked themselves, and an all-out struggle began. Here, along the Aisne, between the woods and across the spurs and through the trim little stone villages, a new phenomenon was seen as both sides gritted their teeth and clung to their positions: trench warfare. Here the first hint of the War's great stalemate was given. By October 1st, when the battle had continued for a fortnight with mounting losses and no perceptible gain to either party, Haig commented: "In front of this Corps, and for many miles on either side, affairs have reached a deadlock, and no decision seems possible in this area." He was right. The Allied and German High Commands would have to try a different strategy, and neither was slow to do this. The "Race to the Sea" began.

OCTOBER 1

[6] *British Official History*, 1914, I, 331.

73

"... a grim slugging match under the chilly autumn rain ..." A German transport column smashed by the fire of French 75-mm. guns.

SEPTEMBER 3
SEPTEMBER 24

So ended the month of September. In the east, Fortune smiled equivocally. East Prussia was cleared of Russian troops, but Rennenkampf's Army had escaped the German claws; the Austrians had lost Lemberg; Przemysl was invested; the southern Russian armies were threatening Silesia. A new Austro-German campaign would evidently have to be mounted. But in the west, Germany's plans were in ruins. No amount of skillful resistance along the Aisne, no degree of vigor or ferocity at Nancy or Verdun, could alter this. The Allied victory may have ended in a grim slugging match under the chilly autumn rain; it may have been cheated of spectacular climacterics such as the rout of the Grand Army after Waterloo, or the laying down of arms at Appomattox. But it was nonetheless real. It spelled the collapse of the *only*

74

plan by which Germany had hoped to win the swift victory "without a tomorrow" that she needed. Now her prospects were confined to the dreaded war on two fronts, alongside an ally whose defects had been disastrously exposed. A terrible equation was about to be expounded: the balance between the modern world's ability to inflict damage and the capacity of its swollen populations to endure that damage. Before this ominous balance could be disturbed, some new advance would be needed on the technological front, which now became, and remained, as decisive as any battlefront. Neither side was backward in seeking both strategic or tactical remedies and the technical solutions of their dilemma. But these would require time; and during that time it was impossible to forecast how many men would die.

4 THE PLAN FAILS

"Good-morning; good-morning!" the General said
When we met him last week on our way to the Line.
Now the soldiers he smiled at are most of 'em dead,
And we're cursing his staff for incompetent swine.
"He's a cheery old card," grunted Harry to Jack
As they slogged up to Arras with rifle and pack. . . .
But he did for them both by his plan of attack.

SIEGFRIED SASSOON, "THE GENERAL," 1917

For Harry and Jack, Philippe, Fritz, Ivan, Mahmud, and Khudadad, the War was now about to don its familiar features, to become the vortex in which, one by one or by thousands, they would be swept away. In the west, until the Battle of the Aisne, no matter how stern the struggle on the battlefield, no matter how arduous the human effort put forth, the decisive point was inside the minds of generals, and their acts were crucial. For a few weeks afterward their role continued to be prominent; but it was at the Aisne that the lineaments of the "soldiers' war" were first seen. Here the unimaginable price that either side was prepared to pay for the gain of a few yards of ground was suddenly realized. Generalship seemed unavailing, either to reduce the price or to increase the

". . . new place names were added to the war's geography . . ." The Germans had passed through Amiens, and vanished again. Now the French returned, and Amiens became, to its sorrow, one of the most famous of the front-line towns. These men look like Territorials, belonging to an older age group than those in the active army.

gain. In the east, seesaw movements of hundreds of miles produced exactly the same results as the inching back and forward of the Western Front. All fronts, all armies, all commanders, encountered the various aspects of a deadlock which was now clenching its grip. Small wonder if, as the dreadful years ticked by, men in all countries shared the bitterness of the English soldier-poet, Siegfried Sassoon; small wonder if an enduring myth was born. It is not the universal folly of that generation's generals which is to blame for what followed; it is the folly of mankind, from which later generations are not exempt.

Nothing could be more absurd than the part of the myth which asserts that the generals of the First World War could imagine no further than an endless series of frontal attacks on heavily defended positions. The whole point of the Schlieffen Plan, which had brought the right wing of the German Army from Aachen to Paris, was a vast flank march of nearly 200 miles as the crow flies, but actually much farther on the ground. The Battle of the Marne was based on a flank attack. Tannenberg was another flanking maneuver. The fall of Lemberg and the subsequent Austrian retreat were brought about by the threat of Russian encirclement of a flank. The German retreat to the Aisne was due to Allied pressure against inner flanks; when this was countered, the first thought of generals on both sides was to act against another exposed flank wherever it might be found. By railway, by automobile, on horseback, but mainly on foot, the two lines of battle extended themselves in the only direction possible: northward, since already their other extremity rested on the neutral frontier of Switzerland. Both contemplated the violation of this neutrality. But Switzerland is not Belgium; her mountains provided a surer guarantee than any fickle treaty. Northward it had to be.

The phrase "Race to the Sea" is misleading. Neither side was at all concerned with the sea; each was looking for the lever by which it might uproot the enemy from forbidding defenses. The "race" began as a crawl, an instinctive edging to the right by the Germans, to the left by the Allies. Von Moltke had been superseded by now, the first and one of the most palpable failures at the topmost level of command. He was replaced by fifty-three-year-old General Erich von Falkenhayn, the Prussian Minister of War, a man of decided ideas who possessed the nerve which von Moltke had conspicuously lacked. His authority gave to what might otherwise have been a somewhat incoherent movement such a degree of control that in the following weeks the French found themselves always "twenty-four hours and an Army Corps behind the

". . . an advance upon Warsaw." German troops marching along a railway track beside a road. On the Eastern Front communications were a constant problem to both sides. Roads were few, extremely dusty in summer, and likely to turn to quagmires with the first rains. Wheeled vehicles would have to follow them; these infantry probably found it easier to march along the ballasted railway line.

enemy." On their side, as Joffre steadily stripped his right and center to feed his left, with De Castelnau coming straight from his furious fights on the Meuse to command in equally stern battles on the Somme, another figure of stature and decision emerged. General Ferdinand Foch, who had begun the War only thirty-seven days earlier as a corps commander under De Castelnau, now took precedence over him, with the task of coordinating the action of all the Allies in the northern sector. These included the Belgians in their fortress of Antwerp, and the BEF, which Joffre began to transfer on October 1st (at Sir John French's suggestion) to the area where it would cover the Channel ports on which it depended for its very existence.

Once again the roar of battle swelled; new place names were added to the War's geography; localities which had hoped to be spared were laid in ruins. On the day that the British Army began to move from the steep slopes of the Aisne to the flats of Flanders, von Hindenburg embarked upon the campaign that was intended to retrieve the fortunes of his Austrian allies—an advance upon Warsaw. At first all went well; in both theaters prospects of a German success which might yet end the War before the close of the year were briefly revived. The great Austrian howitzers which had tumbled Liége and Namur were turned on Antwerp, with the same devastating results. De Castelnau was hard pressed in Picardy. As the British arrived, corps by corps, in Flanders, their advances were successively checked by growing German forces. Warsaw and Ivangorod were both assailed. But the Russians slid out of the net

OCTOBER 1, 1914

SEPTEMBER 28

OCTOBER 9

79

"The great Austrian howitzers . . . were turned on Antwerp . . ." When the bombardment of the city began, thousands of people fled by sea to Britain and Holland. This is the scene near the bridge of boats across the Scheldt to neutral Dutch territory. A group of soldiers (left and center foreground) is trying to force its way through the throng. A British officer stands beside the halted car.

prepared for them, and now unfolded their own threat to German Silesia. The Belgian field army—supported by the bulk of a British Marine division which Mr. Churchill had improvised and rushed to their aid—escaped from the crumbling forts of Antwerp, down the Belgian coast, to link up with the rest of Foch's forces. De Castelnau held on, and the last of the British, Haig's I Corps, arrived at Ypres in time to meet the final great German throw of the year.

Ypres, a quiet, dignified Flemish market town of some 16,000 in-

"The Belgian field army . . . escaped . . . down the coast . . ." A typical level crossing, with the road column halted to let the train pass.

habitants was, strategically speaking, the outlying bastion of the port of Dunkerque. To the north of it lies a region below sea level, depending on a complex drainage system; northeast, east, and southeast, gentle, almost imperceptible undulations ring the town. In any other country but the Flanders plain, these slopes, nowhere more than 180 feet high, would be insignificant; but from their puny crests it is possible to look right back to the moat and ramparts of Ypres, surmounted by the spires of St. Martin's Cathedral and the famous Cloth Hall. These are the

"... students, full of the irrational enthusiasm of 1914 ..." Young German recruits getting ready for the march. Some of them have garlands and ribbons tied to the spikes of their helmets.

"... the battle was in full swing." German artillerymen manhandling a gun into position, November 1914. Note that they are still wearing full-dress uniforms, not the field gray of the infantry.

84

"ridges," shortly to be fought over in the fiercest series of battles of the War, and to be stained with the blood of tens of thousands. In October 1914 Ypres was the objective toward which the German Army strained with the remainder of its might; the Kaiser and his entourage, already cheated of more than one triumphal entry, arrived upon the scene to accompany the German occupation of the town.

The advance began on October 17th, weighted by the presence of four new reserve corps (eight divisions) which had been extemporized by the German War Minister after the outbreak of war. These units were composed mainly of volunteers—a radical departure from normal German recruiting methods. Many of them were students, full of the irrational enthusiasm of 1914; the fate of these relatively untrained "young soldiers' divisions" would be as tragic as that of their British

". . . the British 1st Corps arrived in the line . . ." Lieutenant General (later Field Marshal) Sir Douglas Haig (left) talking to Major General Sir Charles Munro, commanding the 2nd Division, who was wounded at Ypres. Brigadier General Sir John Gough is second from the right, facing the camera; he was killed early in 1915.

OCTOBER 28

counterparts in later years. By the 20th the battle was in full swing. Characteristically, up to that date, despite the increasing strength of the German forces, the Allies themselves, under General Foch's fiery leadership, were trying to take the offensive, and the fighting took the form of head-on encounters. The 20th was the day on which the British I Corps arrived in the line northeast of Ypres; their orders were to press forward, with Bruges and Ghent, about 40 miles away, as their objectives. But the true state of affairs quickly became apparent. By the 28th, after a grim sequence of defensive battles along the whole front from the sea

". . . inflicted prohibitive losses on the Germans." A remarkable picture of British infantry in rough trenches, awaiting a rush of Germans across the open (left middle distance).

to Armentières, the Germans had been stopped—but only just. In the southern sector, the shooting of the British infantry and dismounted cavalry had had its usual effect; from the wet lowland around La Bassée to the excellent defensive positions along the Messines Ridge, they inflicted prohibitive losses on the Germans. Farther north, however, the Belgians and French Marines on the Yser River were severely hammered; the French held Dixmude by the skin of their teeth; the Belgians saved their line by letting in the sea at Nieuport, to flood the low country. It had been a near thing. The disappointment of the German High

Command was not diminished by the knowledge that von Hindenburg was in full retreat before a new Russian advance at Warsaw, and clamoring for help.

On the last day of October, Falkenhayn scraped together the last reinforcements he could find, and sent them eastward. And on that day the Ypres battle came to its second crisis. This time the main attack came

"... the Belgians and French ... were severely hammered ..." This French detachment is moving up to support the Belgians along the Yser Canal.

(opposite) "... the Belgians saved their line ..." King Albert of Belgium (left) talking to a French officer in Furnes, the last corner of Belgian soil unoccupied by the Germans. In the background, French Tirailleurs Algériens.

from the southeast, between Messines and the hamlet of Gheluvelt, on the Ypres-Menin Road. The British line gave way; General Haig mounted his horse and led his staff and escort down the road, as though on parade, to steady the retiring troops. His two divisional commanders both fell casualties to a single shell. Sir John French made a personal appeal to Foch for aid, adding that if it did not come there would be "nothing left for him to do but to go up and get killed with the British I Corps."[1]

Then the miracle occurred. In this war of Army Groups, Armies, Army Corps, Divisions, this war of impersonal masses, one battalion, the 2nd Worcestershire Regiment, about 350 strong, retook Gheluvelt, and the German attack was stopped. It was the last time that such a handful

[1] Foch, *Memoirs*.

88

would be able to produce such an effect—the last flourish of the old British Regular tradition.

Once again, it had been touch and go. Not until the Battle of Verdun in 1916 would the Allied cause in the west be faced with such a rapidly recurring series of crises. The next came, after an "interval" (barely perceptible to the front-line troops), on November 11th, four years to the day from the end of the war itself. A division of the Prussian Guard burst through the ragged British line, a jumble of battered units from both Ist and IInd Corps, north of the Menin Road. All through the war, responsible for many of its frustrations, the spectacle would be seen of troops of both sides, successful in their first hard task of breaking the enemy's front, hesitating, pausing in confusion, lacking direction, losing their impetus, and halting with victory in sight. This was such an occasion. "Among the garden enclosures," says one German regimental history, "the leaderless lines abandoned the forward movement and drifted to the right. . . . As no reinforcements could be got to the attackers, the assault came to a standstill at the third of the British lines. The scattered groups dug themselves in." In fact, there was no "third" British line; there were only a few "strong points," constructed for all-round defense at the insistence of General Haig, and the line of British guns. A wounded German officer who was captured and led through the British artillery position asked, "Where are your reserves?" His answer was a wave of the hand, indicating the guns themselves, some firing at point-blank range. "What is there behind?" he inquired. The reply was, "Divisional headquarters." "God Almighty!" he exclaimed. By so narrow a margin was disaster averted. In the evening, in a down-

". . . the Ypres battle came to its second crisis." British Light Infantry resting, and taking cover from shrapnel, behind a wall during the First Battle of Ypres.

pour of blinding rain, a few small British groups counterattacked, and regained important parts of the lost ground. One of the heroes of the defense, Brigadier General FitzClarence, was killed, but his efforts, and those of his remarkable soldiers, had defeated the cream of the German Army: "They had little else except heavy casualties to show for their final and desperate attempt to break through."[2]

The significance of the First Battle of Ypres can hardly be overrated. The intentions of both sides were thoroughly aggressive, though tempered by the experience they had undergone. Thus Foch tells us that, on the Allied side: "The idea dominating our tactics was that, in view of our feeble armament, notably in artillery and machine guns,[3] we were powerless to break through the front of an enemy who had had time to organize the ground, construct trenches and protect them with wire entanglements. Our plan, therefore, was to forestall him, assail him while he was in full manoeuvre, assault him with troops full of dash before he could organize his defence and bring his powerful armament into play." The battle, says Foch, "was an attempt to exploit the last vestige of our victory on the Marne."

The Germans recognized the offensive character of the Allied operations, and met them with stronger offensives of their own. Falkenhayn tells us: "Not only had the danger that the Germans would be finally cut off from the Belgian coast again become acute, but also the danger of an effective encirclement of the right wing. They both had to be removed unconditionally." German objectives were twofold: to consolidate their grip on the captured territory of Belgium and northern France, and to prepare from that region "the drastic action against England and her sea traffic with submarines, airplanes and airships . . . as a reply to England's war of starvation. . . ."

The fighting, as may be supposed, was of the bitterest kind. The losses of the young German reserve divisions reached such proportions that the battle became known as the *Kindermord von Ypern*—"The Massacre of the Innocents at Ypres." The soldier-writer Rudolph Binding wrote on October 27th: ". . . these young fellows we have, only just trained, are too helpless, particularly when the officers have been killed. Our light infantry battalion, almost all Marburg students . . . have suffered terribly from shellfire. In the next division, just such young souls, the intellectual flower of Germany, went singing into an attack on Langemarck, just as vain and just as costly." On November 1st he

[2] *British Official History.*

[3] On October 30th the Germans used 260 heavy guns; the BEF never deployed more than 54.

wrote: "I can see no strategy in this manner of conducting operations." On the 8th he added: "We are still stuck here for perfectly good reasons; one might as well say for perfectly bad reasons." One platoon of the Gordon Highlanders counted 240 German dead in front of it on one day.

The ordeal of the Allies was equally severe. Because the whole strength of the Expeditionary Force was committed to this battle, because it drew in more soldiers than any previous single engagement in British history, and because the casualties were so high, a tendency immediately appeared to treat the First Battle of Ypres as a specially British affair. The French, not unnaturally, found this annoying. Foch wrote: "On October 31st the French held about fifteen miles of the front, the British twelve. On November 5th, the French held eighteen miles and the British nine. It can be seen that the French troops, both as to length of front occupied and numbers engaged, had to sustain the major part of the battle. It would therefore be contrary to the truth to speak of the battle and victory of Ypres as exclusively British." This argument, with its references to relative numbers and lengths of front, would be repeated more or less acrimoniously throughout the War. At "First Ypres" it was fair enough; the French were the mainstay of the battle, whether stiffening the resistance of the Belgians in the north or supporting the hard-pressed British in the center, or endeavoring to push forward their own vain offensives.

As always, when the troops of several nationalities are involved, there was some bickering; complaints of being "let down" were frequently heard. But, as a matter of hard fact, this battle afforded the best example of close cooperation between nationalities of the entire War. As local commanders responded to the urgent appeals of their neighbors, irrespective of nationality, formations became thoroughly mixed up, with French battalions, regiments, or brigades interspersed among the British, and vice versa. This could only have worked with good will. The name of General Dubois, commanding the French IX Corps, deserves to be remembered as that of a man who set loyalty to the Allied cause as a whole above any other consideration.

As the battle wore on, the condition of all combatants became steadily more depressing. By November 11th, the day of the final crisis, the *British Official History* records: "For the infantry in the front line and the fighting staffs there was nothing to do but lie at the bottom of the trenches and in the holes in the ground, which, when they had a few planks, a door, or some branches, and a few inches of earth over them, were in those days called 'dug-outs.' The British battalions had now been fighting continuously for three weeks, practically without relief or rest, under all the hardships of wet and cold in the open, and to many of the infantry it seemed that the end was now at hand. Without losing heart or faith in the final victory, they had ceased to feel that their lives were any longer their own."

Inevitably, there were failures of morale in all the armies. Haig startled King George V later by telling him "of the crowds of fugitives who came back down the Menin Road from time to time during the Ypres Battle, having thrown everything they could, including their rifles and packs, in order to escape, with a look of absolute terror on their faces, such as I have never before seen on any human being's face." No human beings had ever before had their nerves exposed to such laceration; the wonder is that flesh and blood could stand it—and far worse things still, as the War continued. But for Britain the ultimate significance of "First Ypres" lay in the losses sustained. They amounted to 58,000 officers and men, bringing the total for the War so far to 89,000—more than all the infantry of the first seven Regular divisions. "The old British Army was gone past recall, leaving but a remnant to carry on the training of the New Armies; but the framework that remained had gained an experience and confidence which was to make those armies invincible."[4]

For both sides, the battle ended in frustration, a deadlock which found its perfect expression in the now continuous trench lines, stretching from the sea to Switzerland, haphazard, just as the ebb and flow of action had left them, presenting the unique spectacle of a Continental war in which no flanks existed anywhere. The nature of this conflict was now becoming plain, and thoughtful men were appalled at what they perceived. Rudolph Binding, in his gloomy billet in Flanders, found time to set his feelings down: "When one sees the wasting, burning villages and towns, plundered cellars and attics in which the troops have pulled everything to pieces in the blind instinct of self-preservation, dead or half-starved animals, cattle bellowing in the sugar-beet fields, and then corpses, corpses, and corpses, streams of wounded one after another—then everything becomes senseless, a lunacy, a horrible bad joke of peoples and their history, an endless reproach to mankind, a negation of all civilization, killing all belief in the capacity of mankind and men for progress, a desecration of what is holy, so that one feels that all human beings are doomed in this war."

It was of the nature of the whole experience that, while the Battle of Ypres ascended to its pinnacle of ferocity, savage fighting also proceeded

[4] *British Official History.*

(pages 94 and 95) "... in his gloomy billet in Flanders . . ." As the line stabilized, the Germans had occasion to regret the deliberate burning of houses and villages, which could have given them shelter during the winter. These men were no doubt just passing through the wrecked farmyard—hence their cheerfulness.

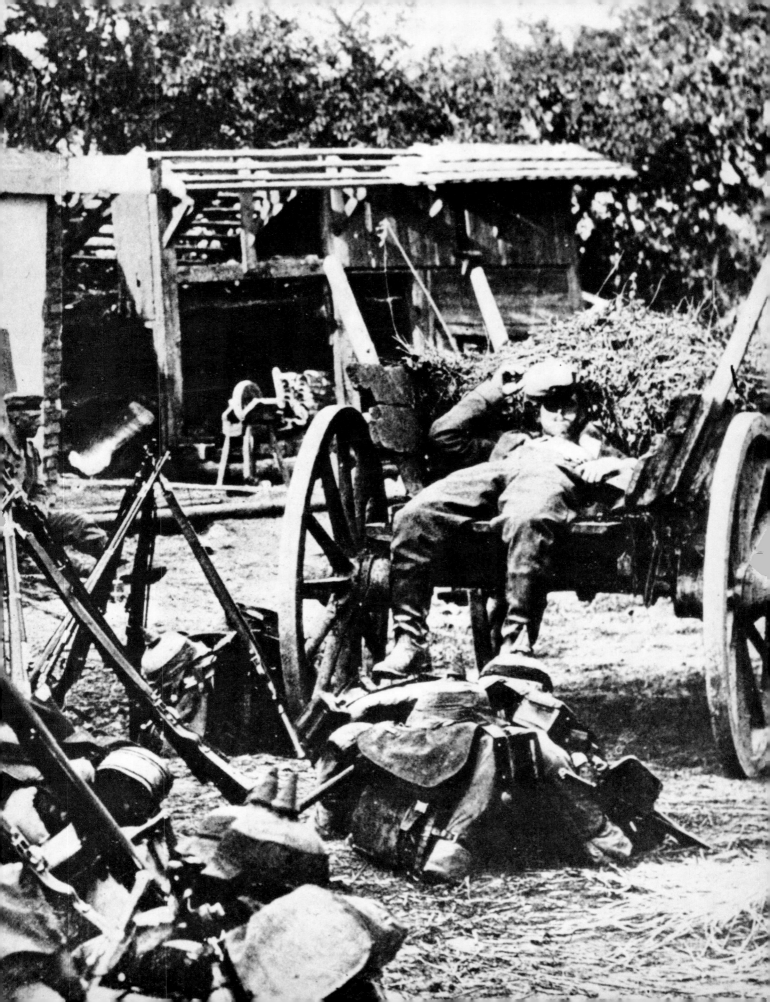

in the east, and no sooner was either dreadful encounter ended than the remorseless interior momentum of events brought on another. All through November the Eastern Front flamed furiously. The victors of Tannenberg found the going harder now. Von Hindenburg's offensive against Warsaw was launched on November 11th, on the day when the Prussian Guard came crashing down the Menin Road; its success was no better than theirs. Indeed, on the right flank of the German line, near Lodz, three German divisions were encircled by the Russians, who anticipated a Tannenberg in reverse, and brought up special trains to take away the prisoners they expected to capture. But the job was bungled, and the German divisions broke out, creating a convenient legend that covered the failure of their main operation. To the north and south of Hindenburg's attempted drive, the Central Powers found themselves in even worse difficulties. At one end of the front, the Russians again forced their way into East Prussia, while at the other they drove the Austrians back to the crests of the Carpathian Mountains, capturing the Dukla Pass. But they could advance no further. Already

(above) ". . . drove the Austrians back to the crests of the Carpathians . . ." An Austrian 305-mm. (12-inch) howitzer in action in the Carpathians in 1914.

(opposite) ". . . the crests of the Carpathian Mountains . . ." A view near the summit of the Dukla Pass.

NOVEMBER 30

shortages of ammunition and technical equipment were having a serious effect on the Russian Army; for the recruits in the depots only one rifle was available for every ten men. The low level of education of many junior commanders was another grave drawback. Uncoded wireless messages continued to provide the enemy with vital information. Considering all these disadvantages, added to their terrible losses—the Germans claimed 135,000 prisoners in the Warsaw offensive, and admitted to 100,000 casualties of their own, of whom 36,000 "were laid to their last rest in the fighting area"—the Russian achievement in 1914 was astounding. It was to have a decisive effect on the next year's campaigns, when the German High Command took the decision to transfer the main weight of its operations to the east, and the Western Allies responded with all-out attempts to take advantage of the shift.

Indeed, its effects were felt before 1915 was born. The first major movements of German forces from west to east began on November 17th, when failure at Ypres was accepted; eight divisions were transferred during the next three weeks. This did not escape the notice of the French Intelligence. Nor was Joffre the man to let such an apparent opportunity slip by. On November 30th he ordered his armies, from Flanders to the Vosges, to prepare to take offensive action; the French attacks began on December 8th, when Foch opened what later became known as the First Battle of Artois, the first of many costly disappointments in that drab region. The weakened BEF made pathetic efforts to join in the French attack; their complete failure added an unnecessary footnote to the depression which surrounded the ending of the year. Nor were the French themselves more fortunate. Six Armies went into the attack. "In all cases," says Joffre, "the results obtained were very poor. . . . It was evident that we should have to make stupendous efforts if we were to succeed in uprooting the Germans from our soil." In this winter fighting, the gloomy omens for 1915 could be perceived.

(opposite, top) ". . . the Russian achievement . . . was astounding." This astonishing picture shows one of the innumerable Russian infantry attacks in mass taking place. It can only have been taken from the German (or Austrian) front line, by a very cool photographer, at the moment that the defenders opened fire. The first casualties may be seen, some in the act of falling, in the leading Russian rank.

(opposite, bottom) ". . . from Flanders to the Vosges..." General Joffre and General de Maud'huy mounted on mules to reach French positions in the Vosges.

"... deliberate building of an Imperial German Navy ..." The Kaiser, with Grand Admiral Alfred von Tirpitz (center), the creator of the High Seas Fleet, and Admiral von Holtzendorff.

"... a new battleship of revolutionary design ..." H.M.S. Dreadnought in 1907.

SEA-POWER AND SIDE SHOWS 5

. . . too many British historians and self-styled experts in strategy have . . . made preposterous claims for sea power, claims both contrary to common sense and founded on distortion of history.

CYRIL FALLS, THE FIRST WORLD WAR

For 111 years the supremacy of the Royal Navy on the world's waters was not seriously put to the test; in all that long span of time between Trafalgar (October 21, 1805) and Jutland (May 31, 1916) the British were not engaged in one major fleet action. By 1914 the consequences of such unchallenged sway were taken for granted; yet three forces were already at work which spelled its undoing. One of these was political: the Kaiser's deliberate building of an Imperial German Navy which could have no significant role other than as a threat to Britain's sea power. The decline of Anglo-German relations during the decade before the war was attributable to this factor above any other. Lloyd George (then Chancellor of the Exchequer) has recorded that, in July 1908, he and Sir Edward Grey, the Foreign Secretary, lunched with Count Metternich, the German Ambassador in London, and discussed how relations might be improved by a reduction of naval expenditure by both countries. Metternich gave only the most evasive replies to the British ministers. Even so, his report angered the Kaiser, who noted on it: "The Ambassador has overlooked entirely that he was not permitted, even if entirely non-committally and only as a private opinion, to (agree) to the insolent demands of the English Ministers to make their peacefulness dependent on the diminution of our sea force. . . . It must be pointed out to him that I do *not* wish a good understanding with England at the expense of the extension of the German fleet." Assisted and inspired by Admiral von Tirpitz, the Kaiser clung to his policy of naval expansion, thereby removing the last possibility that Britain would move away from her "Entente Cordiale" with France, and stand aloof in a European war.

The second and third forces at work against the Royal Navy were, as may be supposed from the nature of the era, technical. In 1906 Britain launched a new battleship of revolutionary design, combining firepower, armor, and speed in proportions never before known. This was H.M.S.

Dreadnought, a vessel whose appearance, like that of the *Merrimac* in Hampton Roads in 1862, made all existing battleships obsolete, and created a disturbing parity between the large shipbuilding nations. The construction of a modern first-line battle fleet had thus to be undertaken from scratch. At the same time, the third factor, the value of battleships themselves, was being placed in doubt. They remained the ultimate expression of naval power, but no one could predict what the effect on their fighting capacities would be of submarines, torpedo boats, mines, and flying machines. A curious contradiction prevailed in official naval circles everywhere: a determination to have modern capital ships—as many of them as possible (Britain had 29 in 1914, Germany 17, France 10)—coupled with a deep fear of exposing them to the unknown, unseen perils of the new weapons. Few admirals were now prepared to echo Farragut's "Damn the torpedoes! . . . go ahead! . . . full speed!" in Mobile Bay.

It was, then, under clouded auspices that sea power sought to find expression in August 1914. Some of the earliest events were inauspicious. Only two days after war was declared, a British light cruiser was sunk by a mine. On August 11th the German battlecruiser *Goeben* and the heavy cruiser *Breslau* escaped from the Mediterranean through the Dardanelles to Constantinople, where they played a notable part in hastening Turkey's entry into the War on the side of the Central Powers. Much criticism was directed at the British admirals in the Mediterranean for permitting this to happen. The sad fact is that British and German ships were in full view of each other on August 4th; the Germans had just bombarded the French bases of Bône and Philippeville on the North African coast. They could have been tackled *flagrante delicto,* but Britain and Germany were not formally at war until midnight. Such chances rarely return; this was one more item in the bill for last-minute vacillation by the British Government.

Outward appearances, however, can be deceptive in the case of such an intangible as sea power, working, for the most part, invisibly and at long distance. The achievements of the Royal Navy on the outbreak of war were immediate and positive, yet mainly to be expressed in negatives. Its early mobilization and assembly at war stations conferred a prompt advantage, which the Germans did not choose to dispute; this was the first negative, immensely significant. The next followed directly from it: despite the qualms of Lord Kitchener and other members of the British Government—and, indeed, the apprehensions of the British

Admiralty itself—there was no question of a German invasion of England. The fear of invasion continued to exert influence throughout the War, and diverted much manpower from where it was most needed, but the actuality, ruled out from the very beginning by naval supremacy, would inevitably have been far more damaging. The reverse side of this achievement—negatively expressed again—was that the BEF was able to proceed to France without any interference whatever, and that, during the whole war, not a single troopship was lost in the Channel. In the same way, with the aid of Allied naval forces, the mobilization of the Empire went forward uninterruptedly; Australians and New Zealanders were carried to the Middle East, Indians to France, and Canadians across the Atlantic to England (31,200 men and 7,000 horses left the St. Lawrence on October 3rd). As Falls says, "*Pace* the critics, the Navy must have been doing something."

Although some German surface raiders escaped the British net for a time—most notably the light cruiser *Emden* under her brilliant captain, von Müller, which enjoyed a remarkable career in the Indian Ocean until destroyed on November 9th by the Australian cruiser *Sydney*—British trade across the world went on virtually unhindered. German trade, on the contrary, was swept from the seas. Finally, but not least important, the German High Seas Fleet, that powerful barb aimed at the very vitals

". . . unknown, unseen perils . . ." A remarkable photograph illustrating a new extension of the art of war: the British submarine C 25 being attacked by a flight of German aircraft off Harwich. The pressure hull of C 25 was so damaged that she could not submerge; Leading Seaman Barge, manning the Lewis gun on the conning tower, unaware of this, called out: "Never mind me, sir. Dive!" as he fell mortally wounded. C 25 was taken in tow by another submarine and brought into Harwich despite a second attack by the aircraft.

NOVEMBER 9

of England, was constrained to lock itself in its harbors behind its mine-fields, to begin a process of slow rot which ended, in spite of some brave adventures, in mutiny and scuttle.

The nonappearance of the German High Seas Fleet came as a distinct surprise to the British. In part, it was due to a deceptive advantage the Germans enjoyed: the great defensive strength of their short North Sea coastline, protected by a screen of islands and shoals, and possessing the three large ports of Emden, Wilhelmshaven, and Hamburg, with all their facilities for maintaining fleets. The British naval bases, on the other hand, were ill placed; in fact, they were survivals of centuries of struggle with France or Spain, disposed to counteract threats from the Bay of Biscay or the Atlantic, and to give the Royal Navy easy access into those seas. New bases, facing toward Germany, were still incomplete; the most important of these were at Scapa Flow in the Orkney Islands at the northernmost tip of Scotland, Rosyth in the Firth of Forth near Edinburgh, and Harwich in East Anglia, covering the English Channel. None of them, in the early days of the War, provided a safe anchorage for Britain's most priceless asset, nor were their installations adequate to service it. Of all this, Admiral Sir John Jellicoe, commanding the British Grand Fleet, was uneasily aware. It preyed upon his methodical, cautious mind, along with the general sense that the great fleet entrusted to him owed some positive act to the Allied war effort.

Partly to satisfy this feeling—widely shared among naval officers—and partly because he actually felt safer at sea than in his barely protected harbors, Jellicoe carried out a number of sweeps with his whole fleet in the North Sea. No contact was made with the enemy. Something else would evidently be needed. This was soon provided by a suggestion put forward to Winston Churchill by Commodore Tyrwhitt, commanding the Harwich Striking Force (light cruisers and destroyers), and Commodore Roger Keyes, commanding the submarines also stationed at Harwich. They proposed to make a surprise attack on the German light forces which habitually patrolled the area to the north of the island of Heligoland. This proposal involved a deep penetration into German-defended waters, risking an engagement with heavy units of the High Seas Fleet. It was a bold concept, but boldness was required at this stage. Sir John Jellicoe, on being informed, offered support from the light cruisers of the Grand Fleet, and three more battle cruisers to augment the two originally earmarked to back up the raid. "He did more. He sent Sir David Beatty."[1] Vice-Admiral Sir David Beatty, who had been

[1] Winston Churchill, *The World Crisis*.

"... a remarkable career in the Indian Ocean ..." The German light cruiser Emden (3,000 tons, ten 4.1-inch guns, speed 24 knots), wrecked on Cocos Island reef after her fight with H.M.A.S. Sydney, from whose decks this picture was taken. Emden sank or captured twenty-four vessels in ninety-seven days (without so much as injuring one civilian) and paralyzed shipping in the Indian Ocean.

(pages 106 and 107) "The nonappearance of the German High Seas Fleet came as a distinct surprise ..." German battleships in line ahead in the North Sea.

". . . a surprise attack on the German light forces . . ." A British destroyer flotilla at sea.

(below) ". . . battle cruisers . . . to back up the raid." Admiral Beatty's battle-cruiser squadron: H.M.S. Lion leading, with Princess Royal, Indomitable, New Zealand in line astern.

present with Churchill at the Battle of Omdurman in 1898, proved to be one of the boldest and most aggressive of British naval leaders of the War. He was just the man to command such an enterprise as this.

The action of the Heligoland Bight took place on August 28th, and "produced results of a far-reaching character upon the whole of the naval war." [2] The weather was overcast and gloomy. The British Admiralty displayed incompetence in relaying signals. The high speed at which all units maneuvered created problems that had evidently not been sufficiently studied at prewar exercises. The presence of British submarines turned out to be an embarrassment to their own surface craft. But Beatty's audacity and relentless pursuit of the offensive counteracted all these drawbacks; the Germans were surprised and never recovered their poise. Three German light cruisers and a destroyer were sunk; three more cruisers were severely damaged, with many casualties. Only one British cruiser was even badly damaged, while losses amounted to 35 killed and about 40 wounded. It was a striking gesture. "The Germans knew nothing of our defective Staff work and of the risks we had run," wrote Churchill afterward. "All they saw was that the British did not hesitate to hazard their greatest vessels as well as their light craft in the most daring offensive action and had escaped apparently unscathed." Admiral von Tirpitz has recorded the effect on the Germans: "The Emperor did not want losses of this sort. . . . Orders were issued by the Emperor . . . to restrict the initiative of the Commander-in-Chief of the North Sea Fleet: the loss of ships was to be avoided, fleet sallies and any greater undertakings must be approved by His Majesty in advance. . . ."

The moral victory won by the British far outweighed the arithmetic of profit and loss; in the months to come this sort of uplift would be sorely needed. Just over three weeks after Heligoland, British public opinion sustained a shock at the sinking, one by one on the same day, as each went to the assistance of the others, of the three old cruisers *Hogue*, *Cressy*, and *Aboukir*. All were victims of *U.9*, under the able but fortunate Commander Weddigen; such a succession of sitting targets is rarely offered to a submariner. On October 27th the modern battleship *Audacious* was sunk by a mine. Worse was to follow. On November 1st the German China Squadron, now operating on the west coast of South America under the skillful leadership of Admiral Graf von Spee, encountered and destroyed a British cruiser squadron under Vice-Admiral Christopher Cradock. The German ships enjoyed both a tactical and a

[2] *Ibid.*

numerical advantage—so great, indeed, that the question has been asked ever since, why Cradock chose to engage them. Their two heavy cruisers, *Scharnhorst* and *Gneisenau*, both crack gunnery vessels, caught Cradock's *Good Hope* and *Monmouth* silhouetted against the sunset off Cape Coronel on the Chilean coast; the three light cruisers in attendance, *Leipsic*, *Dresden*, and *Nürnberg*, utterly overmatched the British *Glasgow* and armored merchantman *Otranto*. All was over within an hour: *Good Hope* and *Monmouth* were sunk with no survivors, Cradock going down in his flagship; *Glasgow* escaped by the skin of her teeth. *Otranto* had been sent away at the outset of the action. Von Spee's victory was complete, a deep injury to British pride and prestige.

The reaction of the British Admiralty was instant. Prince Louis of Battenberg, First Sea Lord at the outbreak of war, had now been replaced by the ferocious Sir John Fisher.[3] He and Churchill "acted like two twin thunderbolts of war in the vastness and rapidity of their remedial measures."[4] Vice-Admiral Sir Doveton Sturdee was given the mission of destroying von Spee. To carry out this task he had a squadron

[3] Battenberg, a talented officer, later became the victim of a shameful press campaign against his German birth.
[4] Cruttwell, *A History of the Great War*.

(opposite) ". . . one of the boldest and most aggressive of British naval leaders . . ." Admiral Sir David Beatty.

(below) ". . . British public opinion sustained a shock . . ." R. Mc-Whirter, Ship's Carpenter of H.M.S. Aboukir, torpedoed on September 22, 1914. He was picked up by H.M.S. Hogue, only to be torpedoed again almost immediately, and was then rescued for the second time and taken aboard H.M.S. Cressy—and torpedoed once again —the third time in one day.

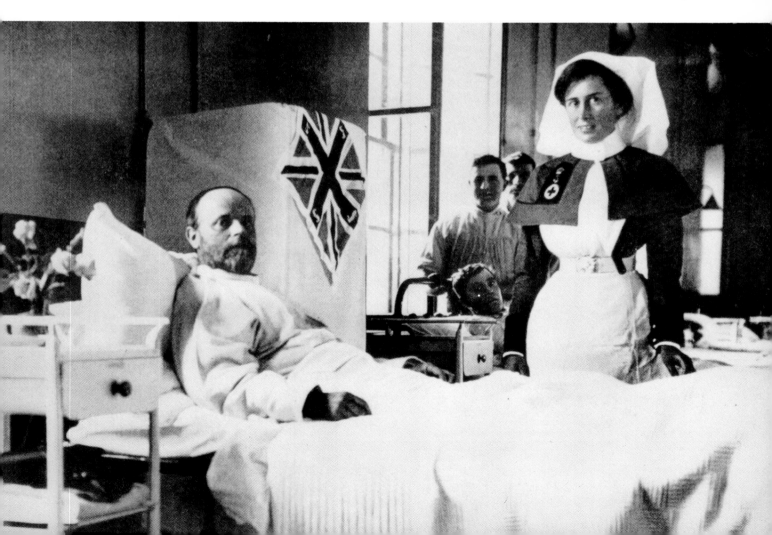

as superior to the Germans as they had been to Cradock: the battle cruisers *Invincible* and *Inflexible;* the armored cruisers *Carnarvon, Cornwall,* and *Kent;* and the light cruisers *Glasgow* and *Bristol.* Sturdee found the enemy—or rather, von Spee found him, to his great dismay— on December 7th at the Falkland Islands wireless station. The sight of the tripod masts of the British battle cruisers in the harbor "was equivalent to a sentence of certain death." The British took longer over it than von Spee had done at Coronel, partly because of Sturdee's determination not to risk damage to the big ships borrowed from the Grand Fleet, but also partly due to ominous defects in British gunnery and ammunition— factors which would recur. In five hours of running battle, *Scharnhorst* and *Gneisenau* went down with their colors flying, fighting bravely to the last. Von Spee and his two sons, together with some 1,800 German sailors, went down with them; only about 200 men were saved from both ships' companies. A little later, *Nürnberg* and *Leipsic* followed them; only *Dresden* survived. The British squadron was hardly touched. The long arm of sea power had stretched out in dramatic vengeance.

The interior dynamic of world conflict brooks no check. "So the circle widened," wrote a British historian,[5] "until a war, begun by a squalid murder in Bosnia, ended with British soldiers fighting in Syria, on the Caspian, at Archangel, in East Africa, the Alps and the Caucasus." That is one way of putting it; alternatively, it is a matter for awe to see how race after race was drawn in. Japan's entry into the War on August 23rd brought its impact not only to her own people but also to many unfortunate Chinese. Pacific islanders soon found themselves under new masters. The Turkish Empire carried into battle not only European Turks but also Anatolians, Iraqis, Palestinians, and Arab tribesmen. All the martial races of India responded to the summons of the drum. All

[5] Keith Feiling.

(opposite, top) ". . . the battleship Audacious was sunk by a mine."

(bottom) ". . . some 1,800 German sailors went down with them . . ." Survivors of Gneisenau in the water. Boats from H.M.S. Inflexible are picking up the German sailors; the photograph was taken from Invincible, whose boats were similarly engaged.

113

over Africa, races and colors were joined in combat under many flags: Afrikaaners from the Union, Rhodesians, Nigerians, Senegalese, Congolese, Kikuyu—down to a small, wretched, oppressed tribe called Bastards.

Not only for reasons of prestige: but for more practical ones too, it was inevitable that Allied sea power, chiefly British, should be turned immediately against Germany's overseas possessions. Wireless stations, bases, harbors, coaling points for commerce destroyers—these were the targets that first attracted expeditions. Some were quickly snapped up: Togoland surrendered on August 27th, Samoa on the 29th, New Guinea on September 17th. Others put up a stern, exhausting struggle: in East Africa, the Germans continued fighting until November 23, 1918, twelve days *after* the Armistice. All in all, campaigns against German colonies and on secondary fronts gave employment, from first to last, to 3,576,391 soldiers of the British Empire, not to mention the French, Russian, Belgian, and other Allied forces engaged. This figure of over 3.5 million needs to be compared with the 5,399,563 British soldiers who fought on the Western Front. It will be seen that the diversion of strength was considerable; it is not to be wondered at that it should have produced some of the bitterest controversy of the War, not stilled to this day. If one recognizes now the inevitability of some of the "sideshows," one must recognize also that the conduct of others was insufficiently related to the progress of the War as a whole. The strongest condemnation has been made by the British Official Historian, who wrote: ". . . they were a drain on the resources of the British Empire, without being a corresponding embarrassment to Germany, and had no other effect on the progress and outcome of the war."

NOVEMBER 7

Japan's war aims were limited and precise. Her prospective area of expansion was China; her most dangerous potential enemy was Russia, with whom she now found herself linked in an uneasy alliance. Her most promising field of activity was against the German naval base of Tsingtao in China's Shantung Province. This was attacked in September, and surrendered on November 7th after an old-style siege in which Japanese heavy artillery played much the same part as that of the German howitzers at Liége, Namur, and Antwerp. The Germans exacted a stiff price (in relation to the forces engaged) for this victory; the Japanese rested content with it. They steadfastly refused to be drawn into the European theater, though in 1917, when Russia was swept by revolution, they took further measures to "protect their interests" on the Asian mainland. For the rest, the Allies owed them a debt of gratitude for the security their

navy brought to the Pacific Ocean, for their help in escorting the convoys of Australians and New Zealanders to the Middle East at a time when the Royal Navy was widely extended, and even for helping to put down an almost forgotten but dangerous and savage mutiny of Indian troops at Singapore in February 1915.

Rebellion and treachery were also at work in South Africa—with more effect, for there they substantially delayed the effective participation of the Union in the War. Their origins were not far to seek: they lay in the war between the British and Boers that had only ended in 1902, and whose verdict had never been accepted by some Afrikaaners. The Prime Minister of the Union, General Louis Botha, and his chief supporter, General Jan Smuts, had both been celebrated commanders against the British. Now, in 1914, both were convinced that South Africa's way forward lay in association with Britain and in full participation in the Empire's war effort. The section of Afrikaaner opinion which already called itself Nationalist opposed the Botha-Smuts policy. Over 11,000 rebels came out in arms against the Government, and though the revolt never had the slightest chance of success it was not until February 1915 that it was finally stamped out, so that South Africa could begin to participate effectively in the War. But already, in the firm measures taken against the rebels, the stature of two great Imperial statesmen was to be perceived: Botha and Smuts, whose example played a large part in the reshaping of Britain's relations with her chief Dominions.

Delays in South Africa were somewhat offset by speedy Allied victories in West Africa (Togoland and Cameroons). On the east coast, however, the British ran into difficulties. The defense of the colony of German East Africa, now known as Tanganyika, was entrusted to Lieutenant-Colonel Paul von Lettow-Vorbeck, who showed himself to be one of the most remarkable soldiers of the War. With forces which never (according to German records) exceeded some 3,500 whites and 12,000 Africans (askaris), von Lettow-Vorbeck, up to the time of his surrender, gave employment to 372,950 British troops, white and black. Admittedly, sickness in that tropical, disease-ridden climate was responsible for an overwhelming proportion of this great number; British battle casualties in East Africa during the whole War amounted to only 10,717,

"...one of the most remarkable soldiers of the war." General von Lettow-Vorbeck, commanding the German forces in East Africa (second from right), on a visit to a plantation.

while the sick numbered 336,540. But disease knows no flag, and that von Lettow-Vorbeck was able to triumph over it, as well as over the greatly superior forces arrayed against him, shows that he was a commander of the highest caliber. He made his mark early, with the repulse of a seaborne invasion mounted from India against the port of Tanga on December 5th. This success came as a timely encouragement for Germany.

DECEMBER 1914

Yet despite the useful role of Germany's own colonies in diverting Allied strength from the Western Front, it was above all to her new ally, Turkey, that she was obliged in this respect. The immediate agent of Turkey's participation in the War was Admiral Wilhelm Souchon, commanding the *Goeben* and the *Breslau*. The arrival of these two ships at Constantinople on August 11th produced effects more striking than the influence of any individual vessel since the C.S.S. *Alabama*. By a legal fiction they were incorporated in the Turkish Navy, over which Souchon was given command. Another German admiral was in charge of coastal defenses. The Chief of Staff of the Turkish Army was a German officer; its training was in the hands of yet another German, whose reputation grew with the progress of the War—Liman von Sanders. All this was in accordance with the policy of Turkish War Minister Enver Pasha and his ruling "Young Turks" party. Enver and Souchon concocted a plot to hasten the German-Turkish alliance that both desired. On October 29th, on a flimsy pretext, the Turkish fleet (including *Goeben* and *Breslau*) bombarded Odessa, Sevastopol, Theodosia, and Novorossisk, and sank certain Russian ships in the Black Sea. Turkey's die was cast. Aimed primarily at Russia, her intervention aroused deep consternation and ire in Britain, concerned by its effects upon the large Mohammedan populations of the Empire.

OCTOBER 1914

Three new "fronts" were at once produced by Turkey's action, though one did not become operative until the following year, when a fourth was also added. Enver's ambitions were directed above all to the Caucasus; he planned to strike into Georgia and raise a revolt of the Transcaucasian peoples against Russian rule. Disregarding "the fact that the troops would have to live on the country in winter; night temperatures twenty degrees below freezing-point; bitter winds, amounting to gales on the higher ground; the inadequacy of a mere 50% superiority in infantry for such an ambitious venture,"[6] he plunged into a disastrous winter campaign in the mountains. In a four-day battle, starting on New Year's Day, at Sarikamish, the Russians smashed this offensive; out of

JANUARY 1, 1915

[6] Cyril Falls, *The First World War*.

95,000 Turks who had begun it, only 18,000 survived. "The rest were frozen hard as boards, but for stragglers who had found shelter in hamlets on the slopes. . . . Turkish strength and fighting power were affected for the rest of the war."[7]

Foiled in their drive eastward, a glittering offensive prospect was opened up to the Turks in the south, toward the Suez Canal. Considering the immense significance of this prize, it is remarkable how slowly and feebly the Turks moved against it. The blame for this, too, must be laid at the door of Enver's grandiose Caucasian schemes, which sapped Turkey's military resources. In November 1914 the British garrison in Egypt was weak; Regulars had been withdrawn and replaced with partly trained Territorials and Indian detachments. Anxiety was acute. Not even the presence of the *Emden,* flushed with success in the Indian Ocean, was allowed to interfere with the rushing of Australian and New Zealand troops to the Canal zone. The arrival in December of the "Anzac Corps," the Australian and New Zealand Army Corps, 38,835 of all ranks, together with complete divisions from India, made the Canal secure. When a small Turkish force did attack in February 1915, it was swiftly defeated. But this was the genesis of the "Egypt and Palestine" front, which ultimately gave employment to no fewer than 1,192,511 British troops.

Finally, there was Turkey's "Achilles' heel"—the flank she exposed in the southwest toward the Persian Gulf. Here, also, the British had important interests, in the Anglo-Persian oil installations centered upon Abadan. Partly to protect these, and partly to encourage an Arab revolt against Turkish domination, a small expedition was organized from India to go to the Shatt-al-Arab, the joint estuary of the Euphrates, Tigris, and Karun rivers on the Gulf. This force arrived even before Turkey's entry into the War, but no move was made until November 6th, when the Anglo-Indian troops landed. On the 17th a Turkish counterattack was defeated, and on the 22nd the British moved up to Basra, twenty miles inland, where a base was formed. Shortly afterward a further advance of fifty-five miles to Qurna was made, as a defensive precaution. All idea of making any attempt upon Baghdad was utterly disclaimed, yet these were the first stages of an "inching" process that would finally carry the British, with many vicissitudes, up to and beyond that famous city. This campaign—"Mesopotamia"—would ultimately draw in 889,702 men. Taking the War as a whole, Turkey absorbed the attentions of some 2.5

[7] *Ibid.*

million British troops alone, to say nothing of the French and Russians who also fought against her.

Christmas came, and the war which was supposed to be over was only just getting into its stride. To both sides and all participants it had brought nothing but horror, squalor, and frustration, setting at naught the extraordinary heights of endurance and bravery of which men of all nations had shown themselves capable. Looking about them, in the brief pause of this first winter, the thoughtful everywhere could "feel a sort of poison creeping into their systems."[8]

But the poison had not yet sunk in completely. On Christmas Day 1914 a strange phenomenon was seen. A British officer recorded:

"On Christmas morning I awoke very early, and emerged from my dug-out into the trench. It was a perfect day. A beautiful, cloudless blue sky . . . Everything looked merry and bright that morning—the discomforts seemed to be less, somehow; they seemed to have epitomised themselves in intense, frosty cold. It was just the sort of day for Peace to

[8] Rudolph Binding.

". . . the first stages of an 'inching' process . . ." An essential feature of all maneuver in Mesopotamia (the Land Between the Rivers) was control of the rivers themselves. This is the British gunboat Firefly in action on the Tigris.

be declared. It would have made such a good finale. . . . Walking about the trench a little later . . . we suddenly became aware of the fact that we were seeing a lot of evidences of Germans. Heads were bobbing about and showing over their parapet in a most reckless way, and, as we looked, this phenomenon became more and more pronounced . . . until, in less time than it takes to tell, half a dozen or so of each of the belligerents were outside their trenches and were advancing toward each other in no-man's-land. . . . I clambered up and over our parapet, and moved out across the field to look. . . . It all felt most curious: here were these sausage-eating wretches, who had elected to start this infernal European fracas, and in so doing had brought us all into the same muddy pickle as themselves. This was my first sight of them at close quarters. Here they were—the actual, practical soldiers of the German army. There was not an atom of hate on either side that day; and yet, on our side, not for a moment was the will to war and the will to beat them relaxed. It was just like the interval between the rounds in a friendly boxing match. . . . I strolled about amongst them all, and sucked in as many impressions as I could. . . . Suddenly, one of the Boches ran back to his trench and presently reappeared with a large camera. I posed in a mixed group for several photographs, and have ever since wished I had fixed up some arrangement for getting a copy. . . . Slowly the meeting began to disperse; a sort of feeling that the authorities on both sides were not very enthusiastic about this fraternising seemed to creep across the gathering. We parted, but there was a distinct and friendly understanding that Christmas Day would be left to finish in tranquillity."[9]

"Tranquillity": this also would be part of the price which the world would pay. Nor would such feelings ever again be able to triumph over the rising tides of hate whipped up by the universal suffering of the War.

[9] Bruce Bairnsfather, *Bullets and Billets.*

ATTRITION OR EVASION? 6

It was in 1915 the old world ended.

D. H. LAWRENCE

Autumn merged into winter; winter passed into spring. There was no respite, no interval in the thunder of the guns. The initiative seized by the Germans at the very outset of the War remained with them. It rewarded them with the only important victories gained in 1915; but it disappointed them too, because once again the victories fell short of being decisive. Not that von Falkenhayn ever truly hoped for a decision; his resolve to make Germany's main effort in the east, rather than in the west, was arrived at, with misgivings, on the insistence of Conrad and Hindenburg. The most that Falkenhayn hoped for was, he says, "that the success would be big enough to check the enemy for a long time." Even this measure of success was not achieved, for the Russians would score some of their most signal triumphs in 1916. On the other hand, their losses in 1915 undoubtedly hastened their ultimate collapse, and not even the 1916 counterstrokes availed against it. Nevertheless, the final outcome showed that the German High Command had badly erred. As one of their distinguished military writers[1] wrote in 1926: "There is no doubt as to what the proper course should have been in the spring of 1915. . . . The British Army should have been so defeated that it could never develop into an efficient 'million army.' It should have been like a newly sown field struck by a heavy hailstorm, which never recovers to bear a full crop; the result would have been certain if such storms of hail and battle had been repeated several times in 1915, when their fury would have been intensified by the hatred of the British which justly filled every German heart."

This analysis goes to the heart of the matter. For the Allies the two key factors of 1915 were the emergence of Britain's "million army" and the manner of its handling under the exigencies of the French alliance. The concept of the "million army" struck the British imagination with all the force of novelty, but in fact it was not new. The idea had been incorporated in Lord Haldane's Army Reforms. But it was not Lord Haldane's system; it was Lord Kitchener's personal appeal to British manhood which resulted in the formation of the "New Armies." Many Regular soldiers scoffed at them. "His ridiculous and preposterous army

[1] General von Moser, *Das militarisch und politisch Wichtigste vom Weltkrieg.*

121

(pages 122 and 123) **"The concept of the 'million army' . . ."** Scene at the Central Recruiting Office at Great Scotland Yard during August 1914. On Saturday, August 1st, the officer on duty attested eight men. On August 4th, when the office re-opened after the Bank Holiday weekend, it took him twenty minutes and the help of twenty policemen to get through the volunteers to his own desk. By September 5th over 250,000 men had volunteered.

of 25 corps is the laughing-stock of every soldier in Europe," wrote Henry Wilson. In retrospect, this last appeal to the voluntary system of which Britain was so proud is revealed as a costly anachronism, a damaging misuse of the national resources. But as Lord Esher subsequently commented: "Since it was conceded that the War should be fought under a system of voluntary enlistment and unequal sacrifice—a concession for which England was destined to pay, and is still paying a heavy price—it is more than doubtful whether armies could have been raised by any method other than the one he chose." Certainly Britain's response to Kitchener's appeal was marvelous. On one day, September 1, 1914, 30,000 men enlisted. During that year a campaign involving 54,000,000 posters, 8,000,000 personal letters, 12,000 meetings, and 20,000 speeches produced 1,186,337 recruits; by September 1915 this figure had risen to 2,257,521. Already, by October 1914, 18 New Army divisions had been formed, over and above Territorials and Regulars. Equipping these human masses was another matter.

So was the question of how they should be used. By January 2, 1915, viewing the complete failure of Joffre's attempts to shake the Germans from their positions in the west, Kitchener wrote to Sir John French: "I suppose we must now recognise that the French Army cannot make a sufficient break through the German lines to bring about the retreat of the German forces from Northern Belgium. If that is so, then the German lines in France may be looked on as a fortress that cannot be carried by assault and also that cannot be completely invested, with the result that the lines may be held by an investing force, whilst operations proceed elsewhere." In due course Kitchener would be cruelly disillusioned; but the idea which he expressed here, the lure of "operations elsewhere," remained to bedevil British strategic thinking for the rest of that war and much of the next. It formed, indeed, the hard core of what Major General J. F. C. Fuller—no apologist for official Allied staff policies—called "The Strategy of Evasion."[2] It held out no appeal to General Joffre. "The best and largest portion of the German army was on our soil," he wrote, "with its line of battle jutting out a mere five days' march from the heart of France. This situation made it clear to every Frenchman that our task consisted in defeating this enemy, and driving him out of our country."

French strategy bore the hallmark of inevitability. The loss of the northeastern provinces, with their large populations and economic resources—most notably the great manufacturing center of Lille, the

[2] Major General J. F. C. Fuller, *The Conduct of War 1789–1961*, London, 1961.

YOUR COUNTRY NEEDS "YOU"

"... Lord Kitchener's personal appeal ..." Besides this poster, placards announced: "An addition of 100,000 men to His Majesty's Regular Army is immediately necessary in the present grave National Emergency. Lord Kitchener is confident that this appeal will be at once responded to by all those who have the safety of our Empire at heart." The response to this call produced the "First Hundred Thousand," or "First New Army," which officially came into existence on August 21st, two days before the Battle of Mons.

"... Kitchener would be cruelly disillusioned ..." Lord Kitchener, with Britain's Foreign Secretary, Sir Edward Grey, in Paris, 1915.

Briey iron basin—added grave material damage to the psychological hurt the French nation had sustained. The pronounced bulge of the German line, the "jutting out" characteristic of which Joffre spoke, offered a standing temptation. All through the year his efforts would be concentrated on the flanks of this bulge, in Artois and Champagne. His object was to slice it off at the base by concentric offensives; he recognized that these would require every man and gun that France could muster. This in turn drew him into an unceasing pressure upon his British allies to help in two ways: by taking over more front to release French formations for the offensive, and by making supporting attacks themselves. Corollary to both these pressures was his aversion to any maneuver or campaign that might divert strength from his main blows. Thus, a British proposal to begin the year by clearing the Belgian coast was peremptorily refused, while the large detachments of British forces to other theaters during the year incurred his rooted opposition.

The flaw in Joffre's reasoning lay not in its overall conception, but in its execution; that is to say, in the unique essence of the War on the Western Front. For the German decision to turn eastward implied, as Falkenhayn noted, "the decision to act purely on the defensive in France, with the most careful application of every imaginable technical device. Trench warfare in the real sense, with all its horrors, began." And so the incredible spectacle unfolded: of trench-locked armies; of millions of men facing each other at distances varying from a few yards to nearly a mile; of a more-or-less continuous line of entrenchments stretching some 450 miles; of a devastated war zone on either side of the line of battle growing more and more like a lunar landscape, where nothing moved in the daytime, night was filled with feverish activity, and the sounds of war were never stilled; and of an immutability, a dreadful equilibrium it seemed nothing could alter, no effort, no matter how prodigious and heroic, could overcome, throughout the next three years.

Undoubtedly the Germans, whose offensive doctrines presupposed areas of intense defensive activity, were better equipped than the Allies for this style of warfare. Equally undoubtedly, the British, in contrast to their earlier high proficiency, were now at a disadvantage compared with the French. Trench warfare brought needs of its own to multiply the already staggering munitions demands of all the combatants: picks and spades and machines to dig the trenches, timber to shore them up, pumps and pipes to drain them, duckboards to floor them, concrete to fortify them, barbed wire—millions of miles of it—to protect them, sandbags to crown and plug them, telephone cable to connect them,

(above) ". . . barbed wire—millions of miles of it . . ." Barbed wire filling a mine crater. Bitter fighting took place for the possession of these craters, and, until they filled with water, dense thickets of wire helped to discourage enemy attacks.

(left) ". . . telephone cable to connect them . . ." These men are using a "fullerphone," devised to enable the field telephones to be used without danger of being overheard by the enemy—a frequent occurrence with the earliest models.

". . . a war of high explosive . . ." German 380-mm. (15-inch) gun on railway mounting, Western Front.

". . . the same dilemmas . . . the same impasse . . ." A quiet moment in a French trench in 1915. The officer is dictating orders; the two men in the foreground take a "time out of war" for fishing.

grenades to fight in them, mortars to bombard them, rockets and lights to signal from them, tunneling equipment to undermine them. It was a whole dimension of war which, if not new, was now to be entered on a scale never before dreamed of. In turn, all this reacted on the more familiar categories of weapons: the machine gun was found to be the

ideal firearm for defending trenches, artillery the only means of cutting wire and destroying machine guns and the trenches themselves. Because of its killing power under these conditions, the machine gun captured popular imagination as the villain of the War; but the truth is that it was artillery which caused the highest death roll and which also provided the most continuous onslaught upon the nerves and senses of men. The First World War was above all an artillery war, in particular a war of high explosive; the bombardments became more and more furious, the individual explosions more devastating, the destruction more complete.

These conditions, and this description, applied universally. Everywhere that men could dig a trench, fringe it with wire and arm it with machine guns, while other men attacked it with artillery, the same dilemma was seen, the same impasse reached. But it was on the Western Front, where the densest masses faced each other uninterruptedly along a line which had no flanks, that trench warfare reached its apotheosis. In 1915 all its weird techniques were developed rapidly, and as each problem neared solution, another appeared; every answer brought a counter-

"Everywhere that men could dig a trench . . ." Austrian trenches on the Eastern Front: a quiet sector, despite the somewhat dramatic attitudes of some of the men. Note the undamaged houses, general absence of shell holes, and cart moving openly in the background. But the front lines were usually much farther apart in the east than in the west.

response. The trench lines multiplied; what had been a thin crust became a thick layer; heroism withered in this fiery maze. The French armies which stormed into the attack time after time in Artois and Champagne all through the year were not short of heroism. But this quality itself, in 1915, proved to be a dubious asset, multiplying the mortality with little visible reward.

It is necessary for historians, in order to trace the outlines of this monstrous, perpetual-motion conflict, to identify particular phases of it as "battles." Thus the bitter fighting that continued along the Aisne, lapping beyond the edges of that pleasant region, all through the autumn and winter of 1914, is known as the "First Battle of Champagne," while the simultaneous abortive attempts of General Foch's Army Group to advance farther north are called the "First Battle of Artois." A "Second Battle of Champagne" and a "Second" and "Third Battle of Artois"

(opposite) "The trench lines multiplied . . ." Germans deepening and clearing mud out of a trench in the Argonne. One section of the trench is riveted with wattle.

(left) ". . . abortive attempts . . . to advance . . ." French machine gunners in Artois; two of the men are wearing anti-smoke goggles.

followed during the next year. But these are titles only; they represent swelling tides in an ocean that was never still. For the soldiers, the difference between a "battle" and an "interval" was one only of degrees of misery and danger. "First Champagne" dragged on until March 1915. Here for the first time was heard that terrifying "drumfire," as the 75's worked up to their 25-rounds-a-minute maximum, which was to signalize so many of the crises of the War. But neither the deluge of shells nor the astounding élan of the French infantry availed; at a cost that some French authorities have placed as high as 240,000 men, they gained no more than a few unimportant hamlets. An attempt to wipe out the dangerous Saint-Mihiel salient on the flank of Verdun was equally unsuccessful. And so, for a few months, the roar of battle was allowed to die down to a rumble in this sector.

The consequences of this failure were felt on the Northern Front, where the British and French armies mingled. As Champagne insatiably swallowed up French reserves, General Foch's pressure upon the Germans naturally fell away, but his pressure upon his British allies sensibly increased. Neither he nor any other French general (nor, indeed, the Germans) had any high regard at this stage for the offensive capacity of

". . . Champagne insatiably swallowed up French reserves . . ." French infantry marching up between the vineyards.

the growing but inexperienced British forces. Nevertheless, their full participation in operations was clearly a necessity; it was agreed that the British should both release French divisions in Artois and join the French in a new offensive from Arras. But never were the interwoven strands of war more evilly knotted, nor was the weakness of Great Britain to be more painfully exposed. The grand strategists in London were by now deeply committed to "operations elsewhere"—the Gallipoli campaign, which, it was at last realized, could not be conducted simply as a naval venture, but must also be supported by a considerable land force. The only unit of any substance available for this enterprise was the last of the British Regular divisions, formed from overseas Imperial

132

garrisons: the 29th Division. This division had been promised to Sir John French, permitting him to agree to Foch's request that he should extend his front. But under the stresses of Gallipoli, Lord Kitchener diverted the 29th Division from France. Sir John French now had the choice of abandoning his own attack or refusing to relieve the French; and if he adopted the latter course, Foch made it clear that he, for his part, would be unable to attack. To such a pass had Britain come in the spring of 1915 that the destination of a single division could vitally affect her entire strategy.

It is hard to see reason in what followed; this was a low ebb of Allied generalship. The French, much irritated, broke off their attacks, but the British Commander in Chief, partly for reasons of prestige, partly to stimulate the uncertain morale of his army, decided to take the offensive alone. His chances of achieving anything significant without French support were negligible; dire shortages of all kinds of munitions made it likely indeed that he might suffer a severe reverse. At the very least, there was bound to be a serious wastage of precious matériel, and a long casualty list. Yet Joffre and Foch shrugged their shoulders and allowed the British to go ahead; nor did any veto come from London. And so, on March 10th, the British First Army[3] under General Sir Douglas Haig was committed to the Battle of Neuve Chapelle.

MARCH 10, 1915

This was the first British offensive of the War and it created the pattern for the major undertakings of the next two years. Under the direction of Haig and his staff, the First Army's preparations were made with great care. A number of important innovations were introduced: rehearsals for the infantry; deceptions with dummies; light railways for supply; a short "hurricane" bombardment (laughable by later standards: Haig possessed only sixty-six heavy guns); artillery timetables; aerial photography of the enemy trenches. The result was an immediate and striking success in the opening phase of the assault, but then, as was to happen so often afterward, "the whole machine clogged and stopped. It was maddening."[4] The battle continued for three days, until increasing casualties and sheer lack of munitions caused it to be broken off. "Practically all the ground won . . . was won in the first three hours."[5] This, though it could scarcely be recognized at the time, was the mold of the future.

The British lost, at Neuve Chapelle, about 13,000 men (a tiny figure

[3] The BEF was reorganized in two Armies on Christmas Day 1914.

[4] Charteris.

[5] Cruttwell, *A History of the Great War.*

"'Practically all the ground won . . . was won in the first three hours.'" This is the headquarters of the 21st Brigade, British 7th Division. They were evidently expecting to be on the move, and their dejection is quite evident.

by comparison with French losses, but shocking to the British public) and inflicted roughly the same damage on the enemy. For this price they had gained one wrecked village. But the significance of the battle was not to be estimated in such material terms. Enough had been done to fire the British Army with a sense of its own capabilities, if properly reinforced and supplied. The French revised their estimates of their allies and sent a number of senior officers to study British methods; above all, the Germans now knew that they could not afford to neglect the British front. Neuve Chapelle marked the beginning of the redeployment of German forces which would finally draw as many of their divisions to the British sector as there were on the French front, three times its length. In short, Neuve Chapelle marked Britain's debut as a major land power. With whatever satisfaction might be gleaned from that— and in the end it was to be a decisive factor—the Allies had to be content as their spring offensives in the west faded out.

The critical endeavors of the War now shifted to other theaters. But the Western Front, always in ferment, always precarious, first produced another shock. Before we turn to the campaigns which supply the special characteristics of 1915, we must watch Germans and Allies alike make further vain efforts to resolve the baffling mysteries of the new style of war in France and Flanders.

No less than the Allies, the German High Command had been appalled at the deadlock produced by the autumn battles in the west during 1914. While the French hastily expanded their heavy artillery to meet the unforeseen need, and while the British improvised every kind of equipment, the better-prepared German armies were able to cast about for new weapons or variations of older ones. Such an adaptation, which occurred simultaneously to men on both sides of the line, was mentioned to General Haig by a visitor in March: "Lord Dundonald arrived . . . he is studying the conditions of war in the hopes of being able to apply to modern conditions an invention of his grandfather for driving a garrison out of a fort by using sulphur fumes. I asked him how he arranged to have a favourable wind."

There was, indeed, nothing new about the idea of using noxious fumes or gases in war. The Hague Convention of 1907 had accepted their existence, but forbade "the use of projectiles the *sole* object of which is the diffusion of asphyxiating gases." German disregard for international agreements was already evident. As early as September 1914 they were contemplating the use of gas; in October their Second Army was listing "flame or asphyxiating gas projectors" among its "close-quarters" weapons. By January 1915, 6,000 cylinders of chlorine gas were ready for use by Duke Albrecht of Württemberg's Fourth Army, facing the Ypres Salient.[6] Chlorine is a heavy gas, a powerful irritant to the respiratory organs; prolonged exposure to a high concentration of it causes death by asphyxia or, at least, cardiac dilation and severe injury

[6] Ministry of National Defence, *Canadian Expeditionary Force 1914–1919*, Ottawa, 1962.

". . . vain efforts to resolve the baffling mysteries . . ." There is a distinctly "early days" look about this German battle headquarters (General von Below). The Light Infantry detachment in the foreground is working a field telephone.

"... grinding away of streets and buildings into ... spectacular ruin ..." All that was left of the famous medieval Cloth Hall of Ypres (center and left) and St. Martin's Cathedral (right).

to the lungs. Released from cylinders, chlorine was a crude instrument. The force of General Haig's objection to Lord Dundonald's ideas lies in the fact that, despite the advice of their meteorologists, the first location of the German cylinders proved useless because the wind consistently failed to blow in the right direction. By mid-April, 5,730 of them were in new positions north of Ypres, but even so ten days passed without a favorable wind—days of great uneasiness for the Germans themselves. "Almost throughout the forces both leaders and troops regarded with mistrust the still untried means of offense, if they were not entirely inclined against it."[7]

At last the wind changed, and the Germans were able to try out their novelty. Astonishingly, that was all they had in mind: "The battles of Ypres which began on the 22nd April, had their origin on the German side solely in the desire to try the new weapon, gas, thoroughly

APRIL 22

[7] German Official History.

136

at the front."[8] The Allies, equally improvident, had had their warnings, but ignored them. French GQG told one of their divisional commanders: "All this gas business need not be taken seriously."[9] The attack was heralded by a violent bombardment of the town of Ypres, the bottleneck through which all Allied communications with the Salient had to pass. Seventeen-inch howitzers now began the remorseless grinding away of streets and buildings into the spectacular ruin that they finally became— an epitome of war's destructive force. Then, at 5:00 P.M. on April 22nd, the gunfire swelled into new intensity, with the French field artillery adding its urgent clamor. Watchers saw "two curious greenish-yellow clouds on the ground on either side of Langemarck in front of the German line. These clouds spread laterally, joined up, and, moving before a light wind, became a bluish-white mist, such as is seen over water meadows on a frosty night."[10] Almost immediately French troops were seen coming back hurriedly, coughing and pointing to their throats, and evidently terrified.

The blow fell upon the French 45th (Algerian) and 87th (Territorial) divisions, interposed between the left of the British Second Army (General Smith-Dorrien) and the Belgians. Both the French formations broke at once, opening a clear four-mile gap leading straight to Ypres. But the Germans were apprehensive of their own innovation, and advanced only slowly. The nearest British troops were the 1st Canadian Division, which had arrived in France in February; supported by British units as they came up, the Canadians extemporized a new defense line and put in counterattacks. On the 24th the Canadians were themselves in the direct line of another gas cloud, which they faced with the utmost gallantry. But by the 25th it had become evident to General Smith-Dorrien that a withdrawal from the exposed forward positions of the Salient was necessary. This provided Field Marshal French with a long-sought opportunity to get rid of Smith-Dorrien, whom he disliked; he was replaced by General Sir Herbert Plumer. Plumer at once carried out the withdrawal almost exactly as Smith-Dorrien had projected.

APRIL 27

The fighting at "Second Ypres" now settled down into, "for its size, one of the most murderous battles of the war."[11] The 1st Canadian Division, between April 15th and May 3rd, lost 208 officers and 5,828 enlisted men—a third of its infantry. Aggregate British losses amounted

[8] *Canadian Expeditionary Force 1914–1919.*

[9] Reichsarchiv.

[10] *British Official History.*

[11] Cyril Falls, *The First World War.*

"... Aubers Ridge ... a complete failure ..." On the front of the 25th Brigade (8th Division) the British exploded two mines. The craters were quickly rushed, but it proved impossible to support the attack. This photograph shows the 2nd Lincolnshire Regiment attempting to go forward through the craters, still full of British and German casualties. The brigadier was later killed, trying to sort out the confusion. Losses in the 8th Division amounted to over 4,500 in one day.

to 2,150 officers and 57,125 enlisted men; incomplete German figures give theirs as 860 officers and 34,073 enlisted men. There were also French casualties to be reckoned. And for the British there was the further peril that "the ammunition situation was now most desperate." The sadness of these statistics lies in the fact that at least a proportion of this loss was avoidable—that part of it which belongs to the ineffectual attempts to regain lost ground during the later stages. There were reasons for these counterattacks, the most acceptable being "the special political and sentimental value attaching to every acre of the small portion of Belgium remaining unconquered, and the moral effect created amongst neutrals, if not the belligerent nations themselves, by the German paeans of victory on the gain of the smallest parcel of ground."[12] But the exorbitant rate of loss had its less warrantable origins elsewhere: "For ill now, although for weal in the last year of the war, General Foch was the very spirit of the offensive."[13]

[12] *British Official History.*
[13] *Ibid.*

138

The Germans had never intended more than an experiment; the French were in the throes of preparation for their second offensive in Artois; the British were critically short of munitions; and so the battle slowly sputtered out. It had achieved nothing, but it had helped to alter the nature of twentieth century war: "In the face of gas, without protection, individuality was annihilated; the soldier in the trench became a mere passive recipient of torture and death. A final stage seemed to be reached in the whole tendency of modern scientific warfare to depress and make of no effect individual bravery, enterprise, and skill."[14]

MAY 8

In May General Foch launched his attack in Artois. With 18 divisions and 293 heavy guns he assaulted the German positions, the core of which was formed by Vimy Ridge. New and sickening place names entered into French military history: Notre-Dame de Lorette, Souchez. At Vimy, General Pétain's XXXIII Corps fought its way almost to the crest of the ridge, where the whitened skeletons and rotting uniforms of the French dead greeted the advancing Canadians two years later. This was the only success. At a cost of 100,000 men, Foch wound up the battle in June. The Germans had lost about 75,000. The British, still battling at Ypres, made two attempts to help their allies forward: at Aubers Ridge, on May 9th—a complete failure—and at Festubert, a small but deceptive gain, on May 15th–27th. "The results of the fighting," says the Official Historian, "were tantalizing: with more guns and with more and better ammunition . . . the British leaders felt they could have achieved a really useful success." This was the deceit of 1915— this sense of being always on the brink of a decisive action. It affected Germans and Allies alike, and the ensuing disappointment constitutes the true origin of the warfare of attrition. Meanwhile, the British First Army had some 27,000 more casualties to add to those at Ypres. Nowhere had the front line shifted more than three miles.

[14] Cruttwell, *op. cit.*

7 THE GREAT "IF"

There is seldom any lack of attractive-looking schemes in war. The difficulty is to give effect to them. . . .

FIELD MARSHAL SIR WILLIAM ROBERTSON

The arrival of the *Goeben* and the *Breslau* at Constantinople drew Turkey into the War. Once in, the aspirations of Enver Pasha lured her to catastrophe in the Caucasus; in turn, Turkish belligerency and the Caucasian campaign drew the Allies, Britain in particular, into one of

"It was the Australians who went ashore first . . ." The landing at **"Anzac Cove," April 25, 1915.**

140

the most desperate, yet promising, ventures of the whole conflict. On January 2, 1915, as the Battle of Sarikamish gathered way, the Russian High Command sent a telegram to London urgently requesting that the world's greatest naval power should make some demonstration against Turkey. This suggestion immediately touched a responsive chord in those who (like Winston Churchill, the First Lord of the Admiralty, or Lord Fisher) were anxiously casting about for new ways to make naval supremacy effective, and also in those like Lord Kitchener, who doubted the prospects of a decision on the Western Front, and were seeking a different stage on which to deploy Britain's New Armies.

The conjunction of these ideas was not arrived at instantly. Lord Fisher never departed from a predilection for operations in the Baltic;

Lord Kitchener was at first totally averse to any commitment of land forces in the Mediterranean beyond the essential defense of the Suez Canal. But under the steady, unwavering pressure of Churchill, the matching threads were collected together, and spun into the pattern of "Gallipoli." "I did not and I could not make the plan," Churchill afterward wrote. "But when it had been made by the naval authorities, and fashioned and endorsed by high technical authorities and approved by the First Sea Lord, I seized upon it and set it on the path of action; and thereafter espoused it with all my resources."

Steadily the eyes of all concerned were drawn to the Straits of the Dardanelles, the famous Hellespont, the narrow strip of water—swum by Leander and Lord Byron—that divides Europe from Asia Minor, and leads to the Sea of Marmora, the Bosporus, and Constantinople itself. With the isles of Greece behind, the plains of Troy on the right hand, and this glittering prize ahead, it is not amazing that the romantic imagination of men was set alight. More material considerations seemed no less auspicious. "There is little doubt today," wrote the British Official Historian, "that the idea of forcing the Straits . . . was one of the few great strategical conceptions of the World War." Sir William Robertson, who opposed the whole enterprise—and later, as CIGS, any other enterprise that resembled it—has nevertheless provided the crispest summary of its merits: "The advantages to be derived from forcing the Straits were perfectly obvious. Such a success would, as the advocates of the project said, serve to secure Egypt, to induce Italy and the Balkan States to come in on our side, and, if followed by the forcing of the Bosporus, would enable Russia to draw munitions from America and Western Europe, and to export her accumulated supplies of wheat." One logical step further brings us to the overwhelming speculation whether success at Gallipoli might not have averted the Bolshevik Revolution.

Far-reaching plans and "attractive-looking schemes" are one thing; carrying them out is something else. Churchill's inference that the Dardanelles expedition was carefully planned by "high technical authorities" is not borne out by the vicissitudes which affected all its stages— above all, its beginning. There was, indeed, no novelty in the concept of attacking Turkey through the Dardanelles; the British Admiralty and General Staff had studied such a project in 1904, 1906, 1908, and 1911, and had reached the firm conclusion that naval forces alone could not handle the affair. The Gallipoli Peninsula, on the north side of the Straits, would have to be seized, and that would require an army. When

". . . casting about for new ways
. . ." Mr. Winston Churchill, First
Lord of the Admiralty, with Lloyd
George.

the Russian request was received in January 1915, Lord Kitchener
bluntly told Mr. Churchill: ". . . we have no troops to land anywhere."
We have seen what the pressures upon the BEF in France were at this
time, and what weight they lent to Kitchener's verdict. Yet the Government, under Churchill's ardent persuasion, setting aside the reasoned
studies available to it, decided upon an attempt by the navy without
army support. From this decision stemmed endless misfortune; yet,
such are the curiosities of this campaign that it would be an assertive
pundit who laid down that there were *no* chances of success.

The peculiarity of the whole Gallipoli story is the number of times
that the Allies came within inches of success; it is this, as much as anything, that has made its memory so poignant. Churchill, above all, was
conscious of its deceptive promises, and described them in this form:
"Force and time in this kind of operation amount to almost the same
thing, and each can to a very large extent be expressed in terms of the
other. A week lost was about the same as a division. Three divisions in
February could have occupied the Gallipoli Peninsula with little fighting.

(pages 144 and 145) ". . . a magnificent body of . . . Australians and
New Zealanders . . ." Men of the
Australian and New Zealand division aboard a transport.

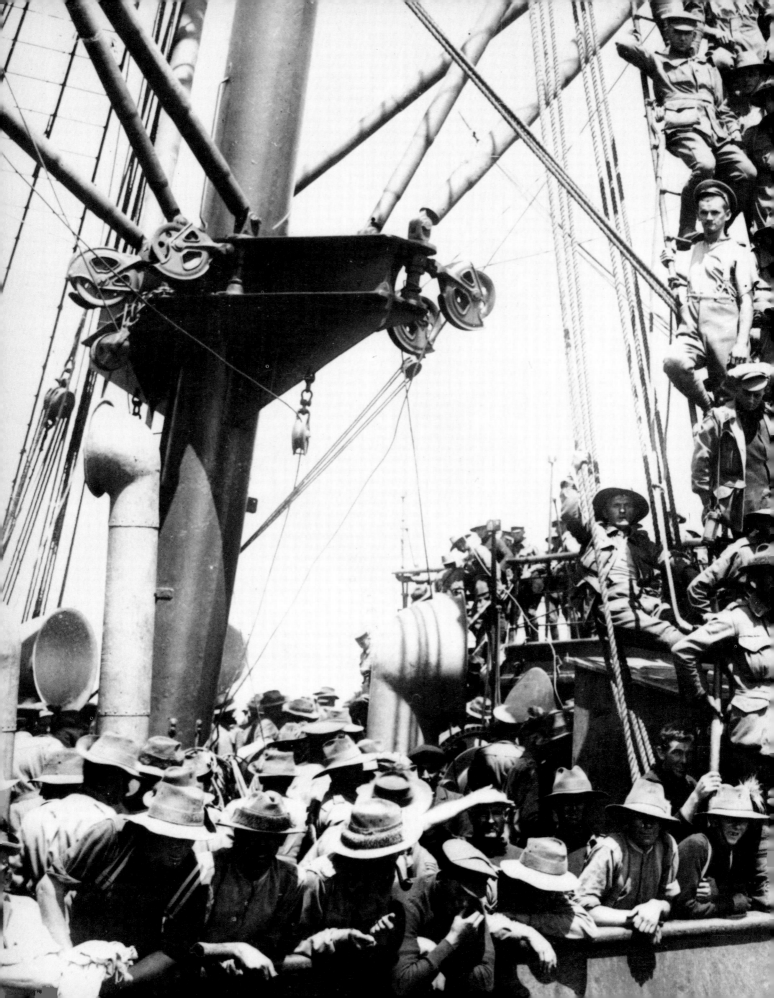

Five could have captured it after March 18. Seven were insufficient at the end of April, but nine might just have done it. Eleven might have sufficed at the beginning of July. Fourteen were to prove insufficient on August 7." Thus a series of "accidents" may be blamed for each successive failure. But can so many breakdowns, so similar in character, truly be called "accidents"? Do they not seem to point to a chronic basic disorder? The Official Historian more soberly remarks: "Many reasons combined to frustrate an enterprise the success of which in 1915 would have altered the course of the war. But every reason will be found to spring from one fundamental cause—an utter lack of preparation before the campaign began."

FEBRUARY 19, 1915

The naval attack by a combined British and French fleet opened on February 19th. Its object was to force an entry into the Sea of Marmora by three deliberate stages: the destruction of the forts and batteries at the mouth of the Straits; the sweeping of the Turkish minefields; the subduing of the forts that guarded the Narrows. For this purpose, ten battleships were available. With two exceptions, these were old vessels "inexorably marked for final extinction within the next year or fifteen months . . . they were surplus and moribund. Yet related to the forts their strength was unimpaired."[1] In our language of today, these ships were expendable—but meanwhile their 12-inch and 9.2-inch guns might do valuable work. The two exceptions were the *Queen Elizabeth*, just-completed prototype of Britain's latest battleship, whose eight 15-inch guns made her the most powerful vessel afloat, and *Inflexible*, a reasonably modern battle cruiser.

The difficulties and drawbacks which surrounded purely naval operations against fixed shore defenses, even if old-fashioned, were at once encountered. One by one the entrance forts were "silenced" during the morning of the 19th, but when the attack was resumed during the afternoon many of their guns were back in action. A further bombardment was planned for the following day, but bad weather forced it to be broken off. The Turks now had a week's grace; when the fleet returned on the

FEBRUARY 25

25th, much of its work had to be done again. Progress, however, was steadily made; the outer defenses were overcome, and landing-parties of marines and seamen were able to move about on the peninsula virtually unopposed. Now the second stage of the task began, more perilous and much harder: the sweeping of the approaches to the Narrows, where fixed and loose mines and hidden torpedo tubes were the main obstacle, themselves guarded by more forts and by mobile batteries which were

[1] Winston Churchill, *The World Crisis.*

146

difficult to spot. All through the first weeks of March this work continued, with small craft playing a major role, until by the 18th all was set for another full-scale attack. But already the true nature of the whole process was becoming evident. Admiral Carden, the naval commander, had given his opinion on March 13th that "in order to ensure my communications line immediately fleet enters the Sea of Marmora, military operations on a large scale should be opened at once." The Government, indeed, had reached this conclusion before the naval attacks even started; the question was to find the troops. The improvidence of allowing the naval onset to go forward, knowing that an army would be needed, but not yet possessing it, may make the student marvel.

Fourteen British and four French battleships advanced toward the Narrows on March 18th. The French moved in to engage the defenses at close range, and in the space of an hour had reduced them to silence; a British squadron now came up to relieve them. As the French, already considerably battered, withdrew, *Gaulois* received a serious hit, which later made it necessary to beach her. *Bouvet* struck a mine, and sank in a few minutes with most of her crew. *Suffren* and *Charlemagne* were badly damaged by gunfire. The British fared little better: *Irresistible* and *Ocean* both struck mines and went to the bottom, though in each case the larger part of the crew was able to get away. *Inflexible*, next to *Queen Elizabeth* the most important unit, was severely hit by shellfire,

". . . one of Britain's most distinguished and cultivated officers . . ." General Sir Ian Hamilton (facing camera center) with Major General Braithwaite, his Chief of Staff, sitting on his right.

and then also struck a mine, compelling her to withdraw to Malta for refitting. It was not immediately apparent, but these losses spelled the end of the naval enterprise as such.

At first, despite the suddenness and severity of the misfortune, the naval leaders were not too disturbed. General Sir Ian Hamilton, one of Britain's most distinguished and cultivated officers, and a friend of Kitchener, had arrived to command such land forces as could be assembled in the Middle East to help the navy. Admiral Carden's health had broken down, and his successor, de Robeck, now told Hamilton: "We are all getting ready for another go and not in the least beaten or down-hearted." In London, when the news arrived, Fisher and Admiral Sir Arthur Wilson met Churchill "with expressions of firm determination to fight it out. . . . The War Council was also quite steady and determined. . . ."

Sir Ian Hamilton was soon undeceived. He wrote to Kitchener on March 19th: "I am most reluctantly driven to the conclusion that the straits are not likely to be forced by battleships . . . and that . . . the Army's part . . . must be a deliberate and prepared military operation, carried out at full strength, so as to open a passage for the Navy." To this Kitchener surprisingly replied: "You know my view, that the Dardanelles must be forced, and that if large military operations on the Gallipoli Peninsula by your troops are necessary to clear the way, those operations must be undertaken . . . and must be carried through." By March 23rd Admiral de Robeck had come round to Hamilton's opinion; the latter commented: "The fat (that is us) is fairly in the fire."

On one point all the prewar studies had been unanimous—and no subsequent critic ever challenged this—that for the success of any combined military and naval attack on the Gallipoli Peninsula, "secrecy and surprise were essential." Already, clear notice had been given of Allied intentions, and more than a month had passed since the navy had begun its bombardments. In January only one Turkish division was stationed on the peninsula, with another on the Asiatic side. In March General Liman von Sanders was placed in charge of the defenses—a potent reinforcement in himself. In April he disposed of four divisions on the peninsula, with two across the straits. Defenses had been constructed at all likely landing points, batteries placed, machine-gun positions dug and concealed, wire stretched across the beaches, running in places under the surface of the water. The Turks were not overwhelmingly strong for what they had to do, but thanks to the leisurely progress of the Allies, they were ready.

How General Hamilton prepared himself in under forty days from his departure from London remains something of a miracle. During that time he had to create a staff and an army; he had to establish his base; he had to draw up a plan; he had to prepare his men for one of the most hazardous feats of war. Every circumstance seemed to conspire against him; it was even found that essential stores from England had to be unshipped and repacked at Alexandria before the army could use them. Above all, however, there was the question of the expeditionary force itself; no study of the Gallipoli campaign is acceptable unless it admits that, despite high courage and wonderful spirit, the units at Hamilton's disposal were an army only in name. The most important was the 29th Division, the last of the British Regulars, formed of overseas garrisons

149

(above) ". . . battleship of Britain's famous 'Fast Division' . . ." H.M.S. Queen Elizabeth in Mudros Harbor.

(right) ". . . everything from ships to horseshoes." Alexandria docks; Indian troops about to embark their mules and fodder.

150

with very few reservists. It was a fine formation—but it had hardly been exercised as a division. There was an improvised Royal Naval Division of bluejackets and Marines, lacking artillery and almost all ancillary services. There was a magnificent body of some 39,000 Australians and New Zealanders, but they were still in the early stages of training and organization. An Indian brigade and a Territorial division (also weak in artillery) completed the available British forces; the French contributed a colonial division, with another to come. An offer of three Greek divisions (with the obvious corollary of Greek entry into the war) brought a hasty rejection from Russia, indeed, from the Czar himself. The Russians had asked for this diversion; they could do nothing to assist it; yet for political reasons they vetoed Greek support. "History in its long record of the short-sighted selfishness shown by individual members of coalitions, devoted in lip-service to a common cause, can hardly provide a more fatal example."[2]

[2] Cruttwell, *A History of the Great War*. The Russians feared Greek designs on Constantinople.

The month sped swiftly by. Each of the actors was occupied in his own way. Liman von Sanders was collecting information, urging forward his defensive preparations. His Turkish allies inflamed their martial ardor by the massacre of three-quarters of a million Armenians in their midst. The Royal Navy was working out the details of landing an army on a hostile shore without any special equipment. The Naval Air Service was probing the Turkish defenses. The Australians, in the intervals of hard training, were terrifying the population of Cairo. Sir Ian Hamilton was searching for everything from ships to horseshoes. Through his whole force ran an extraordinary exhilaration, often matching the feeling, if not the words, of the poet Rupert Brooke: "Oh God! I've never been quite so happy in my life I think. . . . I suddenly realize that the ambition of my life has been—since I was two—to go on a military expedition against Constantinople." But Rupert Brooke died of blood poisoning as the expedition sailed; neither for him nor for his comrades was there more than a distant vision of the Sublime Porte in store.

APRIL 25

It was 5:00 A.M. on the morning of April 25th when Liman von Sanders was awakened with the news that the Allies had landed. Thereafter, reports flowed in briskly, none of them pleasant hearing for the German commander. He had to make up his mind quickly which of several landfalls were real attacks and which were feints; he guessed wrongly. But von Sanders's error scarcely helped the British soldiers; it was part of the irony of the day that such success as it brought forth was obtained largely through accident and at the least likely places.

No more than any other episode of the War can the Gallipoli story be separated from surrounding events. The day on which Sir Ian Hamilton's men clawed their way ashore was also the fourth day of "Second Ypres," marking the second crisis of that battle. Gripped by a desperate shortage of every kind of munitions, pressed by Joffre and Foch to extend its front, and also to join in French offensives, and now hammered at its most sensitive point by the German Army using a terrible new weapon, the situation of the British Army in France was grim indeed. During the testing months of March (Neuve Chapelle), April, and May ("Second Ypres and "Artois"), Sir John French's field guns possessed 8.6, 10.6, and 11 rounds per gun per day, respectively, as against an estimated requirement of 50 rounds per gun per day. His chief heavy gun, the obsolete 4.7 converted naval gun of the Boer War, could fire during those months 5.3, 4.2, and 4.3 rounds per gun per day, as against an estimated need of 25. "It was," says an officer of heavy artillery, "almost 'reasons in writing' for firing away a shell." Even the guns themselves were scarce. When the 27th and 28th (Regular) British divisions relieved two divisions of the French XVI Corps in February, they found that the French had been supported by 120 75-mm. field guns and 30 heavies. The British had only 72 18-pounders between them. The resurrection of the 4.7 told its tale. At Ypres the Second Army was able to deploy only 8 of the "standard" 60-pounders, against 44 4.7s. And the 4.7 had already won the name of "Strict Neutrality" because of its erratic shooting. In the face of these facts, what chance did Ian Hamilton have of properly equipping his force? His first four divisions contained only 118 artillery pieces instead of their "establishment" of 306; this shortage persisted throughout the campaign, and with it a dearth of ammunition. From the beginning, these factors proved decisive.

Hamilton's plan was well considered, as was to be expected of an officer of his distinction. His most important feint was a complete success, his diversions proved immensely valuable, but his entire action was dominated by the need to offset the material weakness of his army by the resources of the fleet. It was this which made the tempting "armchair strategy" of a landing at Bulair, at the neck of the peninsula, impossible; it was this that drew him toward Cape Helles, at the very tip, where naval action—combined with a French landing at Kum Kale, on the Asiatic shore—would be most effective. It was to Helles that he directed the crack 29th Division, to land at five places (so-called "Beaches," identified by the letters S, V, W, X, and Y). The Australian and New Zealand Army Corps (ANZAC) was sent farther up the western coast, to Gaba Tepe; the Royal Naval Division successfully distracted von Sanders's attention toward Bulair with simulated landings.

It was the Australians who went ashore first at 4:20 A.M in the murky half-light of dawn, through which the hilly coast was just becoming visible. At once the strange hazards of this unprecedented adventure were felt. The approach through the darkness produced the complete and hoped-for surprise, but as the boats containing the leading wave of 1,500 men set off for the shore, a strong current carried them 2 miles north of their intended landing point—and in the darkness nobody perceived this. The results were inscrutably mixed: "Anzac Cove," where the Australians grounded, was an unprepossessing place where rugged cliffs loomed over a narrow strip of sand. For that reason it was only lightly defended, and the Australians were able to scramble ashore without much difficulty or loss. But once landed, they were soon entangled in scrubby ravines and rocky gullies. Cohesion was lost; impetus died away. The awakened Turks opened a destructive fire upon the supporting waves. The "buildup" of the beachhead was immensely hampered by the false landfall. Yet the prospects of far-reaching success were there for a brief time—only to be snatched away by the fortuitous intervention of one observant and determined Turk. Mustafa Kemal Pasha, commanding the Turkish 19th Division, with forces never outnumbered by less than three to one, launched a counterattack which stopped the eager but disorganized Australians in their tracks. More, it clenched the Turkish grip on the dominating height of Sari Bair, the bastion against which every subsequent Anzac effort withered.

So unpromising was the position at "Anzac Cove" at nightfall on the 25th that General Birdwood, the Corps commander, even suggested immediate withdrawal. This Hamilton resolutely refused to accept; instead, the Australians and New Zealanders were committed to a furious and laborious battle in which their remarkable fighting qualities were for the first time revealed. General Sir John Monash, then commanding an Australian brigade, wrote: "It was during the next three weeks, when the Turks had got over the surprise and shock of our first wild rush, and came at us, with odds of five to one against us, collecting their reserves from all over the Peninsula, and hurling themselves upon us like fanatics, in their mad efforts to drive us into the sea—it was then that the real fine, brave, steady work was done by the Australians. . . . All that was far finer work than the first mad rush ashore, which was all over in a few hours, while everybody was well and strong, and recently fed, and excited."

It was another story at Cape Helles.

One resemblance, however, persisted: of the five "beaches" assaulted, it was at the least hopeful that success was won, and accidents seemed to assist, rather than diminish, this luck. At Y Beach, the northernmost, where conditions closely resembled those at "Anzac Cove," the attacking battalion landed without much trouble at the foot of steep cliffs, but, like the Australians, incurred loss and confusion inland. So desperate did its position appear the following morning, and so gloomy the general picture, that the unit was withdrawn. At X Beach, some two miles south, a seemingly unpropitious site again proved an advantage; here, too, a relatively easy landing was made, and here one of the few positive gains resulted. Despite counterattacks, the British were able to maintain and enlarge their position and bring much-needed aid to their comrades farther down the coast. Swinging across to S Beach, on the opposite flank, before we turn to the high drama of the main assault in

154

the center, admirable cooperation between navy and army enabled the troops to capture the Turkish defenses and beat off counterattacks without great difficulty. This was almost a model operation; it was doubtless assisted by the successful French landing at Kum Kale, which distracted the Turks on the Asiatic side who might otherwise have concentrated their fire from the rear on the attackers of S Beach.

But these were all minor affairs, diversions and subsidiaries to the principal landings at W Beach and V Beach. The first of these was thenceforward known as "Lancashire Landing," through the exploit of the 1st Battalion, Lancashire Fusiliers. It is no denigration of this splendid battalion to say that its achievement, once again, was due to an accident. And once again, too, the experience of the Australians was repeated on a lesser scale; for as the towing craft cast off the boats crammed with soldiers on entering shallow water, the left-hand company veered away from the main body toward the forbidding headland of Cape Tekke. It was as well that it did so, for W Beach itself was one of the most heavily defended localities along the whole coast. Wire ran down to the water's edge; artillery and machine guns were sited to enfilade the stormers as they struggled through the wire. The Turks withheld their fire until the last moment (a tactic which requires strong nerves, and for which they have been much commended, but which did not generally work out to the defenders' advantage). Here it did; for a merciless converging fire smote the Fusiliers as their boats touched the sand. "Many were shot down in the water, others were hit before they tried to disembark, some were drowned. Nevertheless, undismayed by the hail of bullets and regardless of gaps in the ranks, the Lancashire Fusiliers strove desperately to force their way through the masses of barbed wire which confronted them close to the water's edge, and to press on beyond."[3] The attempt would have been a stark impossibility, a fruitless massacre, but for the company which had taken the wrong direction. Landing where they were least expected, among the rocks at the foot of the cliff, these men were able to outflank the Turkish defenses and bring help without which the rest of the battalion would inevitably have been destroyed. Thus a foothold was won; a supporting battalion came in, and slowly, through a day of furious combat, the beachhead was expanded and gripped.

There remains the epic of V Beach. For this assault, an old collier, the *River Clyde,* was converted into a crude Infantry Landing Ship. Great doors were cut in her sides, gangplanks led down from them, and with

[3] Major General Sir C. E. Callwell, *The Dardanelles.*

155

the aid of lighters it was hoped that the 2,000 men in her hold would be able to rush ashore more quickly than any boats could carry them. Half a battalion in open boats would accompany this onset. It was an ingenious plan, but it did not work. As with the Lancashires, when the boats touched ground they were greeted with a terrible fire; in some of them, every man was hit before he could leap out. Many craft became unmanageable as the sailors in charge were struck down. "Within a few minutes, this portion of the attack had been to all intents and purposes defeated, the troops detailed for the operation were almost wiped out of existence, and the few survivors were cowering at the water's edge under the inadequate protection of the lip scooped by the waves."[4]

The *River Clyde* grounded simultaneously with the disaster to the boats. But at once it was seen that she was still in water too deep for men to wade ashore; a pier of lighters had to be formed against a strong lateral current that constantly swung them out of position, under a murderous fire. Time after time the soldiers in the hold tried to race ashore; time after time gaps in the pier opened up and stopped them; time after time the officers and men of the Royal Navy tried to force the lighters back into position and hold them there. Twice, for long periods until he collapsed with exhaustion, Commander Unwin braced himself against a lighter in the current to steady it, and shouted to the soldiers to come on. Whenever there seemed to be the slightest chance, they did so. Their brigadier was killed; their casualties were frightful. "Air Commodore Samson came flying over . . . at this moment, and looking down saw that the calm blue sea was 'absolutely red with blood' for a distance of fifty yards from the shore, 'a horrible sight to see.' Red ripples washed up on the beach, and everywhere the calm surface of the water was whipped up into a ghastly discoloured foam by thousands of falling bullets. The sun was shining brightly. . . . And so they kept pulling the lighters back into position, and the men kept running out of the ship and the Turks kept killing them."[5] One of the reinforcements who flowed in later wrote: "There, below the pontoon we had to cross from *River Clyde*, the water was six feet deep and so crystal clear that on the bottom we could see, lying in perfect preservation, the uniformed bodies of the soldiers who had been hit or who had fallen in while scrambling ashore ten days earlier." He adds that, with the 88 pounds of equipment that each man carried, once in, "they did not come up again." The regiments

[4] *Ibid.*

[5] Alan Moorehead, *Gallipoli.*

". . . a bitter fight just for a foothold." Interrogating Turkish prisoners after the Third Battle of Krithia, June 4, 1915.

concerned in this tragedy were the Royal Dublin Fusiliers, the Royal Munster Fusiliers, and the Hampshire Regiment.

This was the first day at Gallipoli; there were 259 more days. But everything that happened afterward was clouded by the losses, the failures, and the delusive successes of April 25th. "No continuous line existed, no dominating ground, no depth to give shelter from shell-fire had been won."[6] Sari Bair at "Anzac" and Achi Baba at Cape Helles remained firmly in Turkish hands, overlooking the entire British position. The next phase of the campaign, instead of a victorious march across the

[6] Cruttwell, op. cit.

". . . well-nigh destitute . . ." Soldiers on Gallipoli making hand grenades out of old jam tins filled with rusty nails, bits of shell and barbed wire and other scraps of metal, with an explosive charge. The fuse was fitted through the top of the tin and had to be lighted with a match.

". . . his steadily growing . . . army
. . ." Fusiliers of the 42nd Division
arriving at "W" and "V" beaches,
May 1915.

(pages 160 and 161) ". . . another
major blow." Men of the Royal
Naval Division attacking at Gallipoli.

peninsula, was a bitter fight just for a foothold. By May 31st, the British alone had lost 38,000 men. Trenches, barbed wire, machine guns, and stubborn valor in defense proved to be no less effective at Gallipoli than in France—with these differences: that, if the British in France were poverty-stricken in the matter of equipment for trench warfare, at Gallipoli they were well-nigh destitute; and at Gallipoli disease added a dreadful toll to the casualty lists. Of seven Anzac battalions examined in September, 78 percent had dysentery, 64 percent had skin sores, and 5 percent had weak hearts.

All through May and June, and into July, Sir Ian Hamilton tried to push forward his steadily growing but never strong army. By July 15th he had reached the farthest limit of his gains at Cape Helles—about three miles inland. The Turks, for their part, counterattacked vigorously, and on May 18th launched a mass offensive of their own at "Anzac," which was beaten off with frightful losses to the attackers. The stalemate of the Western Front was exactly repeated. And while the army stuck, the navy, on which it was so dependent, was also weakened. The sinking of the battleship *Goliath* by a bold enemy destroyer at the beginning of May might be regarded as an ordinary mishap of war; but when, on May 22nd, the battleship *Triumph* was torpedoed and sunk in broad daylight and in full view of the enemy, and on the next day another battleship, the *Majestic*, met the same fate, it was clear that a new factor had intervened. U-boats had entered the Mediterranean. This spelled the end of continuous, close support of the army by the fleet. The precious *Queen Elizabeth*, with her mighty armament, was sent home for safety.

MAY 18

". . . an Australian attack from 'Anzac' . . ."

This naval setback was in due course compensated for by the arrival of shallow-draft monitors mounting 14-inch guns. At the same time British submarines, penetrating through the Narrows into the Sea of Marmora, and even into the harbor of Constantinople itself, were performing astonishing feats. The submarine *E 11*, under Commander Nasmyth, sank a transport right inside Constantinople harbor. *E 14* sank another transport with 6,000 troops aboard. In all, British submarines accounted for a battleship, a destroyer, 5 gunboats, 11 transports, 44 steamers, and 184 sailing ships, at a cost of 8 of the 13 submarines which made or attempted the perilous passage of the closely guarded Straits. These heroic exploits did much to encourage the army and its commanders during a bleak period.

By August, Hamilton had received substantial reinforcements, which enabled him to consider another major blow. While pinning the enemy at Helles with a holding attack, he landed a fresh force at Suvla Bay, three miles north of "Anzac." Open beaches, lightly defended, offered excellent landing facilities; self-propelled barges, each capable of holding 500 men, greatly eased the task. In conjunction with an Australian attack from "Anzac," there seemed to be a brilliant opportunity of driving a wedge right across the peninsula. But it was not to be. Once again, Mustafa Kemal was the main agent of resistance to the fiery Australian assault from "Anzac," which reached its bitterest intensity of fighting at "Lone Pine Ridge," where fifteen Victoria Crosses, Britain's highest award for gallantry, were won. The Australians were held—but only just. Even ordinary competence, the smallest amount of dash on the part of the commanders at Suvla Bay, would have made the Turkish commander's efforts of no avail. But this was a Corps of inexperienced, half-trained New Army divisions commanded by elderly "dugout" generals who knew nothing of modern war. The landing itself was effected without any difficulty. Losses were mainly due to distant artillery and snipers. But once ashore, an astounding inertia overcame the troops. Their senior commanders were not on the spot; the junior commanders did not know what they were meant to do ("Ought it not to have been a case of sealed envelopes . . . on a lavish scale?" asks one critic). The majority of them did nothing, and the spectacle was seen of large numbers of men bivouacking and even bathing on the beaches, when only a thin Turkish screen stood before them, and while their Anzac comrades were engaged in furious battle only a few miles away. Such errors are paid for dearly in war; the Suvla fiasco meant the doom of the Gallipoli expedition.

Long before this the first omens had been seen. In May, Lord Fisher, horrified at the implications of the first failures, had resigned from the Admiralty. This step, coming in conjunction with the "munitions scandal," as the press seized upon reports of the grave shortages in France, brought the end of the Liberal Government in Britain. Mr. Asquith, the Prime Minister, formed a coalition with the Conservatives one of whose conditions was the dismissal of Churchill. Thus the expedition lost its most potent supporter. By September, as Russia tottered, and new battles loomed ahead in France, Lord Kitchener, asked if he intended to go on to Constantinople, was saying: "By God, no! By God, no! I have been let into the thing, and never again. Out I come, the first moment I can." In October, Hamilton was recalled. Sir Charles Monro, a Western Front Army commander, went out to Gallipoli to report. He advised evacuation; in Churchill's bitter sentence, "He came, he saw, he capitulated." But a month later Kitchener himself visited the Peninsula, and reached the same conclusion. The only question was whether evacuation would not produce a disaster beside which even the horrors of April 25th would pale.

DECEMBER 19–20 A masterpiece of planning, ingenuity, and deception of a quality the half of which might have transformed some of the earlier operations, turned the evacuations into a wry triumph. On December 19th–20th, Suvla and "Anzac" were abandoned. "Down dozens of little gullies leading back from the front lines came little groups of six to a dozen men, the last (in every case an officer) closing the gully with a previously prepared frame of barbed wire, or lighting a fuse which an hour later would fire a mine for the wrecking of a sap or a tunnel by which the enemy could follow; all these little columns of men kept joining up, like so many rivulets which flow into the main stream, and so at last they coalesced into four continuous lines. . . . There was no check, no halting, no haste or running, just a steady, silent tramp in single file, without any lights or smoking, and every yard brought us nearer to safety . . . each line marched (like so many ghostly figures in the dim light) in single file on to its appointed jetty, the sound of marching feet having been deadened by laying a floor of sandbags; and so on to a motor barge ('beetles' we call them) holding 400. On to these, generals, staff officers, machine-gunners and privates all packed up, promiscuously and quietly. There was a short pause to make sure that no one had been left behind. Not a sound could be heard on the shore except the throb, throb of the beetles' engines, and on the distant hills the spasmodic rifle-shots of the enemy, discharged at our now empty trenches. Then the landing and loading

staff, chiefly naval officers, stepped aboard. 'Let go all over—right away'
was the last order, and slowly we moved out."[7]

The Turks were completely deceived; there was no interference, no
loss at all. And the miracle was that on January 8th–9th, 1916, the whole
process was repeated again at Helles with equal success. And that was
the end of "Gallipoli."

"A masterpiece of planning . . ."
Bringing off guns and personnel
from Suvla, December 1915.

The cost had been high, but in relation to the prize aimed at and to
the normal casualty rate of the war not outstanding. From first to last,
the expedition employed 410,000 British and 79,000 French troops. The
final figure for British casualties was 213,980. Of these, 145,154 were due
to sickness: dysentery was at the top of the list with 29,728 victims,
diarrhea next with 10,373, and enteric fever with 9,423. An indication of
the peculiar and unlooked-for hazards of the campaign is the figure of
15,000 casualties from frostbite, following a severe blizzard in November.

[7] General Sir John Monash, *War Letters*.

The French lost 47,000 men, and in addition there were British naval casualties to be reckoned. On the other side, the Turkish official statement of their losses was 251,000, but Turkish records were not very strictly kept, and some of their authorities place the total as high as 350,000. What is certain is that, coming on top of their dreadful losses in the Caucasus, the damage done to the Turkish military effort was fatal and permanent.

Nevertheless, the Gallipoli campaign was an Allied failure, and for Britain a failure of a special kind. For this was the last attempt in British history to exercise absolute naval supremacy in the traditional manner. Indeed, 1915 was the last year of that supremacy: the paralysis of the Grand Fleet and the growth of the submarine menace during the remainder of the War steadily undermined its strength; the process was completed by the later growth of the American and Japanese navies. Since the British Empire was founded upon naval might, one may truthfully say that the Gallipoli failure marked the beginning of the end of that Empire. But the paradoxical manner of its passing was indicated by the formidable role of the soldiers of the two Dominions, Australia and New Zealand, whose contribution was now seen to be much more than a helpful gesture. Taken in conjunction with what Canada had shown herself capable of at Ypres, it meant that the transition from Empire could add to, rather than detract from, Britain's strength. By 1918 the Dominion contingents had become her spearhead, her "shock troops." But this was a distant consolation when the curtain sadly fell at Gallipoli at the end of 1915.

Quite apart from Gallipoli, 1915 was a bad year for sea power. In the North Sea, across which the German High Seas Fleet and the British Grand Fleet glared at each other in impotent rage, a continuing impasse was reached. Despite admirable Intelligence work, the Royal Navy never found a formula for solving the North Sea problem; on the other hand, partly under the influence of the Kaiser, the German admirals displayed a curious and increasing timidity. The exception was Admiral von Hipper, who, after the Heligoland setback, showed what might be done with battle cruisers and light craft by "tip-and-run" raids. He had caused much alarm in November 1914 when he bombarded the east-coast resort of Yarmouth; in December he was back again, attacking the more northerly towns of Scarborough, Hartlepool, and Whitby. At Hartlepool some 500 civilian casualties deeply angered the British public, and the apparent inability of the navy to prevent such raids did nothing to soothe their feelings. To those who knew the facts, what was more disturbing was that the British had been prepared for this German venture, and had laid a trap for it which failed through bad signaling and through dilatoriness at the Admiralty.

In January a third sortie by Hipper was less fortunate. He was caught at the Dogger Bank by Admiral Beatty's battle cruisers, coming up at the astonishing rate of 28 knots and engaging at 17,000 yards. Two German cruisers, *Blücher* and *Seydlitz*, were severely damaged in the running fight, and *Blücher* was finally sunk. But this was a slender reward; "We ought to have had all four," remarked Beatty later, and this is most probably what would have happened had his own flagship, *Lion*, not been put out of action, forcing him to transfer to a destroyer at the critical moment and thus lose control of the battle. Again there were signaling faults; Beatty's second-in-command misread his instructions and broke off the action. The Germans, however, were so dismayed that they abandoned their active policy for the rest of the year. Only a very few informed observers, assessing correctly the damage to *Lion*, pondered with misgivings upon the accuracy and destructive power of the German 11-inch guns against the thinner armor of the British ships.

JANUARY 24, 1915

Frustrated on the surface, the Germans turned to underwater warfare. On February 4th a blockade of British waters was announced, with the clear implication that this would be carried out mainly by submarines. The United States Government warned Germany that she would be held responsible for losses of American life and shipping. On May 1st the American tanker *Gulflight* was attacked and damaged, and her captain died. Six days later, the Cunard liner *Lusitania*, with nearly 2,000 passengers, was sunk; of the 1,198 who lost their lives, many were Americans. In August more Americans were drowned when another passenger ship went down. The resulting uproar frightened the Germans into a limitation of submarine activity. The British authorities had been alerted to its dangers, and though their immediate remedies left much to be desired, it is likely that without this warning the impact of unrestricted U-boat action later in the War would have been far more serious. But, for Germany, the worst aspect of this abortive expedient was the hardening of American opinion against her, which prepared the way for subsequent intervention.

FEBRUARY 4

MAY 7

Elsewhere, the operations which control of the seas permitted against the German colonies, or which had been brought about by Turkey's entry into the War, continued. German Southwest Africa was overrun by the (mainly mounted) forces of the Union of South Africa,

(pages 168 and 169) ". . . glared at each other in impotent rage . . ." British battleships in line ahead.

(right) ". . . the Cunard liner Lusitania . . ."

(below) ". . . 1,198 who lost their lives . . ." Funeral procession of the Lusitania victims on the way to the graveside.

under the personal leadership of the Prime Minister, General Botha. The remnants of the German garrison capitulated in July. In East Africa, following the collapse of an ill-prepared expedition from India against the port of Tanga, stalemate set in, which lasted through the year. In Mesopotamia political influences—particularly, as the year wore on, the need to offset the influence on the Moslem world of the Turkish success at Gallipoli—brought about the fatal "decision" to make an attempt on Baghdad. In October, the British Cabinet telegraphed that the commanding general "may march on Baghdad if he is satisfied that the force he has available is sufficient for the operation." As the Official Historian remarks, this meant: "We want it done, but the soldiers must take the risk." As a result, against growing Turkish forces, an expedition moved up the river Tigris under General Townshend. On November 21st he attacked the Turkish defenses at Ctesiphon; two days later, with nearly 5,000 casualties out of his total force of 14,000, Townshend had made little progress against an opposition as stubborn as that on Gallipoli. His British and Indian troops were exhausted; he began his retreat to Kut-al-Imara, and there, on December 7th, he was invested. For the time being, the Turks were doing well.

But it was in the Mediterranean again, where we have already observed its most agonizing failure, that sea power was having its largest influence. The command of that sea, despite the intrusion of U-boats, permitted diplomatic essays by the Allies of which the most fruitful was the winning over of Italy by lavish, but regrettable, promises. For some, most notably Mr. Lloyd George, both then and later when he became Prime Minister of Britain, the Italian theater always held out tempting promises. It suggested possibilities of a decisive blow against Austria, a cardinal feature of the policy of "knocking away the props" from under Germany. In fact, this was an illusion; it was Germany that "propped" her relatively feeble allies, cleverly using their forces as diversions of Allied strength. At the same time, the geography of Italy rendered her most unsuitable for great military enterprises. "Faced everywhere by the rampart of the Alps," the Italians found that there were only two sectors where they could deploy in any substantial force: the Trentino, facing northward to the Tyrol, where steep mountains and lack of communications presented every difficulty; and the Isonzo, facing eastward towards Gorizia and Trieste. It was here, against the rocky plateau of the Carso, that the Italians made their chief effort in eleven "Battles of the Isonzo," of which the first four took place in 1915. These four battles cost Italy some 250,000 men. Her gains were very small; the effect on

171

"'. . . the rampart of the Alps' . . ." Italian Alpini moving up a mountainside.

Austria was insufficient even to influence the overthrow of Serbia. Trench warfare conditions, with special impediments created by the mountainous terrain, found the Italians as ill-prepared as any of the Allies. Here, as everywhere, the equation of barbed wire and machine guns against artillery and human flesh produced its inevitable answer and awaited its only possible—technological—solution.

Meanwhile, in the absence of this, the Central Powers, enjoying to the full the advantages of their central position, collected the "honors"

172

"... the Bulgarians struck in ..."
Bulgarian infantry advancing to
attack.

of 1915. The Gallipoli breakdown, coupled with Italian failures, tipped the balance in the Balkans. Nothing less than the capture of Constantinople, or some equally brilliant stroke, could have offset the pro-German influence of the monarchs of Greece and Bulgaria. Greece swung now into quasi-neutrality; Bulgaria, pausing only to gather in her harvest, joined the Central Powers on September 6th. This spelled the doom of Serbia. While Austrian and German forces attacked in great strength from the north, the Bulgarians struck in against her eastern flank. At the end of a long and pitiful retreat through the mountains in the depths of winter, encumbered by a mass flight of the population, the gallant Serbian Army, reduced by half, reached the coast of Albania, and was taken off by Allied shipping to the island of Corfu. It was a sad end to a brave fight.

SEPTEMBER 6

OCTOBER 5

Bulgarians in trenches at Uskub, where they struck at the rear of the Serbian armies.

(pages 174 and 175) "... a sad end to a brave fight." Serbian guns captured by the Austrians, with a group of prisoners passing by.

"'. . . a nice way to make war!'"
French troops marching through
Salonika.

Sadder still was the almost complete inability of the Allies to bring effective help to the Serbs. The best that could be done—and it amounted almost to nothing—was to land an Anglo-French force at Salonika. There was never any hope of building this expedition up or of overcoming its tremendous communications difficulties sufficiently for any major effort, short of powerful Greek assistance, which was not forthcoming. But the decision to abandon Gallipoli released some troops who were reasonably near. The French were particularly keen on the Salonika enterprise, for political reasons of their own, unconnected with the Balkans: it offered employment to the Republican General Maurice Sarrail, who had been dismissed by Joffre from his command on the Western Front, much to the embarrassment of the French Government.

The first French troops landed at Salonika early in October, beginning the process that was to turn that theater into the "greatest Allied internment camp" of the War, according to sardonic German commentators. Ultimately, this front would consume the energies of over 400,000 British troops alone, of whom 481,000 fell sick at one time or another—a ratio of 1,103 hospital admissions per 1,000 strength. In addition, French, Italian, Russian, and Serbian forces were drawn in, swelling the expedition to a maximum strength of over 600,000 in 1917. With the repulse of the first abortive attempt to advance in December 1915, this huge army fell into feeble quiescence, supported only with great difficulty by heavily strained shipping, which at one stage was losing a vessel every other day in the Mediterranean. Yet politics and armchair strategy prevented the removal of this "ulcer"; instead, the accretion of strength which might have followed the abandonment of Gallipoli was diverted into it. This marked a nadir of Allied strategic planning. As Colonel Repington remarked: "The German spies sit in rows on the quays at Salonika smoking large cigars, and note down every man, horse, gun, and ton of stores landed. This is a nice way to make war!"

THE YEAR OF GROPING 8

My victorious sword has crushed the Russians. . . . Woe to them that yet draw the sword against me!

KAISER WILHELM II

While the first cracks were appearing in the fabric of the British Empire, founded on sea power, the empires of the Hohenzollerns, the Habsburgs, and the Romanoffs were busily grinding one another to dust. Three groups of strategists among the Central Powers agreed that the prime objective for 1915 should be to hammer Russia to her knees, but beyond that point agreement faltered, and what ensued was a compromise, a hotch-potch of methods. The German Eastern Front Command (Hindenburg and Ludendorff) believed in a knockout victory; Conrad von Hötzendorf believed in a devastating victory; Falkenhayn believed in a crippling victory. The differences were marginal, but absolute. In the event, it was a Falkenhayn-Conrad plan that was adopted, with Hindenburg and Ludendorff fretfully seeking to transform it into what they had proposed.

One advantage of Conrad's plan was that it would bring direct relief to the most sensitive part of the Austro-German front, where the final upshot of the bitter winter battles had given the Russians a distinct advantage. Hindenburg's attempt to follow up his Warsaw triumph had succeeded to the extent of destroying the Russian Tenth Army with a loss, according to German sources, of 90,000 prisoners alone. Then Russian counterattacks came in, halting the German advance. At the same time (February 1915) the Austrians, on their extreme right, fighting

FEBRUARY 9, 1915

(opposite, top) ". . . to hammer Russia to her knees . . ." German troops on the march on the Eastern Front; note the inevitable dust as soon as the spring mud had dried.

(bottom) ". . . Conrad . . . believed in a devastating victory . . ." Austrian soldiers filling their water bottles; they look cheerful and sturdy, but Conrad's plans were generally brought to nothing by the unreliability of his armies.

"... the bitter winter battles ..."
Russian prisoners slake their thirst
on their journey into captivity.

through deep snow, won a victory which carried them forward over 60 miles with 60,000 prisoners. But the fall of Przemysl, after nearly five months of siege, on March 22nd, released three Russian corps, with which reinforcement they were able to fight their way back to the Carpathian passes, menacing the whole Austro-German line. Conrad's suggestion of a concentrated blow against the front between Gorlice and Tarnow would not only nullify this gain but also imperil the whole Russian position in the mountains and in Poland.

Indeed, Russia's apparent situation in the spring of 1915 was a fraud. Her great gains had left her with a front 800 miles long, and though her army nominally amounted to over 6,000,000 men, it was unequal to holding so vast an extent. One-third of the soldiers lacked rifles; after the awful casualties of the first six months, many of them were untrained conscripts. Russian shortages of munitions were far worse than those that afflicted the British, and aggravated by corruption and inefficiency. Even so, as Falkenhayn realized, it would be a bold man who believed that this limping giant could be absolutely smashed. The vast depths of the Russian hinterland had defeated Napoleon and could do the same again,

180

(left) "Conrad's suggestion . . . a concentrated blow . . . between Gorlice and Tarnow . . ." General Field Marshal Conrad von Hötzendorf (1852–1925), Chief of the Austrian General Staff until February 1917.

(below) ". . . the fall of Przemysl . . . released three Russian corps . . ." Austrian prisoners taken by the Russians in March 1915.

but the clear possibility existed of destroying a large part of Russia's army before that hinterland could be reached.

This concept was the essence of the Austro-German plan. A new German army, the Eleventh, was formed of eight divisions taken from the Western Front[1] and interpolated into the Austrian line of battle. It was commanded by General (later Field Marshal) August von Mackensen, one of the most thrusting commanders of the War, supported by two notable Staff officers, Colonel Seeckt and Colonel Hentsch (of Marne fame). A preliminary diversion would be provided by the Germans in East Prussia, to be developed into a full-scale attack if all went well.

All did go well. By the end of April the Eleventh Army was in position, without arousing undue Russian suspicion; at any rate, the Russians took no precautionary measures, but this may have been due to characteristic sloth and incompetence. The ground was open, with excellent observation; in contrast with the Western Front, No Man's Land was generally 3,000 to 4,000 yards wide. Von Mackensen had about 700 guns, apart from heavy and light trench mortars, and plenty of ammunition. For a 30-mile front, this was not much by Western Front standards: one gun per 57 yards, as compared with densities that rose to one per 5.2 yards on the Flanders front in 1917. But against the enfeebled Russian artillery it was enough. When Mackensen's four-hour bombardment opened on May 2nd, there was scarcely any reply, and when his infantry, which had worked forward under its cover into jumping-off positions close to the Russian line, went forward, they met with little resistance. Their problem, indeed—foreseen and catered for by the German Staff—was to keep the battle moving. In the west, this

MAY 2

[1] Von Falkenhayn wanted fourteen, but Allied offensives prevented their removal.

(right) "A new German army . . . was formed . . ." German infantry in a motor lorry, which is trying to pass horse transport on a typical Eastern Front road.

(opposite, top) "Their problem . . . was to keep the battle moving." A smashed bridge on the Eastern Front.

(opposite, bottom) "Von Hindenburg . . . argued for a blow in the north . . ." Germans in burning Schaulen (Lithuania).

(pages 184 and 185) "Such success brings enigmas . . ." Austro-Hungarian cavalry and German infantry pass each other in the streets of reoccupied Przemysl, June 3, 1915.

". . . by the end of May . . . 153,000 prisoners . . ." Russian prisoners of war taken by the Germans.

proved to be a constant stumbling block for both sides. But this was not the west; in a fortnight the Germans advanced 95 miles, and by the end of May von Mackensen's Eleventh Army alone had taken 153,000 prisoners and 128 guns.

Such success brings enigmas of its own. What form should the exploitation take? Hindenburg and Ludendorff argued for a blow in the

"... every adverse circumstance for the devoted Russian soldiery ..."

north, aimed ultimately at Petrograd, which would automatically produce a Russian collapse in Poland. But Falkenhayn, who faced the implications of Italy's entry into the War, the necessity to win Bulgaria's entry by the conquest of Serbia, and the knowledge of Allied offensive preparations in France, feared the consequences of a drawn-out campaign deep in Russian territory. He settled for a more direct and lesser solution. At the same time, if by chance his aim of neutralizing Russia without her complete surrender should be within sight, feelers were put out for a separate peace between her and the Central Powers. But these

188

were rejected by the Czar. The War continued, with every adverse circumstance for the devoted Russian soldiery and their harassed commanders. Warsaw fell on August 4th, and at the end of the month the burning ruins of Brest-Litovsk were in enemy hands. On September 5th the Czar took personal command of his armies—a step which has been regarded as a considerable acceleration of his downfall, since to many it implied the increased influence of a court which, through the Czarina, was thought to be dangerously pro-German, and that was in any case, also through her, under the malign persuasion of the monk Rasputin.

It was at this stage, with his armies standing 125 miles east of Warsaw, but with the Russian front now straightening and hardening before them, that Falkenhayn determined to break off the campaign. But neither his eastern commanders nor his Austrian allies were quite ready for that. The Austrians insisted on a further offensive in Galicia, but did themselves nothing but harm against reviving Russian counterattacks. In the north, despite the loss of Vilna, and the activities of a German cavalry army of 30,000 men that scythed (like J. E. B. Stuart in the Civil War) across their rear, the Russians were able to stabilize a line along rivers, lakes, forests, and marshes where they could spend the winter and try to recuperate. Angry and disappointed, Hindenburg blamed Falkenhayn's strategy for this result; but the latter was adamant and unrepentant. The greatest single campaign of the whole War was over.

Though its results are not to be measured simply by statistics, the statistics are staggering. At their extreme limit, the Austro-German forces had advanced 300 miles; they had captured 3,000 guns; it has been stated that they inflicted 2,000,000 casualties on the Russians,[2] of whom about half were prisoners. But more important than that—for the distances were nothing in Russia's immensity, and even the loss of life was small beside her huge population—was the psychological blow and its political outcome. The Russians felt themselves powerless, and attributed this sensation mainly to the regime. A mortal blow had been struck at Czarism itself, and many of those who rejoiced at this failed to understand how much else would be dragged down in its fall. Yet, at the end of 1915, Russia was *not* defeated, as her astonishing performance during the next year would show. Falkenhayn had not, as he supposed, achieved "the indefinite crippling of Russia's offensive strength." The losses of his own armies had also been very high, and in the last analysis one perceives that the real victim of the Gorlice-Tarnow campaign was not Russia, but the Empire of Austria-Hungary.

[2] Cruttwell, *A History of the Great War.*

189

"Warsaw fell on August 4th . . ." Entry of King Leopold of Bavaria. The civilian population is conspicuous by its absence, perhaps by order.

". . . the Russian front . . . hardening . . ." A German 210-mm. (8-inch) howitzer in action on the Eastern Front in August 1915.

". . . 2,000,000 casualties . . . of whom about half were prisoners." Russian prisoners pulling their own trolley-mounted machine guns into captivity.

A large factor in Falkenhayn's apprehensions during the last stages of the Gorlice-Tarnow offensive was the evident preparation of the western Allies for a major operation designed both to bring relief to Russia and to capitalize on German preoccupations there. Four German

"The greatest single campaign of the whole war was over." German sledge transport parked outside Warsaw, winter 1915-1916.

divisions were brought back from the east to meet the Allied onset, but, more important still, as delay after delay postponed the attack, the Germans were able to prepare second lines of defense at all the threatened points.

Joffre's plan was grandiose: the main assault would be by 35 French divisions in Champagne, while 18 more French and 12 British divisions concurrently attacked in Artois. By stripping their fortresses, the French assembled 2,000 heavy guns besides their field artillery, another 3,000 pieces. Ten divisions of cavalry were held in readiness to exploit the expected breakthrough. With this unprecedented mass of equipment, there was little doubt among the French commanders that a break-

through would take place; General de Castelnau even prophesied that after the bombardment the infantry would be able to advance with their rifles at the slope—a delusion which similarly possessed General Rawlinson on the Somme almost a year later. With afterknowledge of what actually took place, many critics have jeered at the idea of massing cavalry close to the front of attack, as both French and British constantly did during this phase of the War. The deficiencies of the cavalry arm in modern conditions were evident, but what would one say of generals who aimed at a breakthrough and made *no* provision to exploit it? Cavalry was still the only available mobile arm.

The British entered this great offensive with reluctance. Soldiers and Government alike, after the wretched experiences of April and May, would have preferred to conserve and build up their strength in France for a really powerful stroke in 1916—some adding that this policy might offer just that margin of strength required to carry the Gallipoli campaign through to success. But Joffre "would not countenance it for a moment." His demands were peremptory, and took the usual form; first, relief of French formations. This was done by the creation of a British Third Army in July, which took over from the French Second Army on the Somme. Secondly, Joffre demanded British offensive action, which resulted in the Battle of Loos. Lord Kitchener, the most authoritative opponent of western offensives, was persuaded by the bleak news of Russian and Italian setbacks. Visiting General Haig's First Army Headquarters after conversations with Joffre in August, he repeated to Haig privately what he had already told Sir John French: "The Russians . . . had been severely handled, and *it was doubtful how much longer their army could withstand the German blows.* Up to the present, he had favoured a policy of active defence in France until such time as all our forces were ready to strike. The situation which had arisen in Russia had caused him to modify these views. . . . And he *had decided that we must act with all our energy, and do our utmost to help the French, even though, by so doing, we suffered very heavy losses indeed.*"[3] Not even in the matter of locale was the British Commander in Chief able to assert his views. Joffre insisted that the British should attack side by side with the French, through the ruined mining villages and slag heaps of Loos and Lens, instead of farther north, as both French and Haig preferred.

This was but one of the many contradictions that seriously affected the Allied attack. Delay followed the decision to relieve the French Second Army; more delay followed from the choice of terrain for Joffre's main attack in Champagne. If the Allies felt themselves too weak to attack in midsummer, without these preparations, by the time they did start the enemy was too strong. Furthermore, the delays in Champagne were due to Joffre's selection of an area almost empty of villages and habitations, and therefore also of communications; this was in odd contrast to the densely built-up region in which he asked the British to fight.

[3] Haig's italics.

Tactically, too, the upshot was perverse and discrepant: General Foch incurred heavy losses and failure through massing his reserves too close to the front, where they were cut up by artillery fire; Sir John French suffered the same fate by keeping his reserves too far back. The moral is that of Gallipoli: too many "accidental" features adding up to a fundamental impossibility. But the conjunction of Russian reverses and French desire to liberate lost territory overrode all other considerations. At bottom, there remains the fact of the strategic initiative the Germans had won in 1914; the Allies now were simply dancing to its tune. And this is not a case for mockery; it is precisely for such reasons that the initiative is regarded as a priceless asset in war.

It was not until September 25th that all was ready for the attack. "The greatest battle in the world's history begins today," wrote Haig in his diary. "Some 800,000 French and British troops will actually attack today." "*Votre élan sera irrésistible*," Joffre told his men. Waiting in their assembly trenches under drenching rain, and covered in mud, many of them yet believed him. "Through all the uproar, the bullets and the shells, I go forward like a madman scourged by Furies. . . . There is sulphur in my brain, high explosive in my legs, saltpetre in my quaking chest . . . the feeling that nothing will stop us, nothing. . . . *En avant!*" wrote a French officer. But once again it was all an illusion. In Champagne the deepest French penetration was 3,000 yards; by the third day of the battle their infantry masses were firmly held on the German second position, and their furious onslaught sank into a series of costly and fruitless trench combats. In Artois the story was the same. One division reached the crest of Vimy Ridge, but after two days Joffre ordered Foch to break off the battle, despite the involvement of the British, whom he was urging to continue their efforts.

Beside the enormous French casualties, and the bitter disappointment of their high hopes, the British failure was a small affair. But it contained its own special qualities of tragedy, and had far-reaching effects. The Loos attack was again entrusted to Haig's First Army, this time enjoying far larger artillery support than any hitherto available to the British, though ammunition was still in short supply. Gas was also used, but it was a doubtful asset: ". . . what a risk I must run of gas blowing back upon our own dense masses of troops!" wrote Haig. This was, in fact, what happened on one flank, preventing any progress. Nor was the opposite flank able to advance significantly, but in the center some 8,000 yards of the German front were quickly taken, and for a time there was a distinct possibility of breaking their second line. It was a

195

(pages 196 and 197) ". . . mining villages and slag heaps . . ." British troops in a village in northern France.

question of reserves, and Sir John French, despite Haig's pleas and the urgings of his own Chief of Staff, General Robertson, held the British reserves too far back. When they arrived, it was too late. Consisting of two New Army divisions that had only recently arrived in France—and that had only received their rifles in July—the reserves entered the battle exhausted by long and trying marches, hungry, and ignorant of the situation. In close order, they ran into German artillery and machine-gun fire, which threw them into confusion. It was Suvla Bay again, but far worse; the officers were untrained, and did not know what to do; the whole force began to flow backward, abandoning some of their guns. There was now every possibility of a serious defeat, averted only by the timely arrival of the Guards Division. But the British attack as a whole was wrecked. Haig and his officers were deeply disappointed; and when

"... the bitter disappointment of their high hopes ..." In 1915, as ground attack after attack foundered, men's eyes turned increasingly to the air. This remarkable picture shows the crew of a French machine over Champagne.

(opposite) "... an area almost empty of villages and habitations ..." A French attack waiting to go in behind a barrage in Champagne, September 1915.

(left) "In Artois the story was the same." French infantrymen in a listening post on Vimy Ridge, December 1915. One man is looking through a camouflaged periscope. Both are wearing the recently introduced steel helmets and horizon-blue uniforms.

the news of what had happened seeped through to London, Sir John French, already unpopular in certain Government circles, was held to be to blame, and at the end of the year was removed. By common consent, there being no other officer of comparable stature or experience, General Sir Douglas Haig became Commander in Chief of the British Expeditionary Force.

There was not much else to show for the great Allied autumn offensive. Admittedly, some 25,000 Germans had been captured, and some 150 guns, and in places the enemy had had a bad scare. But against this there had to be reckoned nearly 145,000 French casualties in Champagne and nearly 50,000 more in Artois, with as many British, besides. German losses, all told, may be placed at over 200,000. It was a sad ending, and a bad outlook for the future. As the year drew to a close, Joffre gloomily summed up: "Of all the Entente States, France had furnished the most considerable military effort . . . from the very start she had poured out all she had without counting the cost, and she now began to reach the limit of her resources in men, while the diminution which her effectives would suffer during the course of 1916 already stared her in the face. France needed a period of rest if she was to bring to new offensives renewed strength and increased material resources." This, too, was a vain expectation.

And so the year 1915 ran out, this time without a Christmas "truce" but instead with mounting losses, diminished pity, and diminished hope. The war was being rapidly transformed, and changing all else with it.

THE YEAR OF KILLING: GERMAN GAMBIT $\mathbf{9}$

. . . for England the campaign on the Continent of Europe is at bottom a side-show.
Her real weapons here are the French, Russian and Italian Armies.

GENERAL ERICH VON FALKENHAYN

What was to be done? For both the Allies and the Central Powers, the campaigns of 1915 had been failures. Could this result be reversed in 1916? If not, the destruction of European material and human resources would reach catastrophic proportions. So much was evident, and formed the basis of military planning for the year.

The problem for the Allies was less difficult than for the Central Powers. Russia had been gravely weakened in 1915, but had not been defeated; her huge reserves of strength remained, if only they could be tapped. France also had been weakened, but her army was still the most effective instrument of land war on the Allied side. Italy's will to fight had not yet been impaired, and her warlike capacity was increasing. The forces of the British Empire were at last being mobilized. In manpower and in physical potential the Allies enjoyed great advantages; the question was how to bring them to bear. Then answer was not hard to find. The unanimous resolution of the Inter-Allied Military Conference at Chantilly on December 6–8, 1915, was: "Decisive results will only be

"Italy's will to fight had not yet been impaired . . ." General Cadorna, the Italian Commander in Chief until 1918, arrives at Calais for an Inter-Allied Conference in 1916.

obtained if the offensives of the Armies of the Coalition are made simultaneously, or at least at dates so near together that the enemy will not be able to transport reserves from one front to another."

This policy was the broad intention of the western Allies in 1916, and was evidently correct; simultaneous concentric pressure against the enemy's heartland with all available resources stands out as an obvious and simple need. The tragedy of the War lies in the difficulty of its fulfillment. Some hint of that difficulty may be found in the special problems affecting the French and British contribution. We have seen Joffre's statement that "France needed a period of rest. . . ." This was clearly in conflict with the Chantilly proposition that the "general action should be launched as soon as possible. . . ." To overcome this inconsistency, Joffre urged that his allies, the Italians, and above all the British, should engage in a series of "wearing-out fights" preliminary to the main action. But to this, Haig could not agree.

The British Army in France numbered just over 1,000,000 men on January 1, 1916, divided into 38 divisions of infantry and 5 divisions of cavalry. By comparison with the original Expeditionary Force, this was a vast host, and during the next six months it would be increased by a further 19 divisions. But Haig was very conscious of the weakness statistics concealed; in March he formulated this awareness in a letter to Lord Kitchener: "I have not got an Army in France really, but a collection of divisions untrained for the Field. The actual fighting Army will be evolved from them."

It was this view that guided his response to Joffre's proposals. Haig was in a dilemma. On the one hand, there was his relationship, as British Commander in Chief, to Joffre; he expressed this to Joffre's liaison officer at GHQ in these words: "I pointed out that I am *not under* General Joffre's orders, but that would make no difference, as my intention was to do my utmost to carry out General Joffre's wishes on strategical matters, as if they were orders." At the same time he recognized the French problem. In January he recorded: "I think the French man-power situation is serious as they are not likely to stand another winter's war. There is no doubt to my mind but that the war must be won by the forces of the British Empire."

But if this was the case, was it wise to risk exhausting the British Army in a "wearing-out" fight in which, as Haig also recognized, it was likely that "our troops will be used up no less, possibly more than those of the enemy?" Haig stood out firmly against the "wearing-out fights"; in correspondence and in meetings with Joffre he argued his case forcibly, and won it. He saw the "wearing-out" fight, not as a separate series of operations, but as part of the main battle, as an essential preliminary of it which "should be carried on simultaneously (or nearly so) from the right of the Russians in the Baltic right round via Italy to our left on the North Sea." Nothing less, Haig felt, than this huge combined onslaught could succeed. But as matters turned out, neither Haig's views nor Joffre's were decisive; once again, the Germans stole the initiative.

For the Central Powers, the riddle of 1916 was particularly hard to read. The plan for winning the War in forty days, by attacking in the west, had failed; the alternative plan, for destroying Russia's ability to continue the conflict, had met with equivocal success. For Austria, the temptation to settle at once with perfidious Italy was lively. What should the Central Powers attempt? Another blow at Russia, this time perhaps final? A stroke at Italy? Or another trial in the west? And if they adopted the last of these, at what point in the west? General von Falkenhayn has set out very clearly the considerations which guided his choice. To him, beyond doubt, Great Britain was the "arch-enemy": "Germany can expect no mercy from this enemy, so long as he still retains the slightest hope of achieving his object," which was "the permanent elimination of what seems . . . the most dangerous rival." The question, then, was how to strike at England. This could be done directly, by unrestricted submarine warfare; its results could not be viewed as certainties, since there was no previous experience of such a thing, and there was always the risk that this method would draw in the United States on the side of the Allies. Yet, Falkenhayn concluded, "there can be no justification on military grounds for refusing any further to employ what promises to be our most effective weapon."

What about the land fronts? How would the great German Army contribute to victory in 1916? Falkenhayn at once set aside the secondary theaters—Salonika, Egypt, Mesopotamia. "We can in no case expect to do anything of decisive effect on the course of the war, as the protagonists of an Alexander march to India or Egypt, or an overwhelming blow at Salonika, are always hoping." (It was a grave misfortune for the Allies that similar clarity on this issue did not prevail on their side.) As for the British sector in France, Falkenhayn considered that even the complete defeat of the British forces there would leave him with the problem of then beating the French, and "it is very questionable whether Germany would be able to dispose of the forces required." So possibilities were reduced to an attack on the French front, with the

"To him . . . Great Britain was the 'arch-enemy' . . ." General Erich von Falkenhayn, German Chief of Staff, 1914–1916.

unpleasant reflection, prompted by French experience in Champagne and Artois in 1915, that a major breakthrough was most unlikely, except at a cost Falkenhayn did not care to accept.

Inexorably, the German Chief of Staff was drawn to his false logical conclusion:

"As I have already insisted, the strain on France has almost reached breaking point—though it is certainly borne with the most remarkable devotion. If we succeeded in opening the eyes of her people to the fact that in a military sense they have nothing more to hope for, that breaking point would be reached and England's best sword knocked out of her hand. . . . We can probably do enough for our purposes with limited resources. Within our reach behind the French sector of the Western Front there are objectives for the retention of which the French General Staff would be compelled to throw in every man they have. If they do so the forces of France will bleed to death—as there can be no question of a voluntary withdrawal—whether we reach our goal or not."

The objective upon which Falkenhayn finally fastened his gaze was Verdun.

And so, out of Joffre's desire for simultaneous, concentric Allied offensives, out of Haig's recognition that the British Empire must shoulder the burden of the War in the west, out of Russia's amazing revival, and out of Falkenhayn's proposal to win "with limited resources" was woven the melancholy pattern of 1916.

Secrecy and speed were the German watchwords; long before Joffre's Frenchmen were ready to attack, long before Haig's New Army divisions had shaken down, long before the Russians could draw breath, the Germans struck. On the morning of February 21st, a shell fired by a 380-mm. (15-inch) naval gun burst in the courtyard of the Bishop's Palace at Verdun, some twenty miles away; it was the signal for an unprecedented bombardment, heralding the attack. "It was the artillery that absorbed the maximum German effort."[1] It was by the mincing machine of gun power that von Falkenhayn planned to destroy the French army. The assault itself would be delivered on a limited front by only three army corps belonging to the Fifth Army, commanded by the German Crown Prince Wilhelm. These six divisions, with three more in reserve, would attack on a front of barely 8 miles, but on this front were assembled some 1,220 pieces of artillery, 542 of them of heavy caliber.

[1] Alistair Horne, *The Price of Glory: Verdun 1916*, New York, St. Martin's Press, 1963.

The year 1916, indeed, marked a turning point in the conduct of the War. From the beginning, from the destruction of the forts at Liége, Namur, and Antwerp, it had been recognized that the rôle of the heavy gun in the field would be unexpectedly large. Throughout 1915 the Allies had sought by every means to make good their deficiencies in this weapon. But it was in 1916 that it came into its own, beginning at Verdun. The German siege train for this battle contained such formidable items as: thirteen 420-mm. (17-inch) howitzers—"Big Berthas"—firing a shell weighing over a ton and standing nearly as high as a man, each requiring twelve wagons to transport it and twenty hours to prepare it for action; two 380-mm. (15-inch) long-range naval guns; seventeen 305-mm. (11-inch) Austrian mortars; large numbers of 210-mm. (8-inch) howitzers; even more of the ubiquitous and terrifying 150-mm. (5.9-inch); a number of 130-mm. (5-inch) high-velocity guns, whose alarming feature was the arrival of the projectile simultaneously with the sound of the shot; and finally hundreds of the 77-mm. (3-inch) field guns known to the British Army as "whizz-bangs."

From one of Verdun's defenders we learn what it felt like to be at the receiving end of this battery: "For an eternity we listen to the iron sledgehammers beating upon our trench. Percussion and time fuse, 105's, 150's, 210's—all the calibers. Amid this tempest of ruin we instantly recognize the shell that is coming to bury us. As soon as we pick out its mournful howl we look at each other in agony. All curled and shriveled up, we crouch under the very weight of its breath. Our helmets clang together, we stagger about like drunks. The beams tremble, a cloud of choking smoke fills the dugout, the two candles go out. . . ."[2]

And another wrote: "Above all, the dominant sensation is of the *weight* of the thing coming down. . . . A monstrous creature sweeps toward us, so heavy that its flight alone flattens us against the mud. . . ."[3]

At Verdun, the bombardment aimed at nothing less than annihilation.

For reasons that went deeper than he knew, Falkenhayn had chosen a good place. Ever since the quick collapse of the Belgian forts in 1914, the French High Command had distrusted these means of defense on which, before the War, they had been inclined to lean heavily. The actual fortifications had proved vulnerable to heavy artillery. As fixtures they restricted maneuver; as arsenals their armament was badly needed for the field army. The fortress of Verdun, therefore, had been stripped of its guns; from its forts alone the equivalent of 43 heavy and 11 field

[2] Jacques d'Arnoux, *Paroles d'un Revenant.*

[3] Maurie Genevoix, *Les Eparges.*

206

batteries had been removed. Instead of a fortress, it had been designated a "fortified region," but this nomenclature was largely a fraud. Anxiety about the state of Verdun's defenses began to be expressed as early as June 1915 by those who were in a position to know—officers and soldiers on the spot. A parliamentary mission visited the area in July, and received reassurances from the Army Group Commander, General Auguste Dubail. Yet by November, far from dying away, these reports were becoming more alarming. In particular the depositions of Colonel Driant, Deputy for Nancy and commander of a group of *Chasseur* battalions at Verdun, awakened the liveliest fears. The Minister for War, General Galliéni, wrote to Joffre on December 16th, asking for assurances that the defenses were in order. Joffre replied on the 18th: ". . . I definitely consider that there is no justification for the fears which you express. . . ." Galliéni replied: ". . . The Government has full confidence in you. . . ."

207

Joffre was deeply affronted by these criticisms and by the Government's attention to them; in his letter to Galliéni he added: "I cannot accept that soldiers under my orders should forward to the Government, other than by hierarchical avenues, complaints or protests about the execution of my orders. . . . [Such behavior] can only profoundly disturb the discipline of the army."

Nevertheless, he was sufficiently disturbed himself to send his "Major-General," De Castelnau, to Verdun in January to make a special report. Castelnau did not greatly care for what he discovered, and made strong recommendations which were acted upon immediately. He may thus, says one French historian,[4] rank as "the first savior of Verdun." But time was running out; it was already too late to avert the imminent catastrophe. And Joffre's reputation, which had survived all the disappointments of 1915, never recovered from the shock of what happened at Verdun.

A catastrophe it was, but within its broad outlines may be discerned, alongside French casualness and complacency, a deep, endemic fault in the German system of war. At bottom this stemmed from the contradiction between Falkenhayn's large object—the destruction of the French Army—and the small means by which he hoped to procure it. This in turn inevitably led to a degree of opportunism in German tactics that, while it often paid local dividends, at Verdun as elsewhere later in the War, ensured the ruin of larger projects. The German bombardment on February 21st was more destructive than any yet seen; it constituted a shattering outrage to the human body and spirit. It was meant to annihilate; yet, when it came to following it up, the Germans appeared to lose faith. Very slowly, preceded by large patrols and probing parties, their infantry came forward. Often they found that the bombardment had done its work, but this system did not permit them to exploit it fully or quickly. Elsewhere, they received unpleasant surprises:

"You couldn't kill everyone. And the survivors showed themselves able to bear the *Trommelfeuer*, that tempest of fire, the most inhuman of experiences. Always there was a machine gun in the end of a trench, a grenade thrower in a shellhole, a section which rallied in the hell of a ravaged wood. From the evening of the 21st, the French seemed determined to die on the spot rather than give way."[5]

There were routs, there were panics (especially where the Germans used flamethrowers), there were crippling casualties (Driant's *Chasseurs*

[4] Pierre Dominique, in *Miroir de l'histoire*, June, 1961.

[5] *Ibid.*

lost nine-tenths of their effectives), but except at one point on February 21st the Germans had made small progress, even against the French first line.

Three more days passed before the Germans were able to bring off a solid success, days during which the stunned defenders were able to grip the danger for the first time, and accelerate their countermeasures, so that the German achievements, dazzling though they might seem, proved hollow. It was on February 25th that the second and far more damaging attack procured the sensational triumph: the capture of Fort Douaumont. Here the ill effects of the policy of dismantling the fortress ring were fully revealed. Douaumont, later described by Pétain as the cornerstone of the whole Verdun defense system, had been stripped down to only three guns, served by fifty-six Territorial gunners under a sergeant-major. This was its entire garrison. The North African division around the fort disintegrated under the pressure of German assault. In the obscurity of snow squalls and battle smoke, Pioneer Sergeant Kunze of the 24th Brandenburg Regiment, with nine men of his section, forced his way into Douaumont, unopposed by the French gunners, who did not even see him enter. Joined later by other brave detachments of the same regiment, Kunze's effort reaped a marvelous reward. The great bastion of Fort Douaumont, which, contrary to expectation, had resisted even the heaviest bombardment, was seized without loss, and the way to Verdun lay open.[6]

Such was the situation that greeted General Philippe Pétain, commanding the Second Army (briefly in reserve), when he took up the command at Verdun to which Castelnau had summoned him, on February 25th. "Pétain had a clear intellect and a taste for method. A Northerner, cold and taciturn, he left nothing to chance. An infantryman, he was prudent rather than bold, and careful of the blood of his soldiers. . . . A defensive fighter by temperament, he was the right man in the right place."[7] Under Pétain the defense of Verdun was transformed. The actual fighting, the staving off of the German blows, remained the function of the front-line soldiers, grimly resisting in their torn entrenchments by detachments or by larger units. But behind them Pétain redistributed responsibilities for each sector, rearmed the forts, constructed new lines of trenches, and, above all, established entirely new systems of supply and relief. The morale of the French Army was secured by the constant flow of new formations to the battle, replacing

[6] See Horne, *op. cit.*, for the latest account of this.

[7] Pierre Dominique, *op. cit.*

209

(pages 210 and 211) **The fight for the fort—a drawing on the spot by J. Simont, staff-artist of** L'Illustration.

those that had suffered before they became exhausted. Almost every division in the army sooner or later passed through "the hell of Verdun." To maintain them, Pétain caused thirty-six new bridges to be constructed over the Meuse, laid down a network of light railways, and turned the Verdun–Bar-le-Duc road into the "Voie Sacrée"—the Sacred Route— over which 3,000 (later 3,500), lorries carried 4,000 tons of supplies and 15,000 to 20,000 men every day. Nothing was permitted to interrupt the flow: constant work maintained the road surface; any vehicle that broke down was at once flung into the ditch; no unauthorized use was permitted. All this was made possible because Pétain received the backing and the resources his predecessors had lacked; but it was he who demanded them, and made sure that they were well used.

MARCH 5

With increasing dismay, Falkenhayn began to realize what he had let himself in for. On March 5th the Germans launched a new assault, extending it now to the left bank of the Meuse, at the suggestion and insistence of the Crown Prince. New place names came into prominence: Fort de Vaux on the right, and the grimly styled Mort-Homme (Dead Man's) Hill on the left. This was perhaps the most savage period of all. "Verdun, now, meant hell. No fields. No woods. Just a lunar landscape. Roads cratered. Trenches staved in, filled up, remade, re-dug, filled in again. The snow has melted; the shellholes are full of water. The wounded drown in them. A man can no longer drag himself out of the mud."[8]

So it continued. In April reinforcements enabled the French to counterattack; their gains were wrested back by ferocious new German efforts. Mort-Homme was held by an epic of French endurance. Pétain

APRIL 10

issued his famous Order of the Day: *"Courage; on les aura."*[9] In May he was promoted to command the whole of the Central Army Group, and new personalities appeared on the scene: Artillery General Robert Nivelle to command the Second Army, and the aggressive General Charles Mangin. These were men dedicated to offensive methods, yet not even their dynamic energy could alter the solemn facts. On May 31st General Haig met Joffre, Castelnau, and Foch with the President of France, Poincaré, and the Minister of War, General Roques: "Poincaré said that he had just returned from Verdun where he had seen the senior generals—Pétain, Nivelle, and another general. They told him *'Verdun sera prise'*[10] and that operations must be undertaken without delay to

[8] *Ibid.*

[9] "Courage; we shall have them yet."

[10] "Verdun will be taken."

212

withdraw pressure from that part. . . . From what was said I formed the opinion that Pétain had the 'wind up.' "

Haig was right. Under Pétain's icy outward calm, he did indeed have the "wind up," and not without reason. On June 9th the Germans captured Fort de Vaux. On June 21st 100,000 shells filled with the new phosgene gas fell upon the defenders of Verdun. On June 23rd the French failed to retake Douaumont. On that same day Pétain suggested to Joffre that the whole of the right bank of the Meuse should be abandoned. Half the French artillery was emplaced on that bank; if the Germans continued their advance, the French risked losing all these guns. The stake was enormous; Joffre did not flinch. Despite the misgiving of his normally optimistic staff, he flatly forbade withdrawal. Those around him pointed out the gravity of this decision: *"J'en ai pris bien d'autres,"*[11] he replied.

The decision was justified. He knew that Brusilov had already launched his great offensive on the Eastern Front with remarkable early successes; he knew too that the Italians were conducting a large-scale counterattack on the Trentino, and he knew that the date was fixed for

[11] "I've taken plenty of others."

". . . the aggressive General Charles Mangin." General Charles Mangin (1866–1925). An infantryman, he served mainly in the French colonies. He was present with Marchand at Fashoda in 1899, when France and Britain almost clashed over the occupation of the Sudan; later he took part in the pacification of Morocco. Throughout the war he argued vigorously for the greater use of French colonial forces.

massive British intervention on the Somme with powerful French support. Within a week the conditions laid down at the Chantilly Conference would be fulfilled—if only the defenders of Verdun could hold on. And they could. On July 11th, in view of the development of the Somme offensive, Falkenhayn gave orders for the German attacks at Verdun to halt; the strategic initiative had now passed to the French.

". . . the Battle of Verdun continued . . ." Trucks moving up on the Voie Sacrée.

AUGUST 29

To the accompaniment of the thunders of the Somme away to the north, the Battle of Verdun continued on its devastating course. On July 1st, the opening day of the Somme, a day of catastrophe for the British Army, and the 132nd day of the Battle of Verdun, General Mangin wrote: "I have just retaken [the Thiaumont redoubt] for the fifth time and I hope General Patey's Bretons will stay there; they all went to Confession before the battle. . . ."[12] Throughout July and all through August the attrition of French and German manhood went on. On August 13th Mangin noted: "In two tours of duty of 3 or 4 days, one [German] regiment has lost 80 officers and 3,200 men, that is to say that it was only able to reappear because of large reinforcements. . . . We are a long way below those figures, I am very glad to say. Most of my regiments stay in line 8 to 12 days and only lose 30 percent, which is still a lot. . . ." On both sides the strains on the High Command were considerable: on August 23rd the German Crown Prince at last rid himself of his offensive-minded staff officer, Knobelsdorf, Falkenhayn's nominee. Six days later Falkenhayn himself was replaced, and Hindenburg took over

[12] Charles Mangin, *Lettres de Guerre 1914–1918*, Librairie Arthème Fayard, 1950.

214

with Ludendorff as Quartermaster-General. Despite their titles, their respective rôles were those of Commander in Chief and Chief of Staff. Among the French there were also disagreements. Mangin wrote on September 15th: "Pétain is very defensive-minded; he thinks we should economize our forces. Nivelle and I think it is necessary to gain ground. . . . One must bite in order not to be bitten and also to tie the enemy down here so that he can't go somewhere else."[13]

Pétain's hesitations were slowly overcome by his ardent lieutenants; on October 24th a massive French blow, using 170,000 men, 711 guns and 150 aircraft, retook Fort Douaumont. It was a personal triumph for Mangin, whose plans had been adopted in their entirety by Nivelle: "The total of prisoners is above 5,000. I told Joffre two hours before the attack that I expected to offer him twenty-two Boche battalions in the front line as an opening bid; he looked at me very oddly, probably not being used to this sort of language in such circumstances. 'All the same,' he said to Nivelle as he went out, 'I think he is exaggerating.' Well, I think I've also got the second-line battalions (a total of thirty-eight)." Ebullient, aggressive, methodical, Mangin later explained his system:

"I box in the first line with 75's; nothing can pass through the barrage; then we pound the trench with 155's [6-inch] and 58's [3-inch mortars]. . . . When the trench is well turned over, off we go. Any Boches who are still there are ours. Generally, they come out in groups and surrender. While this is going on, their reserve companies are pinned in their dugouts by a solid stopper of heavy shells. Our infantry waves are preceded by a barrage of 75's; the 155's help to bang down the cork on the reserve companies; the tides of steel join up with the *poilus*[14] 70 or 80 yards behind. The Boche gives up. . . . You see, it is all very simple.

But the year was wearing on. The mud was thickening; the chill of the War's worst winter began to be felt. At the start of November, the French reaped an unlooked-for reward when the Germans abandoned Fort de Vaux. The shameful loss of Douaumont in February was thus avenged. Nivelle and Mangin were still not satisfied; their pressures on Pétain continued. Across a wasteland which Mangin compared to the Sahara, but under gray skies far removed from those of Africa, they pushed on their preparations for another stroke. It came on December 15th, and in three days, on a six-mile front, the French took 11,000 prisoners, 115 guns and hundreds of machine guns and mortars. The

[13] I.e., to the Somme.

[14] Slang for infantryman (U.S. equivalent was "doughboy"); the French soldiers themselves did not greatly care for the nickname, and called themselves *les bonhommes.*

215

(pages 216 and 217) ". . . the attrition of . . . German manhood . . ." German infantry parading before leaving billets for the trenches at Verdun.

"... Hindenburg took over with Ludendorff as quartermaster-general." Field Marshal Paul von Hindenburg (1847–1934) served in the Franco-Prussian War. He had retired in 1911, but was summoned back in 1914 to take command of the Eighth Army, in place of his brother-in-law, von Prittwitz, and in 1916 became virtually Commander in Chief of the German armies. General Erich Ludendorff (1865–1937) was a staff officer for the greater part of his career. He accompanied Hindenburg throughout the war, until his resignation in October 1918.

"... a personal triumph for Mangin ..." French colonial troops (Moroccans) in the ditch of Fort Douaumont after its recapture.

Marshal Henri-Philippe Pétain (1856–1951).

(pages 220 and 221) **In front of Fort Douaumont—a drawing on the spot by Georges Scott.**

Battle of Verdun, begun with an equivocal German success, ended with an equally ambiguous French triumph. Nivelle, its chief architect, had already departed—to the dizzy eminence of Commander in Chief, replacing Joffre. The victory provided a happy augury for his tenure of exalted office. Mangin announced in an Order of the Day: "We know the method and we have the Chief. Success is certain." With this fanfare the tragedies of 1917 were ushered in.

The tragedy which had ended at Verdun on December 18, 1916, cost, at the most sober estimate, some 700,000 casualties to France and Germany. The British Official Historian gives 362,000 for the French, 336,831 for the Germans; figures vary, but are mostly in the region of the 700,000 total. Both sides suffered their main losses in the defensive rôle. That apart, two other lessons stand out: first, that taken in conjunction with the other dire events of 1916, this casualty rate spelled suicide for the two leading powers of Europe; second, that if Verdun proved nothing else, it proved the folly of trying to win an unlimited war "with limited resources." Falkenhayn paid the price of personal dismissal; for his country, the price was very much greater.

(opposite, top) **A group of French soldiers brought straight from the trenches to receive British decorations.**

(opposite, bottom) "... the Germans abandoned Fort de Vaux." **A French machine gun in a sandbagged embrasure of Fort de Vaux after its reoccupation in November.**

"All he knew was that . . . a total defeat would lose the war." Admiral Sir John Jellicoe, Commander in Chief of the British Grand Fleet at Jutland. Jellicoe subsequently became First Sea Lord.

THE YEAR OF KILLING: NAVAL GAMBIT 10

I should assume that the intention was to lead us over mines and submarines, and should decline to be so drawn. . . . This may be deemed a refusal of battle and, indeed, might possibly result in failure to bring the enemy to action as soon as expected and hoped. . . . I feel that such tactics, if not understood, may bring odium on me. . . .

ADMIRAL JELLICOE TO THE BRITISH ADMIRALTY, OCTOBER 1914

The failure at Gallipoli marked the beginning of the end of British naval supremacy, exercised over two centuries; but this was a result that only very slowly became apparent—indeed, not until the Second World War had run some part of its course. Two factors helped to disguise the truth at the time: the completeness of British command of the world's waters and the majestic roll call of the Grand Fleet. Beside this vast array of Dreadnoughts and battle cruisers with their attendant small craft concentrated in their North Sea bases, all misgivings died away. "Only numbers can annihilate," Nelson had said; and here, under Sir John Jellicoe's command, were numbers and power such as Nelson had never dreamed of. When the Grand Fleet and the German High Seas Fleet clashed at Jutland on May 31, 1916, they provided "the culminating manifestation of naval force in the history of the world."[1] Two hundred and fifty-nine warships were deployed at once in deadly grapple. On the British side there were 37 capital ships, 31 cruisers, and 85 destroyers. The failure of this mighty armament to produce a Nelsonian annihilation sent a wave of shock and dismay through the whole British Empire.

This, also, was part of the general failure of comprehension that surrounded the events of the First World War; for as Jellicoe's paper quoted at the opening of this chapter shows, he at least had foreseen the probable stalemate which was as likely to ensue at sea as on land. Indeed, this impasse was written into the whole conception of German sea power, clearly stated in the preamble to the German Navy Act of 1898: ". . . Even if he should succeed in meeting us with considerable superiority of strength, the defeat of a strong German fleet would so

[1] Winston Churchill.

225

substantially weaken the enemy that, in spite of a victory he might have obtained, his own position in the world would no longer be secured by an adequate fleet."

This was a doctrine that could be interpreted in two ways: aggressively, as Grand Admiral von Tirpitz wished; defensively, as the Kaiser

". . . the High Seas Fleet lay in wait . . ." German battleship squadron, Westfalen leading.

APRIL 1916

insisted after the Heligoland and Dogger Bank affairs. Either way, underwater weapons—torpedoes and mines—whether delivered by underwater or by surface craft, could be expected materially to assist the German intention. Tirpitz would have preferred to seek his ends in a great fleet action which, whatever happened to the Germans, would cripple the Royal Navy; Vice-Admiral Scheer, who assumed command of the High Seas Fleet in January 1916, hoped to trap and destroy a part of the British fleet in isolation. With this in mind, he resumed the policy of raiding the British coast. Lowestoft was bombarded in April; in May he went further, and conceived the bold plan of trying to tempt the British battle cruisers to come out by offering his battle-cruiser squadron as a bait. Sixteen U-boats were sent to ambush the Grand Fleet as it came out of its harbors; the High Seas Fleet lay in wait to destroy it by detachments.

226

Two factors combined to play a large part in frustrating Scheer's intentions, but one of them would frustrate the British, too. It was a long time before the Germans realized to what an extent the British Intelligence Service held them in its unblinking eye. "More than perhaps any other Power, we were successful in the war in penetrating the intentions of the enemy," says Churchill. "Again and again the forecasts both of the military and of the naval Intelligence Staffs were vindicated to the wonder of friends and the chagrin of foes." Scheer's chances of surprising the British fleet were thus remote. Equally remote were his chances of damaging them spectacularly by underwater attack—but here the British admirals shared his delusion. Neither Germans nor British had fully studied or drawn the correct conclusions from the Russo-Japanese War of 1904–1905. Neither had absorbed the astonishing truth that of 67 torpedoes fired by the Japanese in the action off Port Arthur on June 23, 1904, none had scored a hit; that only two torpedoes had struck home in the daylight action at Tsushima, and that only four ships were hit (of which only two sank) by the more than 100 torpedoes fired in the night action. When the Grand Fleet came out to catch Scheer on May 30, 1916, all its units passed unscathed through his sixteen waiting U-boats. But as the British were unconscious of the ambush, they were unable to draw encouragement from its ineffectiveness.

North Sea visibility is rarely good for long. On May 31st it was, as usual, patchy—at its best in the morning, before the two great navies came in sight of each other, deteriorating through the afternoon, as the smoke of their guns and funnels mingled with the mist. Surprisingly—but fittingly, perhaps, for the last great action of surface vessels—neither side made any effective use of Air reconnaissance, though the German Zeppelins had carried this to a high degree of efficiency. The two battle fleets were still 200 miles apart, and officers on both sides had almost decided that the whole foray had been abortive, when a chance contact drew the entire agglomeration together like iron filings onto the end of a magnet. Shortly after two o'clock in the afternoon, as Vice-Admiral Beatty's battle-cruiser fleet from Rosyth was turning north to rendezvous with Admiral Jellicoe's Grand Fleet from Scapa Flow, his light cruisers veered aside to investigate a neutral Danish steamer. The light cruiser *Elbing*, belonging to Vice-Admiral von Hipper's scouting group, was carrying out the same mission when she was sighted by the *Galatea*, whose guns opened the Battle of Jutland at 2:28 P.M.

As the light forces now converged upon each other, the Fates dealt out their chances with depressing evenness: on the one hand, when the aggressive Beatty swung his six battle cruisers, fortified by four of the latest and fastest British Dreadnoughts, toward the enemy, it seemed that Scheer's plan for destroying the British in detail might well come off; on the other hand, Scheer did not know that the Grand Fleet was also out, so that the British held the possibility of inflicting a devastating surprise. The course of the battle conformed to this balance of chances; its conclusion was dictated by other factors.

Beatty maneuvered immediately to cut off Hipper from his base, accepting the danger of meeting the whole High Seas Fleet, while Jellicoe increased speed to support him. Hipper turned back to rejoin Scheer, and the two battle-cruiser forces (six British, five German units) were thus running parallel on a course east-southeast when they engaged each other at 3:48 P.M., at a range of 18,000 yards. Within a quarter of an hour the Germans had scored a striking success; within three-quarters of an hour they had reversed the immediate odds against them. Beatty's impetuosity, added to the chronic signaling failures of the Royal Navy, had at once deprived him of the support of his four fast "Dreadnought" battleships under Rear-Admiral Evan-Thomas. Defects in gunnery and equipment now also made their contribution. The German broadsides made the first hits, and minutes elapsed before the British struck back; worse still, through a tactical error, one German ship was not fired on at all. At 4 o'clock the first results were seen: *Indefatigable* blew up with a loss of over 1,000 officers and men. Twenty-five minutes later *Queen Mary*, the best gunnery vessel in Beatty's force, followed her to the bottom with another 1,200 men. This was the first crisis of the battle. The Germans had suffered severely, but thanks to their stronger armor their ships were still afloat and fighting, while Beatty had lost one-third of his battle-cruiser strength. On the other hand, Evan-Thomas's squadron, with its 15-inch guns, was now in action, and Beatty's own spirit was invincible.

The scale and setting of such an action as this is impossible for the layman to grasp. The maximum speed of the British battle cruisers was 27 knots, of the German, 26.5 knots; this is not, of course, to be confused with the average speed in action, but it meant that when the High Seas Fleet appeared on the scene shortly after this, "the opposing forces were now approaching each other at 43 miles an hour." Distances were comparable: Evan-Thomas was eight miles away from Beatty, although under his command; at these speeds the distance could be completely closed in twelve minutes. Decisions needed to be taken quickly. And all the time, amid the smoke of the guns and the huge spray fountains of the "shorts," the "overs," and the "near-misses," the light cruisers and destroyers of both sides were bickering and biting with their smaller armament, threatening to strike home with their torpedoes. When Commodore Goodenough, in the cruiser *Southampton*, sighted Scheer's main fleet at 4:33 P.M., he signaled: "Have sighted enemy battlefleet bearing southeast, course north." The reception of that signal by Beatty and Jellicoe ushered in the battle's second phase.

The question now was whether the British could wield their great strategic advantage in such a way as to redress the tactical mishaps that had befallen them. A new range of problems opened up, falling mainly upon Jellicoe, and very largely due to the inadequacies of British signaling. Beatty's task was relatively simple: to draw the Germans into the jaws of the Grand Fleet. His superior speed had enabled him to escape from Scheer, though Evan-Thomas's squadron, again through a signaling error, turned away too late, and for a time found itself engaged alone against the head of the German line of battle. These were the newest and most powerful ships in the Royal Navy—indeed, in the world. The risk to them was terrible to contemplate; all four were damaged, *Warspite* so severely that she had to leave the action. Their great guns, however, did not leave the German ships unscathed.

"... neither side made any effective use of air reconnaissance ..." An interchange of messages between a U-boat and a seaplane. Both of these proved to be valuable information finders for both sides. Their negligible role at Jutland is one of the freaks of the battle.

"... the best gunnery vessel in Beatty's force ..." H.M.S. Queen Mary, a battle cruiser of 27,000 tons, speed 27 knots, armament eight 13.5-inch, sixteen 4-inch guns. Launched 1912.

(right) "... to the bottom with ... 1,200 men." The smoke and steam from Queen Mary, when she capsized, rose 800 feet in the air.

(opposite) "At four o'clock the Indefatigable blew up ..." Indefatigable's opponent was the battle cruiser Von Der Tann, Germany's first ship of that class. Her displacement was 21,000 tons, length 561 feet. She carried eight 11-inch and ten 5.9-inch guns, as well as torpedo tubes. After her victory over Indefatigable, she sustained heavy damage from the British battleships, and limped home with all her turrets out of action and 600 tons of seawater in her hull.

"'. . . the bow and stern could be seen standing up out of the water . . .'" The end of the Invincible. The destroyer Badger (1st Flotilla) is seen at right in middle distance, about to pick up the only six survivors, four of whom are on a raft between Invincible's bows and H.M.S. Badger. In the disance, the battleships H.M.S. Superb and H.M.S. Canada (4th Battle Squadron) can just be seen engaging the enemy.

It was one minute past six when a visual link was established between Beatty's battle cruisers and Jellicoe's Dreadnoughts; not until then could the commanding admiral take the crucial decision how to deploy his twenty-four battleships. They were advancing in six divisions, each of four ships in line ahead, the whole occupying a front of four miles; to engage, they must turn into a single continuous line, an operation that might take as much as thirty minutes. The question was, in which direction? With these speeds and distances a mistake could have irredeemable consequences. Only from Beatty's visual signal did Jellicoe receive the vital information he needed, and at once took the decision to deploy to port, that is, toward the east. From this he would gain two immediate advantages if the Germans held their course (and there was nothing to warn them not to): he would threaten their line of retreat and he would "cross their 'T'"—the most important tactical consideration of all.

"Have sighted enemy battlefleet . . ." The German Dreadnought Kaiserin, belonging to the 3rd Squadron at Jutland. She displaced 24,700 tons, with a length of 564 feet and a speed of 23 knots. She carried ten 12-inch guns, fourteen 5.9-inch guns, five 20-inch torpedo tubes, and a crew of over 1,000.

Visibility, made murky by the funnel smoke of over 250 ships and the cordite fumes of their guns, was beginning to fail. The maneuvers of the next forty-five minutes were confused; the results of the twenty minutes of actual fighting during this time were contradictory and perplexing. At first the main stress fell upon the light craft, cruisers and destroyers, operating between the giants. The Germans obtained the first advantage, severely damaging the cruiser *Chester;* this was reversed by the arrival of Admiral Hood's 3rd Battle-Cruiser Squadron, which quickly reduced the cruiser *Wiesbaden* to a shambles. The abrupt appearance of Hipper and the head of Scheer's line out of the smoke and mist once again tilted the balance, the British cruiser *Defence* was destroyed and *Warrior* wrecked.

Then, at 6:23 P.M., *Agincourt,* at the rear of Jellicoe's line, opened fire, shortly followed by her neighboring Dreadnoughts. As the heavy

". . . Beatty's own spirit was invincible." Vice-Admiral Sir David Beatty's flagship, Lion, hit on "Q" turret at Jutland. Escorting destroyers of the 13th Flotilla to the left. H.M.S. Lion was launched in 1910: 26,350 tons, 27 knots, eight 13.5-inch, sixteen 4-inch guns.

British shells fell upon and around his leading ships, Scheer realized that the worst had happened: he was heading straight into the very trap that had haunted German naval thinking. He lost no time in deciding what to do; indeed, nothing else remained for him but to turn away as quickly as possible and try to escape. This the High Seas Fleet now did, greatly aided by the declining visibility, and encouraged by one last impressive success in the very moment of acutest danger. Admiral Hood's flagship, *Invincible,* suddenly blew up, the third British battle cruiser to suffer this fate on that day. "Several big explosions took place in rapid succession;

233

masses of coal dust issued from the riven hull; great tongues of flame played over the ship; the masts collapsed; the ship broke in two, and an enormous pall of black smoke ascended to the sky. As it cleared away the bow and stern could be seen standing up out of the water as if to mark the place where an Admiral lay."[2] There were only six survivors out of her crew of 1,026 officers and men; a grim epilogue to Fisher's dream, which had given his country fast ships with superior gun power, but without adequate armor.

By 6:45 P.M. contact between the main fleets had been lost, yet the battle was not over. Scheer's first turn was to the south, then westward toward England. Ten minutes elapsed before Jellicoe knew what Scheer was doing; then he, too, turned south. After twenty minutes on the westward course, Scheer made another 180-degree turn, and steered east again, hoping to cross the tail of Jellicoe's fleet and damage it further in his retreat. Instead, he ran into its very center. For the second time that day Jellicoe was in the happy position of crossing the enemy's "T," with all the advantages of the light in his favor. Heavy injury was done to the German ships at this stage. Once again Scheer had to bolt for the west. This time he covered his maneuver by an operation which had assumed an almost mystical significance in naval thinking: he ordered his destroyers to carry out a mass torpedo attack on the British line. Jellicoe's response to this has drawn down on him the most serious criticism of his conduct of the battle. To avoid the torpedoes, he turned his line of battleships *away*.

Jellicoe's most trenchant critic was to be Winston Churchill; characteristically, it was also Churchill who provided the most penetrating explanation of the admiral's frame of mind, and the nature of the dilemma that faced him: "Nothing like this particular event had ever happened before, and nothing like it was ever to happen again. The 'Nelson touch' arose from years of fighting between the strongest ships of the time. Nelson's genius enabled him to measure truly the consequences of any decision. But that genius worked upon precise practical data. He had seen the same sort of thing happen on a lesser scale many times over before the Battle of Trafalgar. Nelson did not have to worry about under-water damage. He felt he knew what would happen in a fleet action. Jellicoe did not know. Nobody knew. All he knew was that a complete victory would not improve decisively an already favourable naval situation, and that a total defeat would lose the war. He was prepared to accept battle on his own terms; he was not prepared to force

[2] Official narrative.

234

one at a serious hazard. The battle was to be fought as he wished it or left unfought."

Being the world's greatest sea power did, after all, confer one particular advantage: one held the options in a naval action. Jellicoe's turn defeated the intentions of the German torpedo boats; no hits were scored by the thirty-two torpedoes they fired at the Grand Fleet. But contact with the Germans was lost again, and night was approaching fast. Yet the hazards of the days were still not over. At 7:45 Beatty was able to report the position of the High Seas Fleet, and its course— southwest. At 7:50 he urged that the Grand Fleet should follow him to cut the enemy off, but by now the failing light made this practically impossible. Nevertheless, by eight o'clock Germans and British were converging at an angle that must surely bring the British across the German "T" for the third time that day. The squabbles of flanking forces, however, warned Scheer of the danger, and again he turned away to the west.

Jellicoe now lay, with his entire fleet, between the Germans and their bases; it was his firm intention to remain there and bring them to action again the next day. The Germans, for their part, were determined to use the darkness to escape. The only things that could have prevented them were continuing accurate information about their position or a night action. The first of these Jellicoe did not have; the habitual signaling faults of the Royal Navy now proved decisive; failures to report contact by vessel after vessel left Jellicoe ignorant of the movements of his enemy. As for night action, this was against every canon of belief and training in the Royal Navy: ". . . unlike the German, they had no adequate illuminants, neither starshell nor an effective method of controlling their searchlight beams, a policy that was not altered until a decade after the war."[3] These factors were decisive; despite a series of brief, destructive actions, during which both sides suffered further loss, the Germans were able to pass their whole fleet across the British rear during the night without Jellicoe ever understanding what was taking place. At a little after four o'clock on the morning of June 1st, a message from the Admiralty, giving the true position of the High Seas Fleet, brought with it the bitter realization that the battle was over and that the enemy had got away.

The disappointment at this result was intense, and colored the tone of the British communiqué, which contrived almost to give the impression that the British had been defeated. They had not; all that they had

---

[3] Captain Geoffrey Bennett, D.S.C., R.N., in *History Today*, June 1960.

failed to do was to annihilate the enemy. The cost had been high, and feeling was intensified by the dramatic end of the three battle cruisers; the German damage did not fully transpire until later. The final tally was:

CASUALTIES:	Killed	Wounded
British	6,097	510
German	2,551	507

SHIPS:	British	German
Battle cruisers	3	1 (sunk after battle, owing to heavy damage)
Pre-Dreadnought Battleships	–	1
Cruisers	3	4
Destroyers	8	5

But more significant than these figures is the fact that at 9:45 P.M. on June 2nd Admiral Jellicoe was able to inform the Admiralty that his battle fleet was ready to go to sea at four hours' notice; Scheer was not able to report the same thing until the middle of August. The superior construction of the German ships had saved them from sinking, but it could not save them from injuries that made them unfit for action for a long time.

(opposite, top) ". . . Southampton sighted Scheer's main fleet . . ." The light cruiser Southampton, flagship of Commodore Goodenough at Jutland. She displaced 5,400 tons, had a maximum speed of 25½ knots, and carried eight 6-inch guns; she was launched in 1912.

(bottom) "The cost had been high . . ." The armored cruiser Black Prince, launched in 1904. Black Prince, all alone, fell in with the retreating German fleet during the night, and mistook them for the British. The Germans made no such error, and Black Prince was blown out of the water by the successive broadsides of the German Dreadnoughts.

237

On August 19th Scheer made one more attempt to inflict the weakening upon the Royal Navy that he had failed to accomplish at Jutland. Once again he placed great dependence upon his submarines; once again he was frustrated by British Naval Intelligence. And this time his use of Air reconnaissance proved deceptive: Zeppelin reports led him to believe that he was in the presence of the Grand Fleet when, in fact, it was the British light forces from Harwich which were approaching him. Again he turned for home, and again Jellicoe's caution prevented the British from catching him. But this was the last sortie of the High Seas Fleet until it steamed into Scapa Flow to surrender on November 21, 1918. It was a New York newspaper that arrived earliest at the correct assessment of Jutland:

"The German Fleet has assaulted its jailor; but it is still in jail."

The jailor was content with this situation. The alarming defects revealed in the Royal Navy were summed up by Beatty in a comment after the battle: "There is something wrong with *our system.*" There was indeed: ship construction, gunnery, quality of heavy shells, signaling, tactics—all had been proved defective. Even so aggressive a commander as Beatty himself, who succeeded Jellicoe in command of the Grand Fleet in November 1916, came to the conclusion that it was no longer correct to look for action with the Germans. Fortunately, they shared the same view. By January 1918 Beatty was "informing a naval conference . . . that the German battle-cruiser squadron must now be considered definitely superior to our own, and that the new armour-piercing shells ordered after Jutland would not be ready until the summer of 1918. The sombre conclusion was drawn that if trade were to be adequately protected 'the correct strategy of the Grand Fleet is no longer to endeavour to bring the enemy to action at any cost, but rather to contain him in his bases until the general situation becomes more favourable to us.' And these words were written only a month after he had received the reinforcement of six most powerful American super-dreadnoughts."[4]

This point emerges: for the Germans there was an obvious victory to be gained by injuring Britain's main weapon by the sacrifice of a secondary one; for the British, the destruction of the secondary German weapon held out no such advantage. And the destruction of Germany's main weapon was something that only the army could do—at a frightful cost.

[4] Cruttwell, *A History of the Great War.*

"The cost had been high . . ." Repairs to the British light cruiser H.M.S. Chester after Jutland. Scouting ahead of the 3rd Battle Cruiser Squadron, Chester was suddenly caught by the fire of three light cruisers of the German 2nd Scouting Group. "Nearly all her guns were broken up, and her deck became a shambles." First-Class Boy John Travers Cornwell won a posthumous Victoria Cross for standing to his gun though mortally wounded; he was sixteen years old.

(below) "The cost had been high . . ." Repairs to "Q" Turret of Admiral Beatty's flagship, H.M.S. Lion, after Jutland.

11 THE YEAR OF KILLING: ALLIED GAMBIT

So numerous were the combatants, so heavily had they been armed by the growth of warlike industry, that, whether or not the deadlock was broken, the losses and all the miseries of war were certain to increase. In fact it proved to be a year of killing.

CYRIL FALLS

The fierce struggles of the middle period at Verdun formed only part of the picture of a hell-bent world. Those shattering bombardments, those awful losses, constituted but one strain in the crescendo of 1916

that was now preparing. The next "players" to join in were the Austrians, whose Chief of Staff, Conrad von Hötzendorf, had never been fully persuaded by Falkenhayn's strategic reasoning, and clung to his own idea of smashing Italy. His attempt failed, but not before it had done severe damage to the Italians.

Conrad's attack was launched on the Trentino front on May 15th. In five days he advanced five miles. By June 10th, when he had to stop the offensive, it had made a maximum penetration of twelve miles; 45,000 prisoners and 300 guns were taken, and the Italians lost in all some 150,000 men, the Austrians about 80,000. But the Italians, on their own horseshoe frontier, enjoyed that same advantage of interior lines as did the Central Powers as a whole on the larger scale. Only the sheer weight of the Austrian offensive had surprised them; their reserves were at hand, and these, judiciously used, stopped Conrad's armies on the edge of the mountains. Despite their showy victory, the Austrians had failed to

MAY 15, 1916

"... picture of a hell-bent world." Nightly firework display on the Western Front; a German starshell bursts over no-man's-land at Ploegsteert, March 1916.

(above) ". . . the Italians lost . . . some 150,000 men . . ." Italians outside their dugouts on the Forcellina di Montozzo, West Trentino.

(right) ". . . the center of interest . . . had shifted to the east." German cavalry (Dragoons) passing through a Russian village in early 1916.

break out of the Alpine barrier; ". . . the strategic situation had not been seriously altered."[1] Indeed, when General Carlo Cadorna launched his counterattack on June 16th, the Austrians had to abandon much of what they had won in order not to suffer losses as serious as those they had inflicted. But Cadorna had not done with them yet.

For the time being, however, the center of interest had shifted to the east. The most energetic Russian general of the War, and one of its greatest military figures, was Brusilov, now commanding the Southern Group of Armies on the Carpathian front. Discontented with the rôle allotted to him in the projected Russian offensive—conforming to the Chantilly agreement—and believing that he could turn the difficulty of the terrain to his advantage, Brusilov obtained permission to launch a large-scale attack. His preparations were methodical and efficiently carried out; tactical surprise was achieved by calculated dispersal of reserves at more than twenty places. His strategy has been described as "like a man tapping on a wall to find out what part of it is solid stone and what is only lath and plaster."[2]

The Russian attack was launched on June 4th. During the succeeding days it proved that a staggering amount of the Austrian front was no more than "lath and plaster." On both flanks of the attack the Russians made tremendous and immediate gains. The Austrian units facing them melted away, leaving only a few isolated crags of German resistance; Conrad must have bitterly regretted the six good divisions he had sent to Italy. In three days the Russian Eighth Army alone took 44,000 prisoners. In three weeks the grand total had swelled to 200,000; by the end of the campaign, in September, the Russians had taken 450,000. This loss, added to other casualties, ". . . made inevitable the break-up of the Austrian Empire."[3] But Russia herself paid the price of 1,000,000 casualties in four months, a final blow to the morale of her army. By the end of the year it was estimated that at least 1,000,000 deserters were absent from the ranks, most of them living quietly at home. What intensified the significance of this injury was the fruitlessness of the victory. "No one at Russian Headquarters had dreamed of such a success. It was in some ways a serious embarrassment."[4] Brusilov's achievements were not exploited by the other Army Groups; against resistance stiffened by growing numbers of Germans and by German methods, the

[1] Cyril Falls, *The First World War.*
[2] Cruttwell. *A History of the Great War.*
[3] *Ibid.*
[4] *Ibid.*

impetus of his advance steadily declined. What made the whole thing even sadder was that Romania, hovering on the edge of joining the Allies, left the decision until too late; instead of reinforcing a great success in June, she offered herself up in August to an impending German vengeance.

The orchestra still lacked one instrument. Russians, French, Italians, Germans, and Austrians, all were bitterly engaged; there remained the British, with an army which had grown to 58 divisions in France, 1.5 million men. What part would they play?

JULY 1

The answer to that question was provided on July 1, 1916, a day marked by probably the greatest single catastrophe of the whole War. At 7:30 A.M. on that day, eleven British divisions advanced simultaneously against the German positions on the north bank of the river Somme. By nightfall their losses totaled 57,470 men and officers, of whom nearly 20,000 were dead. Except on the right flank, the gains of ground were minimal; some divisions were stopped in their tracks, shot down on their start lines, unable to make any progress at all. One eyewitness account will have to serve here for the whole tragedy; it comes from Brigadier General F. P. Crozier, then a battalion commander in the 36th (Ulster) Division:

"... I glance to the right through a gap in the trees. I see the 10th

". . . The most energetic Russian general of the war . . ." General Brusilov.

". . . the center of interest had shifted to the east." A Russian staff conference in the field. Note officers of the French Mission on the right of the picture.

Rifles plodding on and then my eyes are riveted on a sight I shall never see again. It is the 32nd Division at its best. I see rows upon rows of British soldiers lying dead, dying or wounded in No Man's Land. Here and there I see an officer urging on his followers. Occasionally I can see the hands thrown up and then a body flops to the ground. The bursting shells and smoke make visibility poor, but I can see enough to convince me Thiepval village is still held, for it is now 8 A.M. and by 7:45 A.M. it should have fallen to allow of our passage forward on its flank."

Here and elsewhere, the unbelievable situation developed according to the same pattern: "The extended lines started in excellent order, but gradually melted away. There was no wavering or attempting to come back, the men fell in their ranks, mostly before the first hundred yards of No Man's Land had been crossed."[5] "As a display of bravery it was magnificent, as an example of tactics its very memory made one shudder. . . ."[6] Thiepval, an objective of the first day of battle, was captured by the British on September 27th, the 89th day; the whole battle lasted for 141 days.

It was a long time before the grisly facts about July 1st penetrated the British consciousness. Neither Haig nor General Rawlinson, commanding the Fourth Army, which fought the battle, nor any other officer at first grasped what had happened. One war correspondent[7] wrote in his newspaper: "It is, on balance, a good day for England and France."

[5] *British Official History.*
[6] Spears: *Prelude to Victory,* Cape, 1939.
[7] Philip Gibbs.

(opposite, top) ". . . preparations were methodical . . ." Russian mechanized transport in February 1916.

(opposite, bottom) ". . . isolated crags of German resistance . . ." German troops on the Eastern Front; note their long column stretching away to the horizon, the parked transport, and the absence of any road.

(pages 248 and 249) ". . . an army which had grown to . . . 1.5 million men." A North Lancashire Territorial battalion parades for trench duty in April 1916 (wearing their recently issued "battle bowlers" somewhat self-consciously).

But when at last the British public learned what the loss of life had been in that short span of time, the paroxysm was tremendous. Its effects were felt all through the Second World War, influencing British strategy; they are still felt in Britain today. One reason for this was the special nature of the army that marched into the holocaust. For this was, above all,

"Except on the right flank . . . gains . . . were minimal . . ." A water-logged mine crater at Mametz, one of the few objectives taken and held on the first day; it was captured by the XVth Corps, whose losses for the day, in three divisions, were over 8,000, "due almost entirely to machine gun fire."

"Kitchener's Army"—the eager, devoted, physical and spiritual elite of the British nation who had volunteered at Lord Kitchener's call. The massacre of this breed of men was the price the British paid for the voluntary principle, the principle of unequal sacrifice.

Because of July 1st, because of the shock, and because of the quality of the men who fell, the full truth about the Battle of the Somme has

(opposite, top) ". . . eleven British divisions advanced simultaneously . . ." 1st Lancashire Fusiliers fixing bayonets before their disastrous assault on Beaumont-Hamel, July 1, 1916. The battalion had 483 casualties that day, of whom 180 officers and men were killed. They formed part of the 29th Division.

(opposite, bottom) ". . . eleven British divisions advanced . . ." 16th Middlesex (29th Division) preparing to attack Beaumont-Hamel on July 1, 1916. This battalion lost 549 men that day, 183 killed.

"... the whole battle lasted for 141 days." A sentry on duty in a trench at Ovillers, July 1916, while his exhausted comrades sleep.

been largely obscured. It cannot be grasped without paying full and due attention to the 140 days which followed that dreadful opening; during them the British Army inflicted their first major defeat upon the Germans, and carried forward by a huge stride the process of grinding-down which ultimately brought Germany's collapse. In the course of this the British assumed the leading rôle on the Western Front that Haig had foreseen for them, but whose cost his fellow countrymen had never dreamed of counting. This dates from his reflection on July 2nd, as information—mostly incredibly bad—filtered in to him: "The enemy has undoubtedly been severely shaken. . . . Our correct course, therefore, is to press him hard with the least possible delay." The student will here detect an unmistakable echo of Grant's decision, as the Federal army reeled back from the bloody Battle of the Wilderness in 1864: "Forward to Spottsylvania." Grant has been as severely criticized as Haig. Nevertheless his decision marked the beginning of the end of the Confederacy.

252

For four and a half months the Battle of the Somme raged on. A large French contingent under General Foch fought on the right of the British; in the early stages their activity came largely as a surprise to the Germans (who thought that France had been rendered helpless by Verdun), and Foch's troops were able to make advances which contrasted sharply with the British failures. Then, as German resistance stiffened against them, and while the British applied themselves to learning the lessons of the battle, the French in turn found themselves stuck; their final losses amounted to 195,000, on top of their Verdun casualties. They had achieved much, but one of the most depressing features of the whole battle is the relative lack of coordination between their efforts and those of their British allies; only twice, on July 1st and on September 15th, did the Franco-British forces achieve full unity of action.

At the root of the whole British situation, and of the disaster which had befallen them, lay the rawness of the troops; it was the attempt to impose an inflexible procedure as a compensation for lack of training which produced the July 1st losses. Haig's opinion that he did not have an army, but "a collection of divisions," is borne out by the German official monograph on the battle, which says: "The British Army . . . had not yet reached a sufficiently high tactical standard. The training of the infantry was clearly behind that of the German; the superficially trained

"... the 140 days ..." Border Regiment dugouts in Thiepval Wood, August 1916.

"... the 140 days ..." 8th Seaforth Highlanders holding a stretch of front line in the desert facing toward Martinpuich, August 25, 1916. Martinpuich was captured on September 15th.

British were particularly clumsy in movements of large masses. On the other hand, small bodies, such as machine-gun crews, bombers, and trench blockers and special patrols, thanks to their native independence of character, fought very well. . . ." Slowly, at high and constant cost, these qualities were cultivated and extended. The rigidity of the early days was abandoned as the soldiers learned their trade. The first hint of what they might be able to do was given on July 14th—only a fortnight after the great disaster—when 22,000 of these same raw soldiers, under their same unskilled staff officers, were assembled silently on tapes in No-Man's-Land in the darkness of the night, within 500 yards of the German front line, which they proceeded to capture in one rush at dawn. The French General Balfourier on their right, when told of what the British proposed to do, had proclaimed it utterly impossible. Rawlinson's Chief of Staff, Sir Archibald Montgomery, retorted that if they didn't manage it, he would eat his hat—never supposing that this would be conveyed literally to the Frenchman. When he heard what had happened, Balfourier exclaimed with relief: "Alors, le général Montgomery ne mange pas son chapeau."[8]

JULY 14

This was an admirable and brilliant feat of arms which in any other war might have expunged much of the misery of July 1st. But in the conditions of 1916 the success won proved as deceptive as that of the French earlier. It was a set principle in the German Army not to yield ground. Every British (or French) gain was followed by immediate counterattack;

[8] "Then General Montgomery won't be eating his hat."

254

if the first failed, another was instantly put in. Thus every yard had to be fought over time and again. This was what gave the battle its peculiarly horrible character, and this was what ultimately broke the German spirit. What the Germans had intended to do to France at Verdun, the British did to them on the Somme. From end to end of the long front, from Gommecourt to Thiepval, to Beaumont-Hamel, Pozières, Fricourt, and Mametz, all the way to Combles, where the British and French met, and on from there, the battle raged incessantly. Its "hard cores" were the bastions of Thiepval and Beaumont-Hamel on the left, the open ground around Pozières in the center, and the deadly triangle of Bazentin-le-Petit Wood, High Wood, and Delville Wood on the right. Every one of these place names became an evil memory for British troops, and every one had its moments of glory for particular units: Thiepval for the Ulstermen, Beaumont-Hamel for the Newfoundlanders and Highlanders, Pozières for the Australians—whose dead lay thicker there than on any other battlefield of the war—and Delville Wood for the South Africans. The county regiments of Britain fought over them all.

By the beginning of September the price of this style of warfare was becoming apparent, as were some of its results. At the same time a grave strategic necessity was also exerting its pressure. On August 28th Joffre told Haig: "A great Coalition battle will begin during the first weeks of September." Romania had at last declared her hand; on the preceding day she had entered the War on the Allied side. The final offensive flickers of Brusilov's mighty effort were about to be seen. Cadorna was on the point of launching his own major effort of the year on the Isonzo; the date he aimed at was September 15th. This also was the date that Joffre and Haig were working to. Haig informed his Army Commanders

"... learning the lessons ..." British machine-gunners in gas masks at Ovillers (captured July 15th–17th).

on August 31st: ". . . the C.-in-C. has decided that the attack projected for the middle of September is to be planned as a decisive operation and all preparations made accordingly."

Among the preparations was an entirely new weapon, the long-overdue technical solution to the joint problem of barbed wire and machine guns: the tank. This was the product of the meeting of several minds, but the operative impulse had been given by Winston Churchill in March 1915. Essentially, it comprised the linking of two ideas: the use of armor plate to protect men while advancing and the use of caterpillar traction to enable them to surmount obstacles. Eleven months after Churchill's order to "proceed as proposed," the first trials were held. Officers from Haig's staff observed them; he was impressed by their reports, and immediately wove the new weapon into his battle plans. He was distressed to learn that this was premature; neither the tanks nor

"Every . . . gain was followed by immediate counterattack . . ." Germans in the open, running forward to counterattack on the Somme. Note the ground, still grassy, but becoming pitted with craters, quite bare and devoid of cover. From the trenches (white lines) on the far slopes such a rush as this (whether German or British) could be swept with machine-gun fire.

their crews would be ready to take part in the opening of the battle on July 1st. If they had been, a different story might have emerged.

Nevertheless, Haig continued to hope. Disappointed in July, he might be luckier in August. But production difficulties persisted, and crew training presented further problems. On August 11th he recorded a letter from the Ministry of Munitions telling him that tank accessories could not be delivered until September 1st: "This is disappointing as I have been looking forward to obtaining decisive results from the use of these 'Tanks' at an early date." More than a month would still elapse before he could discover whether his hopes were justified, and even then, far from possessing the 150 tanks which he had asked for in April, all he would have would be 49. But since this was a full-scale venture by the whole Alliance, in which his French, Russian, Italian, and now Romanian Allies would be fully committing themselves, it was unthinkable that

"... ugly but remorseless progress ..." A Mark I "male" tank at Thiepval, September 25, 1916. Note the distinguishing 6-pounder gun in sponson, "tail," or two-wheeled "hydraulic stabilizer" to help steering, and wire-netting antibomb "roof."

Britain should hold anything back, no matter how small, unready, or untried it might be.

SEPTEMBER 12

On September 12th the Allied army at Salonika passed to the offensive. On the same day in Transylvania, Romanians and Russians linked to win the last significant success that would come from that quarter. (In the Dobruja, on the other hand, the first small gains of Field Marshal von Mackensen's troops provided a different omen.) On the 15th Cadorna

SEPTEMBER 15

opened the Seventh Battle of the Isonzo, the first phase of a campaign that would continue well into November. It was also on that day that the British and French undertook their last joint assault on the Somme. Seventeen of the 49 tanks available with the British either became "ditched" or broke down mechanically before they could get into action. Various mishaps befell the remaining 32, but at one point along the vast battlefront, at Flers-Courcelette, 13 of them were briefly in action together in mutually supporting combat. The effect they produced was immediate; its consequences reached far into the future. It was summed up at the time by a message from a contact airplane that exultant press correspondents translated as: "Tank walking up the High Street of Flers with the British Army cheering behind."

The tone of this message was in keeping with the prevailing view of the new machine. It was compared with every kind of mythical or actual monster; its ugly but remorseless progress was generally considered a joke. Philip Gibbs wrote: "When our soldiers first saw these strange

258

creatures lolloping along the roads and over old battlefields, taking trenches on the way, they shouted and cheered wildly, and laughed for a day afterwards." Colonel Swinton, one of the tank's begetters, remarked that among the "real truths" circulating about them were: "That the Tanks carried a crew of 400 men, were armed with 12-inch guns, had a speed of 30 m.p.h., were constructed in Japan by Swedes, and—dire insult . . .—were officered by airmen who had lost their nerve."

It is all very understandable—and rather sad. The fact is that the Mark I tank, 7 feet 4½ inches high, 32 feet 6 inches long, with a crew of eight, and a six-cylinder 105-horsepower Daimler engine, maximum speed 3.7 mph (on rough ground, ½ mph), armed with two 6-pounder guns ("male") or two machine guns ("female"), was a weak and variable instrument. Neither its performance nor its numbers could sway the decision of 1916. The gap punched at Flers was stopped up, and once again the great Allied offensive degenerated into a swaying ding-dong struggle, with the Germans being driven steadily back—the hard way. Many officers, including the German High Command, were completely unconvinced by the tank's achievements on September 15th. Among the exceptions was Haig. He told Swinton "that though the tanks had not achieved all that had been hoped, they had saved many lives and had fully justified themselves; that he wanted five times as many . . ." Even so, the first important successes of the tanks were still a long way off. It was not until fourteen months after their debut that they first showed what they could do if used on a large scale—at Cambrai. The main reason for this is that until then they did not exist on a large scale. Seven months after Flers, the British Army possessed only sixty, and many of these were patched-up veterans of the first engagement. The tanks that went into action at Cambrai in November 1917, moreover,

". . . the Somme dragged on." Troops obtaining water from butts on a light railway, Battle of the Transloy Ridges, October 1916. Water supply was a continuous nightmare on the Somme, where few streams bisected the battlefield.

were mostly Mark IV's, a much-improved model, though still far from perfect. The reason production had been so slow during that interval was this jump through two modification from the Mark I of September 1916, with consequent retooling. The reason for that jump was the experience gained on the Somme, which made possible both the brilliant feat at Cambrai and the role of the tanks in the final victories of 1918.

Meanwhile, the Somme dragged on. The fortress of Thiepval fell on September 27th. By October 1st the British had taken nearly 27,000 German prisoners, but their own casualties during the next month alone were over 60,000. By the beginning of November British GHQ arrived at "a low estimate" of German casualties of over 600,000. On November 13th Beaumont-Hamel was captured. Some of the British commanders wished to attempt to exploit this success, but conditions by now made fighting impossible. A few days later the battle ended in a wilderness of mud at least the equal of Verdun, and now equally swept by the icy winds and snow squalls of the approaching winter. Those who survived and were able to make comparisons generally agree that conditions on the Somme at the end of 1916 surpass all other sensations of horror.

SEPTEMBER 27

NOVEMBER 18

". . . the Somme dragged on." Raiders away! Canadians on the Ancre making for the German trenches, October 1916.

"Our vocabulary is not adapted to describe such an existence, because it is outside experience for which words are normally required," says the *British Official History*.

What was the tally? At the end of the battle British GHQ placed its own casualties at over 460,000; this figure was later corrected to 415,000. The French lost 195,000. German losses will never be known, partly because of the destruction of records, but mainly because during this period the Germans resorted for the first time to deliberate subterfuge to conceal the damage done to them. In view of their methods of fighting and of their subsequent behavior, however, the reasonable assumption is that their casualties at least equaled those of the Allies, and may well have surpassed them. All through the battle their fundamental strategy conformed to that laid down by General von Bülow at its very beginning: "The important thing is to hold on to our present positions at any cost and to improve them by local counterattack. . . . The enemy should have to carve his way over heaps of corpses." This dictated the pattern of the whole campaign. But in September, faced by the last great Allied offensive, the new German commanders, Hindenberg and Ludendorff, departed from this principle. The latter tells us: "[We] had to face the danger that 'Somme fighting' would soon[9] break out at various points on our fronts, and that even our troops would not be able to withstand such attacks indefinitely. . . . Accordingly, the construction had been begun as early as September of powerful rear positions in the West. . . ." The decision to build the "Hindenburg Line" marks the first acceptance

[9] In 1917.

(pages 262 and 263) "'Hans is dead. Fritz is dead. Wilhelm is dead.'" German dead in a wrecked machine-gun post at Guillemont, September 1916.

of defeat by the Germans; the retreat into it in February 1917 (the solitary example of such a withdrawal by Germany) marks their full acknowledgment. The reason was the dreadful damage done to their army.

Prince Rupprecht of Bavaria, an Army Group commander, summed this up from his exalted point of view: "What still remained of the old first-class peace-trained German infantry had been expended on the battlefield."

The man in the line expressed himself somewhat differently. On September 30th a soldier of the 66th Infantry Regiment wrote in a letter:

"Dear Wilhelm, I send you greetings from my grave in the earth. We shall soon become mad in this awful artillery fire. Day and night it goes on without ceasing. Never has it been so bad as this before . . ."

On October 3rd an officer of the 111th Infantry Reserve Regiment wrote: ". . . the men go through frightful experiences. There is no longer a question of a dugout for them. There is no longer even a trench, let alone a dugout in the first line. The trenches have been smashed up. The men lie in shellholes. . . . We are going slowly back."

A soldier of the 110th Infantry Reserve Regiment wrote: "We have had dreadful losses again. I shall not get leave I suppose until we have left the Somme, but with our losses what they are, this cannot be long or there will not be a single man left in the regiment."

Another soldier wrote: "It is decreed by [a Higher Power] that we shall be completely annihilated."

A soldier in the 111th Reserve summed it up: "Hans is dead. Fritz is dead. Wilhelm is dead. There are many others. I am now quite alone in the company. God grant we may soon be relieved. Our losses are dreadful. And now we have bad weather again, so that anyone who is not wounded falls ill. This is almost unendurable. If only peace would come!"

"THE OBJECT OF WAR IS PEACE" 12

Even now, this war could have a glorious ending for us. But it won't.

LORD ESHER TO HAIG, DECEMBER 1917

The winter of 1916–1917 was the worst in European memory since 1880–1881. By October rain, mist, and cold were already restricting and transforming the fighting on the Western Front. Snow came in November; ice and snow were constant attendants thereafter. On Easter Sunday, April 8, 1917, Colonel Repington noted in England: "Horribly cold, much snow." The next day, the British Army attacked at Arras in a blizzard. A week later, on the Aisne, the Senegalese infantry were so benumbed that their French officers had to load their rifles for them. For nearly six months, this glacial interlude multiplied the burdens of war for all the soldiers, revealed them sickeningly to the civilians, and worked its depressing effect on the spirits of men everywhere. The hopes of the world were buried in an icy casket.

When at last the frozen year awoke to life, the calamities contained in it were found to surpass all those that had gone before. It was a year of new men, new situations, new desperation. Lord Kitchener was dead, drowned in H.M.S. *Hampshire*. Von Falkenhayn had gone; Hindenburg and Ludendorff reigned in his stead. Asquith had gone; David Lloyd George was now Prime Minister of Britain. Joffre had gone; General Robert Nivelle commanded the French Army. The Emperor Franz-Joseph was dead, after a reign of sixty-eight years. The Romanoff

". . . a year of new men . . ." The Emperor Karl of Austria-Hungary (1916–1918) inspecting his troops.

265

dynasty was at its last gasp. Everywhere the killing of 1916 had produced a deep sickness. The question for all the newcomers in the new year was whether they could find another way, so that the killing might cease. The most obvious way, of course, was to end the War.

The thought was in many minds; but now an obstacle to reasonable action was perceived, which might have been foreseen but was not, and which succeeding generations have not overcome. Modern war had created for itself new terms of reference. Necessarily, it involved the masses in all countries; to induce them to pour out their blood and the produce of their sweat, a special kind of appeal had to be made. This was true everywhere, but it was particularly true in the democratic countries, where the possibility of the masses withholding their contribution was more real. How was the appeal made? Ultimately, "by awakening the tribal instincts latent in man, and, in order to focus these instincts, to transform the enemy into a devil."[1] If the enemy was indeed a "devil," evidently it was a sin to traffic with him. The "devil" has to be overcome entirely. The result? "Inasmuch as war is not now waged for limited objects, nothing but absolute victory seems a justification for breaking it off; and until it has been gained a compromised peace is regarded as an unwarranted defeat by all belligerents."[2] Thus the two most promising avenues toward peace were firmly blocked: the intervention of neutrals and the acceptance of limited gains.

The weakness of the neutral position was revealed in 1916. The most important neutral in the world was the United States of America, lifted above the conflict not only by distance and self-sufficiency but also by the fact that her large population was ethnically linked to all the combatants. The War offended the American consciousness, and none more than the consciousness of President Woodrow Wilson. In January 1916 he had sent his personal emissary, Colonel House, to Europe to test out the ground on which American mediation could bring the War to a conclusion. There was no ground. The rising bitterness and congealing obduracy of both sides ruled out accommodation. Fortified by re-election and appalled at what the year had brought forth, the President tried again in December. Unfortunately, he had been anticipated by the Central Powers, acting on very different motives. All that his second

[1] Major General J. F. C. Fuller, *The Conduct of War 1789–1961.*
[2] Cruttwell, *A History of the Great War.*

(opposite) ". . . the President tried again . . ." **President Woodrow Wilson photographed at the Quai d'Orsay in 1919.**

"The fall of Bucharest on December 6th . . ." Field-Marshal von Mackensen entering Bucharest in December 1917.

démarche produced was the nearest thing yet seen to a formal declaration of war aims by the Allies. And all that this produced, despíte its deliberately confused and evasive wording in key passages, was the conviction among their enemies that a "war of annihilation" was the true purpose of the Allies. Meanwhile the War and its attributes were steadily sapping at the very neutrality of America itself, thus undermining the President's stand. Propaganda was doing its work; the frame of mind of the American people was changing. James Duane Squires recalls "a great meeting in New England, held under the auspices of a Christian Church—God save the mark! A speaker demanded that the Kaiser, when captured, be boiled in oil, and the entire audience stood on chairs to scream its hysterical approval. This was the mood we were in. This was the kind of madness that had seized us."[3]

So much for neutral intervention; the other possibility proved to be as feeble. The fall of Bucharest on December 6th, with the virtual

[3] "British Propaganda at Home and in the United States from 1914 to 1917," quoted by Fuller, *op. cit.*

268

elimination of Romania and the end of Russia's offensive power; the brave defiance of the German soldiers on the Somme, and of the Austrians on the Carso; the mounting toll of the U-boat offensive (monthly British shipping losses rose from 43,000 tons in August to 182,000 in December, and Allied shipping losses to a peak of 849,000 tons in April 1917)—these encouragements, offsetting the damage they had sustained, persuaded the Central Powers that the time was ripe to offer a deal of sorts. But it was so obviously a deal based on the supposition of partial victory—on the "indestructible strength" of the Central Powers—that the Allies barely discussed it. It had an effect opposite to that presumably intended: it served to harden the hearts of the Allied statesmen, even against the efforts of President Wilson.

Indeed, for reasons that could not have been foreseen, this step made the chance of peace even more remote. The very fact that the Germans and Austrians had taken this initiative suggested to many on the Allied side that they were weakening. In March this belief received important reinforcement: through his brother-in-law, Prince Sixtus of Bourbon, then serving in the Belgian Army, the Emperor Karl of Austria-Hungary made an independent approach to France. Here at MARCH 1917 last was a chance—or so it seemed—of breaking the unity of the Central Powers, of detaching Austria from Germany. There was no more ardent advocate of this idea than the British Prime Minister, Lloyd George, and certainly, if it could have been brought about in this way, it would have held more promise than anything else that offered. But the whole thing broke down on two factors: first, that the Emperor Karl, by the very nature of the approach, could say nothing for Germany, and therefore nothing on the subject on which France was now most adamant, the return of her lost provinces of Alsace-Lorraine; second, Italy hastened to make demands upon Austria that even the hopeful and pacific Karl could not accept. This was the price of alliance, with all the compromises of principle that it implies.

There would be other approaches to peace, further tentative discussions and powerful exhortations during the year. The most significant of them were the International Socialist Conference in Stockholm in JUNE 1917 June, the Pope's appeal to the warring powers in August, and Lord AUGUST 1917 Lansdowne's letter to the London *Daily Telegraph* in November. This NOVEMBER 1917 last, coming from a Conservative former Foreign Secretary (and architect of the Anglo-French Entente), and containing the question, "What will be the value of the blessings of peace to nations so exhausted that they can scarcely stretch out an arm with which to grasp them?" had a

269

very distinct impact on public opinion. But none of these appeals was able to divert the relentless course of events. The tide of fear and hatred engulfed them all.

With peace rejected, nothing remained for the embattled populations but to fight it out. And by now this was very much a matter of populations, not simply of armed forces. For the Central Powers, the situation assumed a particularly forbidding aspect: the Allied blockade, imposed from the beginning of the War, and steadily growing in effectiveness, brought hardships which only more slowly affected the maritime nations of the west. By the middle of 1916 it was clear that the German and Austrian peoples were suffering severely at home; censorship could not prevent the news of this from reaching their fighting troops, who were naturally discouraged at what they heard. A letter from Cologne, found on a German soldier in June 1916, reported:

"... the mounting toll of the U-boat offensive ..." A U-boat sinks a merchant ship by gunfire.

"Hunger is making itself felt here. During the week none of the families received any potatoes. The allowance now is one egg per head per week, and half a pound of bread and 50 grammes of butter per head per day. England is not so wrong about starving us out. If the war lasts three months more we shall be done."

A letter from Dresden in May read: "We have had no meat for six weeks; I have lost 10 pounds' weight. I am afraid that it will soon be all over with us; we are on the downward path. There have been riots again in the market."

German ingenuity, organization, and determination grappled with these problems remarkably well. There were certain assets: the flow of Scandinavian ores to German industry was barely interrupted; the great pastoral and grain lands of central Europe continued to produce, though output fell severely, and to these was later added the loot of Romania

"... the Allied blockade ... growing in effectiveness ..." Brass mortars and pestles, collected in Germany for munitions; brass almost vanished from German-occupied lands, even down to doorknobs.

and the Ukraine; the captured territories of France and Belgium helped to sustain the conquerors. German science offered an astounding range of *ersatz* (substitute) products to replace what had vanished. But nothing could avert the effects of the long and bitter winter; in Austria-Hungary, the number of cattle decreased from 17,324,000 in 1914 to 3,518,000 in 1918, pigs from 7,678,000 to 214,000. It became evident that, short of some new and striking factor, there must be a term to the resistance of the Central Powers. But when?

In France, after the shock of the first reverses and the consequent loss of economic resources, a vast industrial effort was made, matching the energies of the French armies on the battlefields. "Having lost in battle some of her most valuable mines, France re-equipped the Serbian Army, took a large part in re-equipping the Greek, provided the British with thousands of aircraft and a still greater number of engines, and yet played a great role in arming the American, despite the tremendous burden of her own large forces."[4] In industry and in agriculture the

[4] Cyril Falls, *The First World War*.

"... the women ... stepped forward ..." These Belgian women are running a British Army laundry at Poperinghe, with soldiers' shirts festooned to dry, September 1917.

women of France stepped forward to uphold their men at the fronts. The prodigious strength of her peasant economy was revealed. Her political weakness, however, came near to betraying her. The year 1917 was one of dire scandals. An ex-premier, Caillaux, was imprisoned for treason; Malvy, Minister of the Interior until August, was convicted of subsidizing with public funds the defeatist organ *Le Bonnet rouge*, which was also receiving money from Germany. The names of the traitors Bolo, Lenoir, and Almeyreda tainted every current in public life. A mood of cynicism and revulsion swept over the French people, finding its overt expression in a mounting wave of strikes during the spring and summer. The Russian example was duly heeded. Lord Esher wrote from Paris in July: ". . . in this country, and especially in Paris which is its storm centre, the spirit of revolution is always near the surface."

". . . the submarine campaign indicated . . . another price . . ." A British liner "dazzle-painted" as camouflage against U-boat attack.

If the knowledge of war had brought disturbances to France and Germany, in Britain these assumed a seismic quality. It was in 1917 that the whole concept of the "limited-liability war" to which the British had always clung vanished once for all. The Somme casualty lists exposed the cost in blood for the first time; the submarine campaign indicated that there was another price also, from which none would be exempt. Writing to his brother in Canada, the historian F. S. Oliver said in February: ". . . I expect we shall be pretty hungry by Novem-

ber. . . ." In September he was able to fill in some of the details of this prophecy: "It sometimes occurs to me to wonder if you, at the other side of an ocean and a continent, can form an adequate picture of the lives of your friends and relations over here; of a London whose wheeled traffic, I suppose, must have been reduced by about two-thirds; whose nights are dark and sometimes almost as silent as the country; where nearly all the necessaries of life, except air and water, have to be bought in the most sparing quantities, and have to be paid for on the average at something more than twice the old prices; where at any public place you are allowed no more than two tiny lumps of sugar (together not much more than half the size of the old-fashioned lump); where coal, coke, matches, and everything of that nature have to be husbanded as if they were heaps of gold.

"Of course, the result of this is not by any means all bad. I never knew till last summer what a delicious thing a potato was, that is, when I couldn't buy any; nor did I ever realise the transcendent luxury of

274

white bread. The stuff you get from the baker really automatically rations the consumer, because it is so abominable now as to destroy any greediness which may still lurk in our natures."

Rationing of food, resisted with horror by many in Britain, was introduced in January, and full control was practically complete in May. By December the food queue was a regular feature of British daily life. The curtailment of supplies of drink—reduction in both quantity and quality of beer and spirits—brought added irritation. On the Labor front, the experience of full employment in a war economy proved hard to assimilate. The trade unions were prompted by natural defensive instincts to press for every advantage that the unusual situation offered, to make demands for wages and conditions of which they had scarcely dreamed before. At the same time they resisted certain innovations that seemed to hold dangerous possibilities—the "dilution" of industry with unskilled labor and the widespread employment of women. The net result of all these discontents during the year was a total of 588 disputes which cost the country nearly six million working days.

There was something else besides. It was not only that sons and husbands were paying a terrible toll of lives; it was not only that "safe" citizens at home were enduring unexpected hardships; over and above that, they were not even safe. The new dimension of war, the Air, had abolished the "right little, tight little island." As early as January 1915, the German Zeppelins had demonstrated this with a raid on the English Midlands. Attacks on London and other cities followed; in all, the Zeppelins made some 40 raids on Britain, dropped 220 tons of bombs, killed 537 people, and injured 1,358. It was not a very impressive record in itself, but it was a portent.

JANUARY 19, 1915

On June 13, 1917, Colonel Repington wrote: "Today 15 Hun aeroplanes, flying high, bombed the East End of London, causing a large number of casualties. People crowded the streets and tops of houses to look on. Nobody seems much concerned, and no panic." On July 7th he himself observed "a great flight of Hun planes, looking like silver swallows, about 12,000 feet up, and appearing to fly slowly. They were in fan-shape formation and were heading south. I saw them very well and counted twenty-six, but a few may have been ours in chase. The shells were bursting all round them, and after reaching Picadilly they turned south-east, and the formation became more broken. . . . In the evening it was said that 37 people had been killed and 140 wounded, also that no serious damage had been done. . . . London will soon be as accustomed to being bombed as Ladysmith was to being shelled."

JUNE 13, 1917

275

Repington was oversanguine. Reporting the same raid to his brother, F. S. Oliver wrote: "There has been a very foolish outcry with regard to what should be done. . . . But there is no getting away from the fact that we ought to defend London better than we are doing, for the moral reason that attacks upon the capital city are in the nature of public humiliations . . . also for the practical reason that London is in a sense our base. . . . Still, it seemed to me that the important thing for the moment was to stop the squealing." The "squealing" did not stop; as the German airplanes returned during the summer and autumn, often by day, later also by night, damage and casualties mounted. These were the famous Gothas, twin-engined aircraft with pusher screws, able to lift their bombloads high, and difficult to attack because of their three gun positions (nose, midship, and belly). Public agitation increased; night after night hundreds of thousands of people flocked for shelter into London's underground railway system; by September the output of the night shift had dropped to 27 percent of its normal figure. Sir William Robertson, coming from a War Cabinet meeting, remarked, "One would have thought the world was coming to an end." On October 2nd Repington found Robertson's deputy, General Maurice, "much concerned at the attitude of the Press towards air-raids and their cry that German towns must be bombed. We have only four bombing squadrons. . . . Trenchard[5] turned up, and was irate about the folly of the same criticism. He says that the long-range bombing squadrons . . . will not be ready till the winter. Somebody decidedly should be hanged for this after three years of war."

The improved aircraft designs of 1917 meant that bombing had "arrived" as an instrument of war. Until then a very chancy affair, thereafter it became more and more precise; the outcry of civilian populations has somewhat disguised the fact that it was developing rapidly as a technique of battle. The setting up under Trenchard of an "Independent Air Force" to carry out long-range bombing of Germany has obscured the steady, continuous, practical work of the Air Forces of both sides in attacking communications, camps, and positions. Trenchard's force came too late to effect much; its significance was as a pointer to the future. The great Handley-Page night bombers of 1918, each capable of carrying sixteen 112-pound bombs and of remaining in the air for eight hours, provided a clear indication of what war would become. Meanwhile, however, they formed only a very small proportion of a Royal Air Force, which had grown from some 60 first-line machines in

[5] Lord Trenchard, founder of the Royal Air Force.

August 1914 to a grand total of over 22,000 in 1918, of which 3,300 were first-line. The advantages of ever-developing design swayed from side to side. At the beginning of 1917 the Germans held a decided superiority, and this was a bleak time for the young semitrained fliers of Britain. By 1918 the balance had swung again, and victory in the Air was a natural concomitant of total victory.

Air raids, shortages, and strikes in Britain; corruption, treachery, and cynicism in France; a growing war weariness in Italy—the catalogue of the misfortunes of the Allies was not yet complete. In Russia the grim winter had struck with even more compelling force against a population which normally lived closer to the borderline of absolute poverty and starvation than did those in the west. On March 8, 1917, riots broke out in Petrograd. They began with the sacking of bakers' shops; they ended with the overthrow of world order. In the absence of any firm or rational lead from the Government, their political character swiftly grew. On March 12th a Soviet of Workers' and Soldiers' Representatives was created which, independently of the constitutional Opposition forces which believed themselves to be in control of events, set to work to subvert the army and seize the key positions of power. For the time being, this organization did not seek or win the limelight; it was the constitutional elements which forced the Czar's abdication within a week, on March 15th. The Russian liberals seemed to be in charge; their antagonism was toward the corrupt, heartless despotism and chronic inefficiency of the Czarist regime, not toward the war against the Central Powers. On March 23rd Colonel Repington noted: ". . . on the whole the change meets with general approval here, and also in America." For a brief moment it seemed that Russia would be revived and strengthened by an upsurge of democratic instinct. Nothing could have been further from the truth.

MARCH 8, 1917

MARCH 15

". . . technique of battle." Almost an epitome of the war, this scene behind the German lines shows horses (basic transport) at left, but with a motor lorry behind; center, the fuselages of two aircraft, one captured from the Allies (foreground), one German (loaded on lorry); right, road repairs in progress, the everlasting labor of all armies.

"... ever-developing design ..."
The Bristol fighter; after a disastrous beginning, due to unfamiliarity with her characteristics, this aircraft became famous. A two-seater, her Rolls-Royce engines gave her maximum speeds of 96–110 m.p.h., a ceiling of 22,000 feet, and an endurance of three to six hours.

"... continuous, practical work ..."
French "Morane Parasoles" in service with the Royal Flying Corps, September 1916.

". . . ever-developing design . . ."
Hauptmann Ritter von Tutschek
(27 victories) in a Fokker triplane.

"... Kerensky was able to launch one last offensive ..." The Minister of War of the Provisional Government, taking the salute in 1917.

"This was the end." Trotsky and Joffe arriving at Brest-Litovsk to make peace with Germany, January 1918.

Looking backward, the span of time between the March and October revolutions seems illusory, contracted, insignificant. While the span lasted, however—seven long months of it—while the Provisional Government remained in being, the omens from the east were contradictory and hard to read. On the one hand, the influence of the Soviets was clearly growing, and within them the influence of the Bolshevik section of the Social-Democratic Party headed by Vladimir Ulyanov, alias Lenin, a revolutionary returned from exile by German connivance. On the other hand, by immense efforts, the new Government, inspired by Minister of War Kerensky, was able to launch one last offensive on the grand scale (44 divisions) against the Central Powers. The Russians struck on July 1st; at first, incredible though it now seems, they gained substantial successes; then, with the aid of four divisions brought from the west in the absence of any Allied activity there, the Germans launched a counteroffensive. The brilliant artilleryman Bruchmüller provided techniques which compensated for numerical inferiority. The Russian armies crumbled away.

JULY 1, 1917

This was the end. From the close of July until October, it became more and more evident that Russian military power had ceased to be; the only question was how soon the effects of this would be exploited by the Germans and suffered by the Allies. Put in a different way, would the loss of Russian help, plus other factors, suffice to bring the Allies to defeat before American support could effectively help them? The United States had declared war against Germany in April. There was hope, but for those who understood the state of America's war preparedness, the year would pass with the sense of a terrible race against time.

APRIL 6, 1917

"General Nivelle had a Plan." General Robert Nivelle in 1917.

THE YEAR
OF CATASTROPHE 13

. . . in my view it was at present a question whether our armies could win the war before our navies lost it.

REPINGTON, JANUARY 24, 1917

General Nivelle had a Plan. There was nothing niggling or small about it. It was a plan for winning the war outright, and by a decision to be gained in a matter of twenty-four to forty-eight hours; it was based upon the twin propositions of great violence and great weight. The centerpiece of this project was to be a "mass of maneuver" of 27 divisions, a battering ram which would thrust right through the German lines and roll them up. Evidently, for such a task, a homogeneous force was essential; equally evidently, such a force could be provided only by France. Thus the essence of the Nivelle plan was yet another attempt by the French Army to win the War mainly by its own efforts. In this it departed diametrically from the decisions taken by the Allies while Joffre was still in command. Arrived at in November 1916, these had once again prescribed a simultaneous onslaught by all the Allied armies, the difference being that, at the urgent representation of the British Government, the British would strike in Flanders instead of nearer to the French front. But that made no difference to the principle of simultaneity of effort—indeed, it assisted by splitting the enemy's reserves. To both French and British Governments, however, the whole concept smacked too much of "the mixture as before," and they could no longer stomach it. So Joffre departed, covered with honors, and promoted to Marshal of France, and his war-weary countrymen found themselves burdened once again with the leading rôle which had already cost them so dearly.

In retrospect, few circumstances of the War seem so curious as the acceptance of this grandiose, impractical scheme by governments grown increasingly cynical about the ability of their military leaders. It was the forty-eight-hour promise that did the trick—the contrast between this and Joffre's remorseless, costly warfare of attrition. In no one was conversion to belief in victory on the Western Front more marked than in Britain's new Prime Minister, Lloyd George. Starting from the attitude

283

that he was "not prepared to accept the position of a butcher's boy driving cattle to the slaughter, and that he would not do it," he had already canvassed a number of alternative strategies. In December Repington noted: "Robertson . . . says that L.G. wants a victory quickly, a victory while you wait. He does not care where. Somewhere where opinion will be impressed, like Damascus. R. has told him that Damascus may come in time, when rail and pipe lines are laid, and meantime what about Beersheba? L.G. didn't fancy that Beersheba would catch on, but Jerusalem might! This is War Cabinet strategy at the close of 1916, and if we can win on it we can win on anything." By January, Lloyd George had changed his mind. At the Rome Conference during that month he argued for a joint Allied offensive from the Italian front; this was rejected by the French and the Italians. On his way home he met Nivelle. He invited the French general to London, and within a week Nivelle's charm, persuasiveness, and command of the English language had done their work. Robertson was told to instruct Haig to conform to Nivelle's plan "both in the letter and in the spirit." All else was to be set aside.

The British generals were less enthusiastic than their Prime Minister. Their own plans for a massive attack in Flanders were already well in hand; mounting losses from U-boat action, a high proportion of which were wrongly attributed by naval Intelligence to the bases at Ostend and Zeebrugge, gave this attack a special urgency. Yet both Haig and Robertson loyally cooperated with the French Commander in Chief. Lloyd George, however, was not satisfied. Distrusting the capacity of his military advisers, enthusiastically admiring the bold designs of Nivelle, but uncertain of his own political security, he decided to make use of Nivelle and his plan for the purpose of surreptitiously reducing the status and authority of the British generals. All he needed was a pretext, and this was not slow in offering itself.

Among the other casualties of the freezing winter was the Nord Railway system, on which the British forces in France depended. A transportation crisis of the first magnitude now arose. Haig and Nivelle were inevitably drawn in, as their experts failed to reach satisfactory solutions, but the accord of the two Commanders in Chief secured an understanding which at least made remedy possible. Lloyd George, however, seized upon this crisis as an occasion for an inter-Allied conference, ostensibly to discuss transportation, but in reality (unknown to the British War Cabinet) to rearrange the command structure of the Western Front. In short, his object was no less than to place Haig and the British armies in France under the direct command of Nivelle. The latter and his staff were warned of this intention, and drew up detailed proposals accordingly. They were not to know that the British Prime Minister was playing a lone hand, not only without the backing of his advisers but actually contrary to their convictions and those of his Government colleagues.

The outcome of Lloyd George's ill-considered machinations was seen at the Calais Conference on February 26–27th. It marked an important milestone in Allied war direction. Prompted by Lloyd George, Nivelle put forward proposals which would have reduced the forces of the British Empire in France to a mere contingent in the French Army and the British Commander in Chief to a glorified Adjutant General. Haig and Robertson were outraged; Lloyd George himself was somewhat taken aback. The French, when they discovered how they had been used, were much dismayed and perplexed. In the event, a compromise conclusion was reached, whereby the British Expeditionary Force retained its identity, under its own C. in C., but Haig was subordinated to Nivelle for the duration of the offensive outlined in the great plan. A second conference in London early in March, by which time the British Government as a whole had a much better idea of the situation, underlined this essential reservation. For a short time Nivelle tried to act as though it did not exist—as though, in fact, Haig was a pure subordinate like any French Army Group commander. The War itself, and a new French political crisis which gravely undermined Nivelle's personal position, made this attempt short-lived. Very soon he found himself in the odd position of seeking Haig's support against his own Government. The damage done at Calais lay elsewhere: in the shattering of confidence between the civil and military heads of the British war effort which was to remain as a permanent factor right through to the end. This was an unlooked-for victory for Germany, a gratuitous gift.

The deep irony of Calais lies, not in the outraged feelings or ill-founded pretensions exposed there, but in the maneuvers simultaneously taking place on the field of battle, which made a mockery of those in the distant corridors and council chambers. For the Germans now were engaged in the delicate task of transforming a strategic defeat into a tactical advantage. The first indications of their withdrawal into the new Hindenburg Line were received on the eve of the Calais Conference: "Important developments have been taking place on the Fifth Army [British] front. The enemy has fallen back on a front of 18,000 yards. . . . Our advanced guards met with little opposition . . . ," Haig noted on February 25th. Aboundingly self-confident, Nivelle and his officers had freely advertised their war-winning plan; their actual preparations in

285

front of the enemy were on a scale which would have made secrecy difficult in any case, but little attempt was made to achieve it. Appreciating what was in store, the Germans very naturally concluded that they could well do without it, and accordingly they began, by deliberate stages, to slip away, leaving a devastated area behind them. What had appeared at first as an isolated phenomenon on the front of the British Fifth Army (Gough) extended right across the zone of the French Northern Army Group (Franchet d'Esperey), robbing Nivelle of one-third of his front of attack. Despite all the efforts of Gough and D'Esperey —and two more aggressive commanders it would be hard to name— the Allies were utterly unable to pin down the German rear guards. Cavalry proved quite useless for this type of pursuit against an unbroken enemy; trench-bound infantry, used to massive artillery support at all times, could not adapt themselves to open warfare conditions; the artillery lurched and floundered along wrecked roads and over the icy mire; "booby traps" made their unwelcome contribution to the blockage.

It was Field-Marshal Haig° who first, among the Allied leaders,

° Haig became a Field-Marshal in December 1916.

". . . a devastated area behind them." Trees felled across a road by the Germans to delay the Allied advance; Spring 1917.

correctly analyzed the German intention: "His objects seem to be: to disorganize our offensive by causing our attacks to be made in the air, and so to cause us loss of time; to wear out our troops by causing us at each stage to renew our preparations for attack . . . to affect the moral of the Allies by disappointment at seeing the enemy able to escape at each successive stage, in spite of the greatest efforts made to prevent this." His conclusion was: "The advisability of launching Nivelle's battle at all grows daily less. . . ." This was the very opposite of Nivelle's own conviction, expressed at the beginning of March. The German withdrawal, he stated, was entirely to the advantage of the Allies, and on this view he based the decision *"de n'apporter aucune modification fondamentale au plan générale d'opérations qui est arrêté."*[1] For a short time longer, Nivelle and his headquarters existed in a world of optimistic dreams that shunned contact with the forbidding realities at the front. But he and his entourage were becoming more and more isolated, lonely and meaningless figures in a new tide of change. The French Govern-

[1] ". . . to make no fundamental change whatever in the general plan of operations which has been drawn up."

ment fell on March 18th, and the new war minister, Paul Painlevé, never a believer in Nivelle, rapidly became the focus of a growing body of opposition to the great offensive. If not the "leaders" of this opposition, the three most powerful figures in it were the Army Group commanders who would have to carry out the attack: D'Esperey, Pétain, and Micheler. As each week passed, their lack of confidence in Nivelle's project became plainer to see: a cruel dilemma for Painlevé, in the face of Nivelle's continued assertions of complete confidence.

APRIL 6

The War Minister made his supreme attempt to resolve the deadlock on April 6th, the day on which the United States declared war on Germany. At Compiègne, the seat of the GQG, President Poincaré, with Prime Minister Ribot and Painlevé, met Nivelle and his generals. Micheler, who had been loudest in denunciation, now made a halting case against Nivelle's plan; D'Esperey and Pétain added professional footnotes, which were naturally diffident, under the eye of the Commander in Chief. Nivelle himself offered to resign, but this was more than the Government could bear. The Compiègne Conference broke up, having taken no decision, but having revealed two distasteful facts: the inability of elected political leaders to control the "technicians" of modern war, and the foolishness of Lloyd George in supposing that the subordination of the British Army to a French general could mean anything less than its subordination to the French Government. The British were not consulted at Compiègne, yet their battle had already begun.

For his British Allies Nivelle had propounded a major diversionary offensive, to be launched a week before his own. The area selected was Arras, immediately to the north of the German sector of withdrawal. Almost the only gratification Haig had been able to extract from the proceedings at Calais had been the agreement to include the famous and fearsome Vimy Ridge among his objectives. This would be assaulted by the Canadian Corps in General Horne's First Army, while General Allenby's Third Army continued the offensive to the south, and General Gough's Fifth Army, farther south still, staged a "diversion within a diversion." Arras was, once again, to be a "set-piece" battle, depending chiefly on artillery (nearly 3,000 guns) and careful preliminary preparation. But the British Army had come a long way in the nine months since it had last launched an attack in this manner and on this scale; the immediate results would be very different.

APRIL 9

The main bombardment opened on April 4th; the offensive went in, through driving snow and sleet, on April 9th. The weather took its toll.

The Royal Flying Corps, numerically superior, but with aircraft for the time being inferior to the latest German types,[2] was much hampered, and able to fulfill its rôle only at the cost of the highest monthly rate of casualties of the whole War: only sixty tanks were available for the battle, and ground conditions prevented many of these from even entering the action. On the other hand, artillery ammunition was now plentiful and much improved in quality; the artillerymen, experienced after the Somme, had reached a high level of proficiency, which was revealed in the precision of the creeping barrage. Infantry assault tactics

". . . the highest monthly rate of casualties of the whole war . . ." This is a "dog-fight." Scenes like this never occurred again after the Great War. The aircraft of those days are regarded as of "low performance" now, but no later types have ever matched their maneuverability, remarkably displayed in this photograph.

[2] Lieutenant Baron Manfred von Richthofen, in his red Albatross fighter, at the head of his "circus," now clinched his reputation; on April 29th he shot down five British aircraft, one of them being his fiftieth victim.

were much improved; the staffs had done their work well, their tour de force being the use of the underground cellars of Arras for concealing some 20,000 reserves, and the construction of galleries that enabled these to enter the line without being seen and without clogging normal communication routes. The opening phase of the attack, in sharp contrast to the tragedy of July 1, 1916, was a triumph which even the weather could not diminish.

The four divisions of the Canadian Corps "went over the top" at 5:30 A.M. on the 9th, covered by the fire of 983 guns and mortars, which had already disgorged about a million projectiles upon the target. By midmorning the Canadians were on their third objective. A sudden break in the clouds, bringing a brief gleam of deceptive sunshine, revealed to both sides the issue of the day: "the Germans saw that the Ridge was lost, the Canadians knew that it was won." By the beginning of the afternoon, they were standing on the crest, looking down on the plain of Douai—"the first Allied soldiers to do so since the far-off days of 1915, when for a few hours the French had held the northern extremity of the heights. It was an extraordinary sight, a glimpse of another world. Behind them lay an expanse of churned-up mud and desolation com-

"... at the head of his 'circus' ..." Richthofen's airdrome with the "circus" lined up; what the picture misses is the variation of bright colors in which each aircraft was painted.

pletely commanded from where they stood. . . . Below and beyond them on the German side lay a peaceful countryside with villages that appeared from a distance to be untouched by war."[3] It was one of the most dramatic moments of the War. Just after four o'clock that afternoon an attempt was made to pass some cavalry forward; it failed, amid the craters, as one might suppose; but the fruit of the Canadian feat was none the less real and permanent. "In previous operations," says the *Canadian Official History,* "objectives had been taken at great cost, only to be lost again through failure to consolidate efficiently against the enemy's counter-blows. Vimy set a new standard. At last an Allied formation had proved its ability to pass 'readily from swift and sustained assault to aggressive and concerted defence.'"

The full value of what the Canadians had done was not seen until the following year, when Vimy Ridge became the backbone of the British defensive system against the great German offensive of March 1918. But the immediate effects were also impressive: in six days the Canadians took over 4,000 prisoners and 54 guns at a cost of some 10,500 men. Farther south, under Allenby, the Third Army captured a further 7,000

[3] Spears, *Prelude to Victory.*

"Lieutenant Baron Manfred von Richthofen . . ." The famous German "ace" with his pursuit flight pilots.

prisoners and 112 guns. The German High Command was deeply shocked. "The consequences of a breakthrough of 12 to 15 kilometers wide and 6 or more kilometers deep are not easy to meet . . ." wrote Ludendorff, ". . . colossal efforts are needed to make good the damage." Prince Rupprecht of Bavaria, the Army Group commander, noted in his diary: "The further question arises. Is it of any use to pursue the war further under such conditions? Only if a peace with Russia is speedily concluded. If not . . . we must admit ourselves to be conquered."

But there were weaknesses on the British side also: both Haig and Allenby observed with dismay that many local commanders, faced with a deep advance and all the forgotten problems of movement, were at a loss. This was scarcely surprising, in view of past experience, and in view of the nature of an artillery battlefield, with all its impediments. The attempts to exploit with cavalry proved to be hopeless. The tanks were far too few and feeble. The Germans hastily organized new defenses, manned by fresh troops and backed by a great arc of newly sited guns. British progress became more and more costly; the Fifth Army's "diversion" at Bullecourt became a bitter name in Australian history. If the battle could be broken off early, the gains won during the first phase would constitute a considerable tactical victory; if not, the ultimate cost might well render much of it void. This was a dilemma which could not be resolved by Haig; the answer would depend on Nivelle.

Nivelle, remarked General Robertson on April 13th, "will fight with a halter round his neck." This was the truth, and not less grimly significant by reason of the fact that the halter was largely manufactured by himself. The French had made no attempt to preserve secrecy—indeed, their massive preparations, with over 50 divisions and 5,000 guns involved, would have made it well-nigh impossible. But the consequence was that the Germans were able to reinforce both infantry and artillery, and to evolve a new tactic of "defense in depth" to foil the French assault. A successful spoiling attack launched on April 4th–5th brought the Germans the unexpected benefit of the capture of a document setting out the precise details and timetables of Nivelle's plan. By the time the attack went in, after several delays, on April 16th, confidence had seriously waned among many of the subordinate officers who would have to lead it. These doubts had not yet filtered through to the mass of the soldiers, buoyed up by Nivelle's confident pronouncements and hoping for nothing better than a quick end to the War, even if it meant one last murderous cataclysm. *"Les poilus,"* wrote Mangin on the 15th, *"sont magnifiques."*

Indeed, it is hard to think of any moment during the whole War when the virtues of the French soldier were more devotedly revealed than in this wretched April battle along the Chemin des Dames. The whole French Army seemed to have caught the spirit of one officer's orders, which concluded: "We are playing our last cards. A higher courage than ever is demanded of all." The weather was deadly, downpours of icy rain alternating with snow squalls, "but," says Spears, who witnessed the attack, "all the water in the world could not damp the ardour of the French troops." As zero hour approached, the excitement of the great masses drawn up along the valley of the Aisne grew with the swelling crescendo of the guns. Then, "at two minutes to six a sudden great hush fell over the battlefield. As at Arras, it gave the impression of Death, a finger to his lips."[4] At six o'clock exactly the barrage pealed forth again, and the infantry were off their marks. The tragic élan of the French divisions was unmistakable; the large colonial contingents from Africa, however, were already half-defeated by the European winter. The Senegalese "advanced when ordered to do so, carrying their rifles under their arms like umbrellas, finding what protection they could for their

[4] *Prelude to Victory.*

". . . the immediate effects were . . . impressive . . ." An almost perfect battle piece at Arras: infantry crossing newly won ground in the file formation that was now habitual, a field battery out in the open (18 pounders), a tank rolling forward; in the distance, a squadron of cavalry; ground surface reasonably "clean" and free from craters.

frozen fingers in the folds of their cloaks. They got quite a long way before the German machines guns mowed them down."[5]

The new method had failed; the old, bitterly familiar story was repeated. Once again the machine guns had survived the bombardment —machine guns in undreamed-of numbers, spaced in depth to trap and decimate the advancing French infantry. "This was the gala day of these infernal weapons; they sprinkled death unhindered, as with a watering-can. Never before had so many been in action at once."[6] The French used eighty tanks to support the attack, but they arrived late across the shell-churned ground, to find the infantry exhausted beyond the possibility of coordinated efforts. "Each individual tank, as soon as it was spotted by the enemy, was enveloped in flame and smoke as salvo after salvo burst about it; then out it would crawl, turning this way and that in a moving fence of explosions."[7] Their casualties were very high. The French Air Force had equally failed to dominate the air; the artillery, after the first phase, was blinded, and often fired on its own infantry. A shortage of signal flares and rockets intensified this misfortune. Other shortages—grenades, for example—were seriously felt. Losses in the infantry mounted steadily, with the usual incidents of particular horror, where whole waves were caught in the crossfire of machine guns, or by the German counterbarrage. It became apparent that, beneath the vast scale of the French preparations, overconfidence had bred a lamentable spirit of slapdash; innumerable details had been overlooked, innumerable difficulties optimistically brushed aside. Nowhere was this more pitifully true than in the medical services, which had been told to prepare for 10,000 cases, had added another 5,000 of their own accord for good measure—and found themselves faced with 90,000 wounded. By early afternoon, German counterattacks were already beginning; by evening, the French had lost much of the ground that they had so hardly gained.

And so it was demonstrated that the War would not, after all, be won in forty-eight hours. Now the question was, could the battle be broken off, as Nivelle had also promised, if the result should be in any doubt? And the answer, as ever—as at Verdun, as at Arras, as later at Passchendaele—was that it could not. Large objectives gave way to small ones; counterattacks transformed small episodes into major conflicts. It was going to be slow work again. Mangin tried to cheer himself with the thought: "It is possible that this battle will enable us to avoid another

[5] *Ibid.*

[6] *Ibid.*

[7] *Ibid.*

"... the medical services ... faced with 90,000 wounded." A French field hospital in a church on the Aisne.

one 15 or 20 kilometers farther on." Indomitable Mangin—it would be a long time yet, before his hopes became more than dreams. Another French commander, talking to Spears, made a different observation: "Looking over the different reports and messages that lay before him spread out on a rickety table in a cellar, he said the fact was that the Germans had industrialized war, and had adapted the system of mass production to their defensive organization." This was the truth, concealed under much superstitious talk about "defense in depth." It was organization and system that saved the Germans here as elsewhere. "Defense in depth" is merely the name that is given to a certain tactical situation when the defense is successful; when it fails, the same situation is said to reveal the value of "infiltration."

For the French Army as a whole, the disappointment was shattering, though the full results would not be seen just yet; for Nivelle it spelled

295

the end. He stands out in history as a supreme example of a man who talked too much. For in the last resort it was not what happened on the battlefield that brought him down, so much as what he had predicted would happen. The French soldier has a fantastic rallying ability, and in the last days of that sickening April he rallied again. The effort was too much for him, but he made it nevertheless. In ten days, "defense in depth" or no "defense in depth," the French penetrated 4 miles on a 16-mile front, besides other gains along the 35-mile total frontage of their offensive. They captured 28,815 German prisoners and about 150 guns. The Germans admitted to 163,000 casualties in the battle. French casualties have remained a matter of dispute to this day, ranging from the 137,000 claimed by the *French Official History,* to a more likely figure of 187,000 given by Parliamentary sources. Even so, the achievement was considerable, and not outstandingly costly by comparison with Joffre's vain holocausts of 1915. "If the Germans had gained as much ground as Nivelle's Armies did . . . and had taken as many prisoners, they would have broadcast the battle to the world as a colossal victory," remarks the British Official Historian. But one thing remained perfectly clear for all to see: this was not the "decisive victory" to finish the War at a stroke that Nivelle had promised. His deeds mattered nothing; he had committed the unforgivable crime of blighting the hopes that he had raised. On April 28th General Pétain became Chief of Staff of the French Armies. His star was evidently in the ascendant; Nivelle was on his way out.

Now what were the Allies to do? Above all, what were the British to do, securely caught in their trench-to-trench advance at Arras, whose whole purpose had been to help Nivelle? For Haig and for Lloyd George dreadful prospects opened up; the collapse of the French plan, to which the British Prime Minister had so firmly attached himself, drew him into brief, deceptive amity with his own Commander in Chief for the last time. Haig learned with horror that a French minister, "who had just passed through London on his way to Russia, had told L.G. that it was the intention of the French Government, if the offensive operations near Soissons by the French did not develop successfully very quickly, to stop them, and do nothing till 1918 when the Americans would be able to help." This was known to be Pétain's theory—"to avoid losses and await American reinforcements." Lloyd George was equally disturbed. On MAY 4 May 4th he met the French Government and Army leaders in Paris, and told them:

"We must go on hitting and hitting with all our strength until the

296

German ended, as he always did, by cracking. M. Ribot accepted my points. He said that to shut ourselves up on the defensive after three years of war would be a reckless and imprudent policy. We must press on with all our forces. But . . . France must, although putting forth her full strength, guard against excessive losses. I repeated that we were ready to put the full strength of the British Army into the attack, *but it was no good doing so unless the French did the same*."[8]

The conference ended in uneasy accord. Outside it, a new element, a frightening new hazard had appeared.

MAY 3

On May 3rd, the day before the Paris Conference opened, the 2nd French Colonial Infantry Division near Soissons, ordered to return to its attack on the strongpoint of Laffaux, where so many of its dead still lay, refused to reenter the line. The outburst of indiscipline was short-lived; the next day the Colonials marched off, and two days later they took Laffaux. But their action was a portent; by May 25th ten similar outbreaks had been recorded. During the next fortnight, another forty-five mutinies took place. Their nature varied from place to place, unit to unit: sometimes officers were attacked; sometimes the men set off in formed bodies on a "march to Paris"; sometimes they simply dispersed, to live like brigands in the woods; more often than not, they simply refused to attack. They would hold the line; they would not willingly let the enemy through; but no more attacks, no more massacres. By the beginning of June there were only two fully trustworthy divisions left on the French central front, covering Paris. The Fall of France had begun.

Faced with this appalling situation, the French Government adopted two far-reaching measures: first, a total secrecy, contrasting markedly with almost every previous French security performance; secondly, the dismissal of Nivelle and the appointment of Pétain as Commander in Chief. Pétain was the only possible choice. He alone among the French generals could persuade the soldiers that their lives would not be trifled with. "On the day when a choice had to be made between ruin and reason, Pétain received promotion," wrote General Charles de Gaulle. It was another way of saying what Pétain's A.D.C., Serrigny, told him in 1942: "You think too much about the French and not enough about France." After so much talk about *La France* and *La Gloire*, the men in uniform were glad to feel that someone was thinking about "the French." Slowly, by concession, by reform of patent abuses (leave was a special scandal), by exhortation and explanation, above all, by obviously caring about his men, General Pétain brought the army back to its

[8] Lloyd George, *War Memoirs*.

obedience with only fifty-five recorded executions.[9] But it was never the same again.

So Nivelle departed; half the year had gone with him. For the weakening of his allies had forced Haig to continue the Battle of Arras almost to the end of May, and two more months would elapse before the British Army could mount another major action. The final cost of Arras was over 158,000 casualties, in a "diversion" the British Official Historian sums up as having "no strategic importance whatever, but of some attrition value." The German casualties would seem to have been about the same, and included 20,000 prisoners. The British had advanced five miles on a frontage of twenty miles, but the ominous fact remained that the main success was won in the opening phase of the battle and that its later stages had procured little except heavy loss. Serious defects were revealed: ". . . the infantry were better at a set piece than at improvising. . . . Staff work was too slow. . . . Delays, accidents, and friction are the commonplaces of war, but they played too big a part here."[10] As they had done against Nivelle, the Germans displayed talents of reorganization which were directly attributable to their superior system.

The posture of the Allies was now critical. The human losses of nearly 350,000 already sustained on the Western Front, depressing though they were, were not the most serious element; it was the loss of time and of the possibility of coordination which brought about the wreckage of the year. One by one the Allies had struck their blows, and one by one they had been defeated. The Italians, almost a month after the launching of Nivelle's Aisne offensive, joined in again on the Isonzo —their tenth battle in that region. In seventeen days gains that were nowhere deeper than two miles cost them 157,000 men, roughly double

MAY 14

[9] Unrecorded, on-the-spot action probably makes the full total very much higher; there were many deportations.

[10] Cyril Falls, *The First World War.*

(opposite, top) "Russia . . . was preparing her last enterprise . . ." German troops cross the Dvina during the 1917 operations against Russia.

(opposite, bottom) ". . . her last enterprise . . ." When the "Kerensky Offensive" collapsed, the Russian Army broke up into bands of irregulars; these Germans are guarding a railway against such a band.

those of the Austrians. In June an Austrian counterattack on the Trentino produced a minor Italian catastrophe. Russia, under the forceful urging of Kerensky, was preparing her last enterprise on the Allied side; it behooved them to cooperate, though only the most sanguine could persuade themselves that the exhausted giant would be able to achieve anything of note. The French were passing through their most acute crisis; a great question mark hung over their entire potential. General Pétain and the French Government assured their British allies that they were determined to take part wholeheartedly in the further operations of the year, but it was evident that Haig's armies would have to bear the brunt of whatever befell.

The British situation itself was by no means brilliant. Thanks to the determined personal intervention of Lloyd George, the reluctant British Admiralty had at last adopted the "convoy" system in April, after a

". . . at last adopted the 'convoy' system . . ." A British convoy steers a zigzag course in a danger zone.

month of disastrous sinking by unrestricted U-boats. Yet it would be several months before the full effect of this step was felt. Losses of British tonnage fell from 526,447 in April to 345,293 in May; in June, however, they rose again to nearly 400,000 tons, and it was not until September that any significant drop was seen. The main curve on the graph was downward, but there were still some ugly bumps to come. The steady pressure of this other "war of attrition" did much to unnerve the British Government and its advisers as the gloomy year wore on. Admiral Jellicoe, now First Sea Lord, told the War Cabinet in June: "There is no good discussing plans for next Spring—we cannot go on." To Admiral

William S. Sims of the United States Navy, visiting him in April, he had said the same thing:

"I was fairly astounded; for I had never imagined anything so terrible. . . .

"'It looks as though the Germans were winning the war,' I remarked.

"'They will win, unless we can stop these losses—and stop them soon,' the Admiral replied.

"'Is there no solution for the problem?' I asked.

"'Absolutely none that we can see now,' Jellicoe answered."[11]

This was shocking news for any American officer to hear. The first contingent of American troops was to arrive in France in June; the clear implication was the possibility of a massacre in mid-Atlantic as gruesome as any on the battlefields of Europe. All in all, the general picture was depressing beyond words; only one ray of comfort existed, summed up by Lloyd George:

"The British Army was the one Allied army in the field which could be absolutely relied on for any enterprise."

The British Army's eyes were now firmly fixed on Flanders.

Few campaigns in history have been the subject of so much misrepresentation as the British campaign in Flanders in 1917, officially known as the Third Battle of Ypres, popularly know as "Passchendaele." It began on June 7th with one of the most dramatic spectacles of the War. Nineteen mines, containing just under one million pounds of high explosive, detonated simultaneously at 3:10 A.M. under the Messines Ridge, the great German bastion which had locked in the southeast flank of the Ypres Salient since 1914. The effect was like an earthquake. Tall rose-colored mushroom clouds ascended into the air; the sound was distinctly heard in London. Before it could die away, it was caught and redoubled in the tempestuous roar of 2,266 guns and howitzers, laying down a barrage 700 yards deep. Behind this, 80,000 British, Australian, and New Zealand infantry advanced to the attack; in some places they moved so swiftly that tanks could not keep up with them. The crest of the Ridge was taken at once; by midafternoon every objective was firmly held. Outpost fighting continued for a week, but all German counter-attacks were failures. Their casualties were 25,000 (7,500 prisoners and 67 guns); the British lost 17,000 men.

Coming on top of the Canadian triumph at Vimy, the Battle of Messines seemed to be a clear pointer to the new skills of the British

[11] W. S. Sims and B. J. Hendrick, *The Victory at Sea.*

JUNE 7

(pages 302 and 303) ". . . a . . . question mark over their entire potential." French infantry (3rd Regiment) in September 1917; few traces of the mutinies may be seen in these cheerful, hardy faces. The French Army was beginning to recover its spirits, under Pétain's careful nursing.

301

"The crest of the Ridge was taken at once . . ." Shattered German trenches on the Messines Ridge, June 1917, with British clearing parties at work.

Army. It brought into prominence for the first time a commander who was to play an increasing rôle during the remainder of the War: General Sir Herbert Plumer, whose Second Army was already a byword for efficiency and happy internal relations. Pot-bellied, round-faced, chinless, white-haired, "Daddy" Plumer looked the opposite of what he was: one of the most modern, resourceful and determined soldiers of the period. His watchwords were Trust, Training and Thoroughness, and none of these was ever neglected by him, or by his excellent staff. His Chief of Staff, Sir Charles Harington, has left a revealing example of Plumer's unshakable moral authority. The mines that gave its special quality of drama to Messines were one of the best-kept secrets of the War. Some of them had been in existence for over a year. As each week passed, the strain of depending upon the secret grew. Then, not long before the battle was due to open, the chief Engineer of the Second Army informed Harington that he had definite evidence that the enemy knew about the mines, and was taking countermeasures. All the labor seemed likely to be wasted; the only thing to do, said the Engineer officer, was to blow them at once. Plumer was asleep (he always went to bed at ten o'clock), and it was not customary to wake him. But Harington went to his room and roused him to ask for permission to blow the mines. Plumer replied instantly, "The mines will *not* be blown; good night"— and went back to sleep.

Haig now made a serious mistake: the first stage of his campaign had passed off brilliantly under Plumer's direction; that officer was very willing to develop his victory; but it was to Gough that Haig entrusted the next stage. Since Gough was new to the area; inevitably Haig's decision produced delay, during which the alerted Germans were able to strengthen their defenses. The insertion of a French Army on the left flank of the British line to join in the attack also led to damaging postponements. Weeks passed while preparations were completed in full view of the enemy. Not the least dangerous consequence of this time lag was the opportunity given to the volatile British Prime Minister and his Government to conceive new doubts and hesitations about the venture. Worst of all, perhaps, was the strategic contradiction which lay at the root of all that was being prepared. Fundamentally, the Flanders campaign had two objectives: to clear the Belgian coast, and thereby remove

". . . every objective was firmly held." A captured "pillbox" on the Messines Ridge, showing the thickness of the structure. Some were completely lifted by mine explosions, and heaved onto their sides. In some the occupants were killed by blast.

the menace of the German U-boat bases at Ostend and Zeebrugge, to which the Admiralty attached such undue importance; to capture or dominate by artillery the railway center of Roulers, on which the whole German position in western Flanders largely depended. As the crow flies, Roulers is twelve miles from Ypres. The advance at Arras—a secondary operation—had been five miles; if the main operation could only double that depth of advance, the German lateral railways would be cut. But Roulers lies northeast of Ypres; Ostend lies due north. The axes of these projected advances pulled away from each other; only immense force, or a correspondingly weakened enemy, could make the pursuit of both at the same time feasible. Gough, on the left, became increasingly preoccupied with the northern line of attack. Haig, from his higher viewpoint, became more and more anxious about the vital "plateau" around Gheluvelt, to the east of Ypres, which could block either maneuver if not quickly seized. But with his habitual deference to the man on the spot, he did not impose his ideas on Gough. The misunderstanding between them—not, unfortunately, the last—proved fatal. Meanwhile time, that most precious of all elements in war, was slipping by. General Charteris wrote on June 21st: "The longest day of the year, and we have not yet even begun the really big effort. . . . We fight alone here, the only army active. We shall do well, of that there is no reasonable doubt. Have we time to accomplish?"

At last the armies were ready. General Pétain had given specific and detailed promises of cooperation (over and above the First French Army placed under Haig in Flanders); the British Government had been reluctantly persuaded, and had given its official authorization. The Italians were about to make another attempt; the Russians, however, had shot their bolt, and were already a beaten force. The weather became steadily worse. The intricate drainage system of the low ground around Ypres was shattered by the long bombardment; the consequent overflow of streams, swollen by heavy rain, turned much of the battle area into a bog, marked day by day in blue on the "swamp map" compiled by Tank Corps Headquarters. They were ordered to discontinue sending this depressing document to Fifth Army and GHQ.

In truth, however, this was not a battle which could have been planned as a major tank exercise: less than 150 were available. Once again, Haig had been disappointed by tank production. As early as February, he had contemplated "an attack by surprise in centre with Tanks, and without artillery preparation, to capture the high ground" in what he already perceived to be the vital sector. This fertile idea had

". . . 7,500 prisoners . . ." Four studies of German prisoners taken at Messines, June 1917.

been quietly eroded, partly by the shortage of tanks themselves, partly by dislike of them in Gough's Fifth Army staff. Once again, artillery and infantry would have to do the job.

The great offensive which marked Britain's acceptance of the main burden in the west opened at 3:50 A.M. on July 31st. Before it ended, on November 12th, it had come to embody for future generations, especially in Britain, all the worst and most repellent connotations of the war of trenches. It was ultimately described by Lloyd George as "the battle which, with the Somme and Verdun, will always rank as the most gigantic, tenacious, grim, futile and bloody fight ever waged in the history of war." And this quality he largely attributed to the "stubborn and narrow egotism, unsurpassed amongst the records of disaster wrought by human complacency," of Haig and Robertson. This view has won wide acceptance. The image of the battle became that proffered by the poet Siegfried Sassoon:

> "I died in hell—
> (They called it Passchendaele); my wound was slight,
> And I was hobbling back, and then a shell
> Burst slick upon the duck-boards; so I fell
> Into the bottomless mud, and lost the light."

Sir Philip Gibbs, the war correspondent, wrote at the end of it: "For the first time the British Army lost its spirit of optimism."

These views and impressions express a great deal of the truth, but not all of it; what they conceal is the working out of an old adage, that "hope deferred maketh the heart sick." In no campaign of the war, except Gallipoli, was hope so constantly deferred as at "Passchendaele."

JULY 31

Each stage of the battle shares this trait. The whole action falls into three well-defined stages, each also having particular characteristics. The first stage contained the three sub-battles of Pilckem Ridge (July 31st), Gheluvelt Plateau (August 10th), and Langemarck (August 16th). The opening day epitomized the whole. Nine divisions of Gough's Fifth Army attacked behind a barrage supplied by over 2,000 guns. The advance of two divisions of the French First Army on the left and of three divisions of Plumer's Second Army on the right provided flank protection. Deterioration of the weather, turning to heavy rain in the afternoon, robbed the Air Force of visibility; General Charteris wrote:

"To show what this means, it is enough to say that during the Messines battle in June we received two hundred of what we call "Now Firing" calls. These are calls sent down by the aeroplanes of fresh targets

308

"Heavy losses of tanks were incurred . . ." Result of a direct hit on a tank during the Third Battle of Ypres.

not previously identified, and which are then taken up by our artillery under direction from the air; on the 31st of July we did not receive a single call of this nature. . . ."

Yet the attack made considerable progress. Despite the discovery that the German artillery had not been dominated as supposed, and despite the great strength of the enemy's reinforced-concrete machine-gun posts, with walls four feet thick ("pillboxes"), the French and the left of Gough's Fifth Army made and held advances of two miles. On the right, however, against the Gheluvelt Plateau, whose vital importance Haig had not succeeded in impressing on Gough, the attack faltered. Heavy losses of tanks were incurred in this sector; indeed, of 48 fighting tanks allocated to the II Corps only 19 were able to enter the action, and of these 17 became casualties. The advance here was no more than 500 yards, with Plumer's men alongside.

In the center the disappointment was sharpest; for here some units found the going so easy at first that they pushed on prematurely to further objectives, outdistancing their supports and losing touch with the artillery. Although a tribute to the spirit of the troops and the leadership of junior commanders, against such foes as the Germans this was a false tactic. For here, as on the Aisne against Nivelle, the essence of the German defense was counterattack. Starting at 2 P.M. with a heavy barrage, German counterattacks developed through the afternoon; the rain which had already fallen on the broken-up battlefield had done much mischief to the British, yet there can be no doubt that the solid downpour which began at about four o'clock worked to their advantage. The advancing Germans were in many places up to their knees in muddy water, their weapons clogged with mud. But they were able to push the British back over some 2,000 yards of ground that had been won earlier in the day.

July 31st ended in perplexity. There was no doubt that a heavy blow had been struck at the enemy: over 6,000 prisoners and 25 guns were taken (many more guns were captured, but most of them were lost again to the German counterattacks). British losses, by Somme standards, or even Arras standards, were not high. All depended on whether the blow could be repeated quickly. No one could have been more eager to press

"British losses, by Somme standards . . . were not high." Battle of Pilckem Ridge; an advanced dressing station at Boesinghe. On the foreground stretcher a Royal Army Medical Corps stretcher-bearer lies wounded himself. The weather evidently is still fine.

forward than Gough. But the rain was inexorable. "The ground is like a bog," wrote Haig on August 3rd. By that time the British Army had lost over 30,000 men without being able to make any significant further advance. The rain, Charteris commented bitterly next day, "has killed this attack. Every day's delay tells against us." The only thing to do was to wait, and hope that the weather would clear. It did not. August 10th

AUGUST 10

AUGUST 10

". . . German counterattacks developed . . ." A wave of German infantry scrambling across a crater field (arms outflung for balance) and through shattered wire entanglements. Slung rifles suggest this is a supporting group.

came, and the battle at Gheluvelt; no less than six German counterattacks on that day reduced the British gains to almost nil. August 16th (Langemarck) offered no better consolation. One of the few bright gleams amid this gloom was the spectacular success of 11 tanks against a particularly strong pillbox position on August 19th at St. Julien. Haig remarked: "All objectives taken, 12 infantry casualties, and 14 men of the Tanks hit. Without Tanks we would have lost 600!" But this was only an incident. By the end of the month, British losses had risen to over 67,000. This was only 10,000 more than those of the first day of the Somme, but it was a high figure, and there was apparently little to show for it.

AUGUST 16

AUGUST 19

Yet the invisible balance sheet was not entirely adverse to the Allies. On August 15th, at Lens (scene of the 1915 fiascoes), the Canadian Corps had opened a successful diversionary attack. Three Canadian divisions took and held "Hill 70," and fought five German divisions to a standstill. On the 18th, Cadorna launched the Eleventh Battle of the Isonzo, at first with some success, though with the usual high wastage of Italian manpower. On the 20th, Pétain made the first of his promised gestures of support on a ten-mile front at Verdun. It was a "limited operation" which revealed the considerable potential of such tactics: the French took 10,000 prisoners. The aspect of affairs at the end of August,

AUGUST 15

AUGUST 18

AUGUST 20

"... the rain was inexorable." This gun is already well bogged by August 9th, the eve of the Battle of Gheluvelt Plateau. The smart officer at right will not remain so for long.

from the German point of view, was anything but rosy. Ludendorff wrote: "The costly August battles in Flanders and at Verdun imposed a heavy strain on the western troops. In spite of all the concrete protection they seemed more or less powerless under the enormous weight of the enemy's artillery. At some points they no longer displayed the firmness which I, in common with the local commanders, had hoped for."

Haig now made a significant change. Dissatisfied with Gough's tactics, as with his strategic assessment, Haig transferred the main control of the battle to Plumer—a confession in itself of his earlier error in distributing command. Plumer's methods were of the same cast as Pétain's: he believed in the deliberate operation for set, prescribed objectives. The difference was that he also believed in repeating such operations as rapidly as possible, until the enemy could resist no longer. But deliberation was, of course, a thief of time. Plumer demanded three weeks in which to make his preparations; during them, almost the whole of the 1917 summer came and went.

The second period of the campaign, which now followed, is its least known, its most interesting, its most hopeful, and ultimately its most disappointing. It contained the three battles of the Menin Road Ridge

"... 394 'Now Firing' calls ..." A good day for aircraft was a good day for balloons as well; this German balloon is about to ascend.

"'. . . a heavy strain on the western troops.'" German antiaircraft gun mounted on lorry, Flanders, August 1917; this was one of the fine days when aircraft could operate.

(September 20th), Polygon Wood (September 26th), and Broodseinde (October 4th). In all these actions the Australian and New Zealand divisions played a vigorous part, becoming now what they were to remain for the rest of the War—the spearhead of the British Army. Meticulous planning, precise attention to detail, concentration of crushing strength at decisive points, these were the ingredients of the Plumer plan. It worked brilliantly. Behind a rolling barrage 1,000-yards deep, the infantry moved on to their fixed and firmly limited objectives, where they remained while the guns changed positions for the next act. This was, inevitably, the German counterattack, now, in contrast to the August fighting, killed stone-dead by the waiting British artillery. The significance of weather is revealed by the 394 "Now Firing" calls from aircraft received by the British gunners on that day. "The enemy's onslaught on the 20th was successful," wrote Ludendorff, "which proved the superiority of the attack over the defense."

SEPTEMBER 20

The treatment was repeated on the 26th. General Birdwood, commanding the Australians, said of the British barrage: ". . . it was perfect, breaking out with a single crash, and raising a dense wall of dust." Once again the infantry swept forward; once again the German counterattacks

SEPTEMBER 26

". . . precise attention to detail . . ." Battle of the Menin Road Ridge: Durham Light Infantry before their attack on September 20, 1917. Note the telescope on tripod, signaling lamps on parapet of trench, and camouflaged (blotched) helmets.

313

collapsed. They found themselves forced to reconsider their methods. "The 26th," says Ludendorff, "proved to be a day of heavy fighting, accompanied by every circumstance that could cause us loss. We might be able to stand the loss of ground, but the reduction of our fighting strength was again all the heavier." The question was, could it be done again? It could, and it was. Broodseinde, on October 4th, marked the climax of the whole campaign. This time the Germans attempted to forestall the British by a major attack of their own; caught in the open by the British barrage, they were then, says Birdwood, "swept away in many individual combats by my Australians." One Australian officer has spoken of the reports of wounded coming back from the front, saying that "they had actually seen the German gun teams hitching up their guns and limbers and galloping away, and that there before them were green fields and pastures, things of course we had never seen before in the Ypres sector." General Monash, commanding the Australian 3rd Division, wrote: "Great happenings are possible in the near future. . . ." The *Australian Official History* sums it up: "Let the student, looking at the prospect as it appeared at noon on 4th October, ask himself: 'In view of three step-by-step blows, all successful, what will be the result of three more in the next fortnight?' "

OCTOBER 4

The answer was obvious to both sides; the German official monograph calls October 4th "the black day"; "we came through it only with enormous losses," says Ludendorff. But what now followed was, for the British, the most harrowing disappointment of all: the weather broke again. Once more the rain fell in drenching torrents—"our most effective ally," Prince Rupprecht called it. The ground became "a porridge of mud." Under these frightful conditions, hardly describable in words, the British passed into the last and worst period of the campaign. This was signalized by the battles of Poelcappelle (October 9th), Passchendaele I (October 12th), and Passchendaele II (October 26th); the village of Passchendaele, scarcely more now than a brick-colored stain on the watery landscape, was captured by the Canadians on November 6th, and six days later the campaign ended. The dreadful cost of this last phase of the fighting, which was also its most depressing to the human spirit, is revealed by these figures in the *British Official History:* Casualties, July 31st–October 3rd, 138,787; October 4th–November 12th, 106,110.

NOVEMBER 6
NOVEMBER 12

OCTOBER 23

The only relief for the Allies was the success of yet another of Pétain's limited attacks, this time on the Aisne, on October 23rd, bringing in 8,000 prisoners. But this was nothing against the general fading of Allied hopes. On the previous day, the Petrograd Soviet had denounced Kerensky. Trotsky was demanding immediate peace; the Bolshevik Revolution was at hand. And on the day after Pétain's victory, Conrad launched Austria's last throw, at Caporetto. The Italians had lost 165,000 men in their last Isonzo attack; demoralization had set in among the soldiers. The Austro-German offensive began brilliantly, and gathered, before it ended, 275,000 prisoners and 2,500 guns. Caporetto was, like Gorlice-Tarnow, one of the most spectacular feats of arms of the War. But spectacle is not everything—indeed, often it is a delusion. Italy came near to collapse, but she did *not* collapse. Whatever the sufferings and losses of the British in Flanders, their achievements there were more solid than the glitter of Conrad's triumph. Ludendorff says: "October came, and with it one of the hardest months of the war. The world at large . . . saw only Tarnopol, Czernovitz, Riga, and later Osel, Udine, the Tagliamento and the Piave. It did not see my anxiety, nor my deep sympathy with the sufferings of our troops in the west. My mind was in the east and Italy, my heart was on the Western Front . . . the wastage in the big actions of the Fourth Battle of Flanders was extraordinarily high . . . it has to be admitted that certain units no longer triumphed over

". . . the last and worst period . . ." A correspondent wrote of "Passchendaele": "For the first time the British Army lost its spirit of optimism." Amid such daily scenes as this, it was not to be wondered at.

the demoralizing effect of the defensive battle as they had done formerly."

But the cost of equally matched bludgeoning on a fixed front was now becoming unbearable. What had taken Wellington and Blücher three days in 1815, what had taken Grant a bloody year in 1864–1865, had now taken three and a half years for the Allies to accomplish only in part—at the price of Russian collapse, Italian disaster, and French decline. Could the British stand the pace? The *British Official History* gives their Flanders casualties as 244,897; this was the figure submitted by G.H.Q. to the Supreme War Council in February 1918, at a time when further demands for an extension of the British front, and for British divisions to form part of a general reserve, required them to make the most of their losses. German casualties must be conjectured; they have never been precisely stated. But all the evidence suggests that they equaled those of the Allies in this battle, and may have exceeded them. In the absence of clear information about the enemy, it was, however, the British losses, coming on top of Arras and the Somme, that counted most. Lloyd George and his Government were appalled at the price of a narrow strip of Flanders mud, and knew nothing of how the German leaders viewed the price of defending it.[12] The further deterioration of understanding between the Government and the High Command was the most serious part of Britain's injury.

The question whether any other means of obtaining victory could be found now raised itself again in the most compulsive form. The tragic year held yet one more deception: during it, the curtain of the future was briefly raised, and then came down again. On November 20th, on the front of the British Third Army under General Sir Julian Byng, facing Cambrai, at 6:20 A.M., a barrage of 1,000 guns burst forth suddenly, and *immediately*, without any sustained preparation at all by artillery, a line of 378 fighting tanks, under an "umbrella" of 289 aircraft, led forward 8 British divisions to attack the German position, which included part of the Hindenburg Line. Major General Hugh Elles, commanding the Royal Tank Corps, informed his men: "I propose leading the attack of the Centre Division." This intention he carried out, in a Mark IV tank, *Hilda*, carrying the largest Tank Corps flag that could be procured. It was an appropriate gesture: ". . . it was generally realised that the Tank Corps had, in this action, a very great deal at stake; it risked not merely machines and the lives of its officers and men, but its very existence. If the tanks failed to make good this time there is little doubt that this type

[12] One German authority called it "The greatest martyrdom of the war."

of mechanical warfare would have been abandoned for some time at least."[13] The tanks did not fail. Everywhere, the surprise and demoralization of the enemy was complete. The German wire was crushed flat by the tanks, huge fascines tumbled into their trenches to enable the machines to pass over; the advance rolled forward to a depth of three to

four miles on a six-mile front, overrunning this section of the Hindenburg Line. Six thousand prisoners and over 100 guns were taken. "By 4 P.M. on November 20 one of the most astonishing battles in all history had been won, and as far as the Tank Corps was concerned, tactically finished. There were no reserves of Tanks, and the crews that had fought all day were now very spent and weary. The infantry were still more exhausted and a further advance was impossible."[14]

November 20th was a triumph, indeed; but perceptible in it already were the outlines of the great deception that was to follow. The tanks themselves had lost 179 of their number on that day: 65 by enemy action, 16 of these the victims of a single brilliantly handled field gun. The cavalry, held ready in masses for exploitation, failed completely. Trench warfare had well-nigh killed the "cavalry spirit"; solitary machine guns could always do infinite damage to horsemen. Worst of all, the key position overhanging the whole left flank of the battlefield, Bourlon Ridge, was still in enemy hands. And "there were no reserves of Tanks."

[13] Clough Williams-Ellis, *The Tank Corps*.

[14] *Ibid.*

". . . the Tank Corps had . . . a very great deal at stake . . ." A tank train waiting to go forward to the railhead for the Battle of Cambrai, November 20, 1917; note the fascines on top of the tank for crossing German trenches.

NOVEMBER 20

317

Out of these circumstances arose a fight which was not at all what Haig had intended. German method rose to the occasion again; reserves flowed to the threatened front. The British Army, exhausted and weakened, and with its own reserves (one hundred heavy guns and five divisions) now in Italy, found itself committed to another grinding contest, yard by yard and trench by trench, against the usual furious counterattacks, along the Bourlon Ridge. This went on for a week, until the sheer absence of reserves compelled it to be broken off; hopefully, the British sat back to count their substantial gains. But now the Germans, in their turn, sprang a surprise. On November 30th, shortly after daylight, with new formations secretly assembled, they struck back in strength. In two days they won back nearly all that they had yielded, capturing almost as many British prisoners as they had lost themselves. With the aid of the remaining tanks, and a splendid feat of arms by the Guards Division, they were held, and the Battle of Cambrai died down after three days, having cost each side about 45,000 men.

NOVEMBER 30

The disappointment on the field of battle was acute, but it was not the worst aspect of the affair. Williams-Ellis wrote: "When on November 21 the bells of London pealed forth in celebration of the victory of Cambrai, consciously or unconsciously to their listeners they tolled out an old tactic and rang in a new. Cambrai had become the Valmy of a new epoch in war, the epoch of the mechanical engineer."

This was correct enough. Cambrai had given an unmistakable pointer to the future. But for the time being those bells, with their premature raptures, constituted the most vivid symbol of the frustrated hopes and miserable deceits of 1917. The War's last Christmas approached in unrelieved gloom.

THE GAMBLER'S FLING 14

. . . it would appear certain that a crushing victory cannot be hoped for against an admirably trained, disciplined, and equipped army of warlike people, unless we have a great preponderance of numbers. There is no chance of this until the Americans come in; and when is it reasonable to think that the Americans will be able to put in that immense army of three millions, fully equipped, each man with a hair mattress, a hot-water bottle, a gramophone, and a medicine chest, which they tell us will get to Berlin and "cook the goose" of the Kaiser? When? If it came next year it might produce the desired military results. But is there the slightest reason to imagine that it will come next year, or the year after, or even the year after that? . . . From a purely military point of view, therefore, I don't see victory approaching.

F. S. OLIVER, MAY 2, 1918

Never had so much talent and so many good intentions been brought to such mockery. The Allies found themselves cheated equally by failure or success. At Salonika a force with a ration strength of over 600,000 was able to put only 100,000 men in the field in 1917, and General Sarrail's attempt to break out of his "concentration camp" in May accordingly failed completely. The destruction of the town of Salonika in August by a disastrous fire only underlined the casual afflictions of this futile expedi-

MAY 1917

". . . the famous city of Baghdad." Indian troops entering Baghdad, March 11, 1917.

tion. In Mesopotamia we left General Townshend besieged in Kut-al-Imara at the end of 1915; he surrendered with 10,000 British and Indian troops in April 1916. Substantially reinforced, General Sir Stanley Maude reentered Kut in December, and in March 1917 he took possession of the prize that had lured Townshend to his downfall—the famous city of Baghdad. This at least was a consolation for disappointed hopes, but a costly one. By December 1, 1917, the ration strength of the Mesopotamia force was 413,432; the collapse of Russia multiplied its difficulties, bringing Turko-German threats to the precious oil fields at Baku, and the possibility of embroilment in Persia. In Palestine, Government pressure, unsupported by adequate fresh forces, compelled the British commander, Sir Archibald Murray, to attempt advances against the Turkish lines at Gaza. A half-success in March proved here, as elsewhere, to be more dangerous than outright failure; Murray was urged on to make another effort in April, which led only to further loss. For this he suffered the penalty of dismissal; the thwarted British Government replaced him by Sir Edmund Allenby.

Allenby promptly renewed Murray's demands for fresh troops, and—more fortunate than Murray—obtained them. Lloyd George wanted " 'Jerusalem by Christmas' as a present for the British nation." For this he was prepared to allow Allenby a ration strength of 340,000, yielding over 100,000 combatants for the new offensive, against a mere 36,000 Turkish effectives. A British participant wrote that "the strength of the British to that of the Turks was that of a tiger to a tom-cat." The tom-cat was duly gobbled up. Swinging round the Turkish defenses at Beersheba, Allenby entered the city of Jerusalem on December 9, 1917. The British

APRIL 29, 1916
MARCH 11, 1917

MARCH 26

APRIL 19

OCTOBER 31

(opposite, top) ". . . a consolation . . ." **Advanced headquarters of a British corps in Mesopotamia, November 1917. Note the signaling by heliograph in progress. The officer on the left of the picture is Captain Kermit Roosevelt, then serving with the Royal Engineers; he later joined the United States forces in France and won a Military Cross.**

(opposite, bottom) "The tom-cat was duly gobbled up." **Turkish machine-gunners awaiting Allenby's attack in their lines at Beersheba; on this occasion the British preferred to go round a flank.**

321

nation had received its Christmas present; "but German plans for a knock-out blow in Europe in March 1918 were not affected in any degree, and . . . from shortage of men the British Expeditionary Force in France very nearly suffered a disaster."[1] Not until Germany herself had met with the shattering of her hopes would her allies utterly fail her, and that was a long way off in a murky future. But when the day came, Allenby, by skillful use of cavalry and air power, and with some aid from the Arab revolt organized by Colonel T. E. Lawrence, would show that Western Front generals were not devoid of art and imagination. Given the due ratio of strength and the right conditions, they could put both to admirable use. Allenby's 1918 victories, like Franchet d'Esperey's at Salonika, take their place among the dramatic spectacles of the War.

It did not require a genius to perceive that these random operations of the Allies, with their equivocal and uneconomic results, were unlikely to bring success. More than anything else, the Allied cause clamored for firm, consistent direction. It was among the British, in particular, that the perception of this need was most acute. Sir Henry Wilson had been preaching the idea of unified command for years; he now found an ardent backer in Lloyd George. The French were somewhat less eager. Until the fall of Nivelle, because of their military predominance, they had, in fact, enjoyed the advantages of exercising supreme command without the need for formal machinery. This, however, was a situation which was not likely to recur; the French problem at the end of 1917 was that of preserving status amid their expanding allies, Britain and America. For the time being, it was the British who held the whole initiative. Unfortunately, there existed a grave divergence of British opinion on this subject, as on so many others.

Lloyd George's motives were mixed. On the one hand, he sincerely supported the principle of unity of command, whose virtues were too evident to need enumeration. On the other, he wished to make use of this principle in order to circumvent and override the two soldiers at the head of the British military effort, Haig and Robertson, whom he so much distrusted and disliked. We have seen the lamentable effects of his first foray against them, at Calais in February 1917; by November he was ready for another attempt. The soldiers themselves believed that Britain's growing contribution to the War and her assumption of the leading rôle on the Western Front entitled her to a larger say in the general direction of affairs than she had yet exercised. Beyond that there was not much clarity. Robertson, working in London in daily contact with the Prime Minister,

[1] Edmonds, *Short History.*

understood better than Haig the dangers latent in Lloyd George's new enthusiasm. He consequently set his face against any organizational proposal, recognizing that it could only weaken Britain's position by exposing the contradictions of her policy. Haig, more empirically, reflected that he had accepted *de facto* unity of command under Joffre and that this would be the best arrangement for the future, if it could be worked. But could it? He also agreed with Pétain's shrewd assessment, that such unity "was possible amongst Allies only when one Army was really the dominant one as in the case of the Central Powers. Our case was different. The British and French Armies were now in his views on an equality. Therefore, he and I must exercise command, and if we disagree, our Governments alone can settle the point in dispute." Thus he, too, reacted against the creation of an organization of control. But such negatives did not add up to any satisfactory, agreed line of conduct. Lloyd George found little difficulty in brushing aside these doubts.

NOVEMBER 5

His opportunity came at the Allied Conference at Rapallo. There he proposed, with the backing of Painlevé, the setting up of a Supreme War Council "charged with the duty of continuously surveying the field of operations as a whole, and, by the light of information derived from all fronts and from all Governments and Staffs, of co-ordinating the plans prepared by the different General Staffs, and, if necessary, of making proposals of their own for the better conduct of the war." To this arrangement the representatives of France, Italy, the United States, and Britain put their signatures; the fifth session of the Rapallo Conference on November 7th transformed itself into the first session of the Supreme War Council. The Council would consist of political representatives of the governments concerned meeting at least once a month, and supported by a permanent body of military representatives, who would be their technical advisers. The location of the whole machinery was Versailles—a minor triumph for the French.

Reactions to the new organization were, of course, varied. Lloyd George derived great satisfaction from his achievement—for a time. The French were fairly pleased; they meant to use every opportunity of making the machine work for them. The Italians (after Caporetto) were not in a position to argue about anything, and merely hoped that the Supreme War Council would help to save them from further disasters. The Americans watched warily, determined not to be trapped in these European machinations and naturally insistent on having a voice in all significant decisions. Sir William Robertson said: "I wash my hands of this business." Haig said: "Judging by the past, our representatives are more

323

likely to be permanent than are those of France and Italy, and we may gain a leading voice on the Council. I doubt much whether it will be a controlling voice however." Nevertheless, he concluded: "The object of ensuring common plans and co-ordination in executing them is of course admirable, and I think that as the Government has apparently decided on this Scheme all we can do is try to work it until and unless we find that it is not possible to do so."

The precise nature of the probable difficulties was instantly revealed. Everything hinged upon the permanent military representatives. Who would they be? What point of view would they enunciate? Lloyd George wanted men who would stand apart from the "official" views of the General Staffs, and act as a critical forum for the inspection and modification of those views. His own nominee for Britain was Wilson, who, he trusted, would maintain policies sharply diverging from those of Robertson, the Government's responsible adviser, and of Haig. But this was a private quarrel, a personal motive which found no echo elsewhere. The Italians appointed their former Commander in Chief, Cadorna, a mouthpiece of their General Staff. The United States carried logic all the way, and appointed General Bliss, the Chief of the General Staff. The French, with a new premier, Clemenceau, one of the most powerful personalities of the War, announced that they, too, would appoint their Chief of Staff, General Foch, and asked that Pétain should be represented also. Lloyd George was horrified. This was the last thing he wanted. He remonstrated with Clemenceau, and made his first acquaintance with the obduracy of that ruthless old man. The most he could obtain was the substitution of Weygand for Foch—a difference of name only, for Weygand was Foch's staff officer, his shadow, and spokesman. Wilson's position, says his biographer, "was, in fact, going to be the exceptional one." He alone would speak without the authority of responsibility. For the second time Lloyd George had placed his country at a grave disadvantage; the ultimate irony was that the organization by which he had thought to create unity, in the event, only institutionalized disorder.

General Charteris dismissed the Supreme War Council with the sentence: "It is utter rubbish so far as fighting is concerned." Fighting of the most critical kind was evidently now imminent. With the collapse of Russia, the German High Command was able once again to envisage a decisive stroke against the western Allies, as it had done in 1914. But, also as in 1914, the time factor was all-important. At the opening of the War it had been a matter of smashing the French before Russia could mobilize; now it was a matter of defeating the French and British before the Americans arrived in force. Could it be done? Ludendorff and the military party insisted that it could, brushing aside the doubts of those who would have preferred to use the Russian collapse as an opportunity of "negotiating from strength" for a compromise peace. Nearly a million men (44 divisions) could be transferred, with all their supporting weapons, from east to west. Tired and dispirited formations could be revived or replaced. The tactics which had crumbled the Russians at Riga and the Italians at Caporetto could be polished and perfected. It was a wonderful opportunity, all the more promising because of Allied weaknesses which were partly cumulative and inevitable, but also partly self-inflicted.

By 1918 the French had reached the end of their manpower potential: 3 divisions were broken up completely and the remaining 100 divisions on the Western Front were reduced to an infantry establishment of 6,000, half the 1914 figure. The British were in an even worse plight. Lloyd George adopted the policy of withholding reinforcements from the Western Front, in case they might be swallowed up in more of the offensives which he so detested. While 5 British divisions remained idle in Italy, and Allenby's expanded Palestine army was encouraged to push on, 141 bat-

"... the German High Command was able ... to envisage a decisive stroke ..." German infantry and artillery massing in Saint-Quentin for the "Michael" offensive in March 1918.

talions in France were disbanded, and at the same time 28 miles of new front were taken over from the French along the Somme. Over 600,000 trained "A" category soldiers were retained in the United Kingdom, over and above Dominion reinforcements. Yet by the middle of February it was already known that the 59 reduced British divisions were faced by 81 German, with the German strength increasing week by week. There was little doubt as to where the impending blow would fall.

"We must beat the British," said Ludendorff, summing up the deliberations of the German General Staff. There were no doubts about this conclusion, but there were differences of opinion about how the job was to be done. A fatal opportunism, a curious inability to grasp firm principle, constantly throughout the War, marred German operations, which brilliant method and inventiveness might otherwise have brought to fruition. So it was in 1918. Ludendorff was unable to bring himself to a clear decision between the two schools of thought which argued on the one hand that more than one blow would be necessary to destroy the British Army and, on the other, that resources and time permitted only one mighty stroke. Ludendorff himself leaned toward the second belief. While he initiated preparations for subsequent attacks, his heart really was in the first—code name "Michael"—with the result that all that followed partook of the quality of improvisation, an attribute which as Haig later remarked in another context, is "never economical and seldom satisfactory."

As the day of battle manifestly drew near, a certain desperation gripped the Allied leaders. The deficiencies of the Supreme War Council in such a crisis were exposed. More was needed from the topmost leadership now than study and advice. Was there unity of direction or was there not? And if so, what form could it take, what would be its actual contribution? Against such an onslaught as the Germans were known to be preparing, the most obviously effective intervention of central leadership would be the handling of reserves. For this purpose, an "Executive Committee" was set up at Versailles under the chairmanship of Foch, with the duty of determining the strength, composition, location, and movement of Allied reserves on the French, British, and Italian fronts. It is a somber thought that after nearly four years of total conflict, the best expedient that Allied deliberation could devise was warfare by committee. It was, said Colonel Repington, a form of lunacy: "This is the gammon that is going on before the great German offensive."

He need not have worried. The field commanders could not stomach it. Both Haig and Pétain stated bluntly that they had not a man to spare for the Versailles reserve, that effectively the Allied reserve was the United

States Army, and that beyond that the most they could offer was the British (5 divisions) and French (6 divisions) contingents in Italy. As regards immediate dangers, they had made arrangements between themselves, and they preferred to depend on these rather than on the slow and chancy interventions of committees. Wilson, very depressed, told Haig that "he would have to live on Pétain's charity, and he would find that very cold charity. But I was quite unable to persuade him."

Strategy and tactics, the highest direction of the War and its smallest details, trust, intelligence, fortitude, and courage—above all courage—all were put to the test on March 21, 1918. At 4:40 A.M. on that day—a morning of dense fog, mingled with smoke and gas—a skillfully "orchestrated" barrage supplied by almost 6,000 guns burst forth on the fronts of the British Fifth and Third armies from the Somme to Cambrai. A British officer of heavy artillery, some way back from the front line, records: "I awoke with a tremendous start conscious of noise, incessant and almost musical, so intense that it seemed as if a hundred devils were dancing in my brain. Everything seemed to be vibrating—the ground, my dug-out, my bed . . ."[2] When the guns had done their work, the infantry of 62 German divisions (43 against the Fifth Army, 19 against the Third) began an advance headed by carefully trained "storm troops," using every device of infiltration against a British defense which was based on mutually supporting posts. In theory, this was defense in depth; in fact, because of shortage of troops and shortage of labor, the depth scarcely existed. On the Fifth Army front, rear lines consisted of little more than markings on the ground. This, added to the chronic absence of reserves (only 8 divisions for the whole BEF), meant that the main British defense would be in the battle zone; the weight of bombardment, added to the fog, meant that the units in the battle zone were half obliterated and largely blinded from the first.

The fate of one brigade belonging to the Fifth Army was typical of many. This was the 41st Brigade (14th Division) belonging to the right-hand (III) Corps of Gough's Army. The brigade had one battalion, the 8th King's Royal Rifles, in the forward zone; the 7th Battalion Rifle Brigade in the battle zone; and the 8th Battalion Rifle Brigade[3] in reserve. The regimental history of the Rifle Brigade laconically states: "About 4:40 A.M. the enemy bombardment opened, a considerable number of gas shells being included. The bombardment included all the back areas . . . which had not previously been shelled since the division had occupied

[2] Arthur Behrend, *As from Kemmel Hill*, Eyre & Spottiswoode, 1963.

[3] "Rifle Brigade" is a regimental title.

the sector. From that moment nothing was heard of, or from, the Seventh Battalion." Thus, immediately, before the assault was even delivered, this brigade had lost two of its three battalions—the Royal Rifles in the forward zone disappeared along with the Seventh Battalion Rifle Brigade in the battle zone. The casualties of the latter battalion for the day are recorded as 20 officers and 525 other ranks *missing*.

The absolute breakdown of communications with the forward troops under the weight of enemy gunfire and because of the fog was the most serious element of the whole situation. It destroyed all the attributes of local command. Under such massive attack, and with such paucity of reserves (Gough had 14 divisions for his 40-mile front, only 3 of them in reserve), command would have been stretched to its limits in any case. Years of offensive strategy had deprived the British Army of adequate training in defensive methods; national temperament added its quota of obstruction: "Elastic yielding was unknown to the British troops."[4] Decimated units fought it out blindly where they stood, until they were completely destroyed. Many heroic small defenses were conducted on these lines, which served to delay the Germans here and there, and inflicted losses on them. But the main impetus of the German tidal wave was barely checked.

MARCH 24

By the 24th the shape and future of the battle were established, though the men involved in such dire transactions found them hard to perceive. The British Fifth Army had been smashed—that much was clear. The line of the Somme had gone; contact with the French on the right was only tenuously maintained. French reserves were coming up, but slowly, and had not yet made their presence felt; on the left of the Fifth Army, disintegrated units were falling back as fast as fatigue would allow them, drawing the right wing of the Third Army with them. The one ray of hope in all this was the firm resistance of the center and left of the Third Army; stronger on the ground, occupying better positions, and less affected by fog, that Army was taking a severe toll of the German attacks. More significantly, its fine defense had brought about a characteristically opportunist shift of German strategy. For it was the attack on the Third Army by the German Seventeenth and Second armies which had been designed to "roll up" the British line; General von Hutier's Eighteenth Army, on Gough's front, had been intended to act mainly as a great flank guard, protecting and supporting the more northward blow. Hutier's success, and the glittering promise contained in it of breaking right through the junction of the British and French forces, tempted Ludendorff into a

[4]Edmonds, *op. cit.*

change of plan. "The object," he announced, "is now to separate the French and British." Conflicting aims and divergent axes of advance would shortly help to nullify the spectacular tactical victory which the Germans had won.

Nowhere was this victory more absolute than in the mind of General Pétain. On the night of March 24th Pétain came to Haig's advanced headquarters, and told him that he had directed the French Armies on the British right "in the event of the German advance being pressed still further, to fall back south-westwards to Beauvais in order to cover Paris. . . . I at once asked Pétain if he meant to abandon my right flank. He nodded assent, and added, 'It is the only thing possible, if the enemy compel the Allies to fall back still further.' "

Haig was appalled. In a flash there opened up to him a vista which not even the brilliant successes of the Germans in the field had yet suggested:

329

"... contact with the French ... was only tenuously maintained." Machine-gunners of the British 20th Division and French infantry. This type of picture was freely used to illustrate Allied "solidarity." In fact, what it reveals is crisis. Differences of languages, temperament, weapons, command, and supply systems always made close cooperation between French and British very chancy.

"Hutier's success and the glittering promise contained in it . . ." General Oskar von Hutier, commander of the German Eighteenth Army in March 1918.

the rupture of the Allied line, and consequent defeat in detail. Pétain, at this stage, was the key man. Only he, on the Allied side, possessed reserves—40 divisions made available by Haig's extension of his front earlier in the year, and by the growing strength of the United States Army. If these reserves were not to be used to hold the Allied line together, the War would be lost. Haig concluded that drastic remedies were essential. He telegraphed immediately to London to ask that the Secretary of State for War and the CIGS[5] should come over at once "to arrange that General Foch or some other determined general, who would fight, should be given supreme control of the operations in France. I knew . . . that [Foch] was a man of great courage and decision . . ."

MARCH 26   Thus, on March 26th, in the little town of Doullens, there came about at last the formal unity of command which had eluded the Allies throughout the War. Created by the stress of battle, it took the only style that battle would permit—command over all armies by one man belonging to the nation which possessed the reserves. And, with one more irony, it was Haig who did most to bring this result about. Foch became effective Commander in Chief; the title itself would follow, and later the rank of Marshal of France; the actuality was what was important now. Clemenceau dryly commented: "Well, you've got the job you so much wanted." Foch replied: "A fine gift; you give me a lost battle and tell me to win it."

He was wrong on both counts: the battle was not lost, and it was not

[5]Wilson was now CIGS; the struggle over the Reserve and the "executive committee" had finished Robertson.

his intervention that "won" it. What counted was his presence and his frame of mind. Foch did not, in fact, produce large-scale French operations in aid of the British. But what he did was to annul Pétain's orders for a possible French withdrawal toward Paris, and set about building a formidable mass of French troops in the Amiens area. Long before these could intervene decisively, the battle had faded out. General Byng, commanding the Third Army, had told Haig at Doullens on the 26th: "In the south near the Somme the enemy is very tired. . . . Friend and foe are, it seems, dead beat and seem to stagger up against each other." The last great stroke of the "Michael" offensive was delivered against the Third Army front on the 28th; it was a complete failure, repelled with crushing loss. Partly this was due to poor tactics, partly to well-handled British defense, strongly aided by Air action; but partly, also, it was due to certain serious symptoms which were appearing in the German Army. On that day, Rudolph Binding, now a staff officer, wrote:

"Today the advance of our infantry suddenly stopped near Albert. Nobody could understand why. Our airmen had reported no enemy between Albert and Amiens. The enemy's guns were only firing now and again on the very edge of affairs. Our way seemed entirely clear. I jumped into a car with orders to find out what was causing the stoppage in front. . . . I . . . took a sharp turn with the car into Albert.

"As soon as I got near the town I began to see curious sights. Strange figures, who looked very little like soldiers, and certainly showed no sign of advancing, were making their way back. . . . There were men driving

MARCH 28

333

cows before them on a line; others who carried a hen under one arm and a box of notepaper under the other. Men carrying a bottle of wine under their arm and another one open in their hand. Men who had torn a silk drawing-room curtain from off its rod and were dragging it to the rear as a useful bit of loot. More men with writing paper and colored notebooks. Evidently they had found it desirable to sack a stationer's shop. Men dressed up in comic disguise. Men with top hats on their heads. Men staggering. Men who could hardly walk . . .

"When I got into the town the streets were running with wine. Out of a cellar came a lieutenant of the Second Marine Division, helpless and in despair. I asked him, 'What is going to happen?' It was essential for them to get forward immediately. He replied, solemnly and emphatically, 'I cannot get my men out of this cellar without bloodshed.' When I insisted . . . he invited me to try my hand, but it was no business of mine, and I saw, too, that I could have done no more than he. I drove back to Divisional HQ with a fearful impression of the situation."

The failure on March 28th drew Ludendorff into further opportunism. He decided to transfer his main effort northward to the Lys front, aiming a blow at the vital railway center of Hazebrouck. This was the proposed operation originally code-named "George"—now, with reduced means,

". . . well-handled British defense . . ." A line of 18-pounders in the open, helping to repel the German attack on March 28, 1918, which proved to be a complete failure.

"Georgette." Meanwhile, attacks toward Amiens continued as a diversion. Against the French, arriving piecemeal, they had some success; against the reinforced British right wing, redesignated the Fourth Army, with the arrival of Rawlinson in place of the unfortunate (now dismissed) Gough they were stopped 9 miles short of Amiens itself. Against the Third Army they had no success at all.

On April 5th, Ludendorff admitted defeat: "The enemy resistance was beyond our powers." The great offensive had failed; all that followed was the random threshing and flailing of men driven desperate. It was "Michael" that mattered; "Michael" was the supreme expression of German military might of the War; and "Michael" was in ruins. True, it had cost the British 163,493 casualties in sixteen days—a rate of loss that makes "Passchendaele" seem child's play—while the French had lost a further 77,000. But the Germans themselves, through ruthless and often extremely clumsy tactics, without benefit of tanks, had lost at least as many; and above all, despite their showy gains on the map, they had suffered what Nivelle's Frenchmen suffered in 1917—the shattering of high hopes. The crack in morale from April onward became decisive—and found its fatal counterpart in the hysterical vacillations of Ludendorff himself.

APRIL 5

All this is easy to say now; yet the next three and a half months would bring to the Allies strains and perils which took on the intensity of the March crisis again and again. The American build-up in France was painfully slow: five divisions at the beginning of February, only seven and parts of two more on May 1st. Not only were the bulk of the Americans unready for action; it was also the set purpose of their commander, General John Joseph Pershing, to form them into a separate Army or Army Group as befitted the stature of the United States; with this in mind, he viewed with apprehension any suggestion of drawing his men into the vortex of battle by detachments. The weakened British and French would, for the time being, have to fight it out by themselves. It was upon the British, still reeling from the disaster in Picardy, that the next blow also fell.

The attack on April 9th, unlike that on March 21st, was delivered on a narrow front, but again with a tremendous weight of artillery, and again with the help of heavy mist. There were other factors to assist the Germans: the Portuguese holding one sector were in a low state of morale, and broke at once; many of the British divisions in the First and Second armies were tired and reduced after their Somme exertions. The features of the Battle of the Lys were its steady extension northward (until it be-

APRIL 9

came, in fact, a fourth battle of Ypres, with Plumer once again controlling the British effort) and the astonishing powers of resistance displayed by the decimated British units. On the first day the Germans made a penetration of some 3.5 miles; during the entire remainder of the month, the best they could do was to gain another 7 to 8 miles, bringing them within 5 miles of Hazebrouck. And there they stuck.

Yet it was a murderous experience for the British soldiers, and a time of terrible anxiety for their commanders. Had the Germans been able to match their Somme achievements, they would have burst clear through to Dunkerque; Calais and Boulogne would have been under their guns. For Haig the personal strain was acute, and for a long time unalleviated by any contribution from Foch. The Generalissimo steadfastly refused to relieve British divisions. Doubting the recovery of the French Army, and its ability to stand up to this pitch of defensive fighting, he told Haig that the British army "must hold on where it stood." Haig accordingly

APRIL 11

addressed his famous Order of the Day to his army on April 11th: "Victory," he said, "will belong to the side that holds out longest." He continued: "There is no other course open to us but to fight it out. Every position must be held to the last man. There must be no retirement. With our backs to the wall and believing in the justice of our cause each one of us must fight on to the end."

The appeal was not in vain. Slowly, as driblets of reinforcements reached them from other theaters (Italy, Palestine, Salonika: the final ironic footnote to those campaigns), the British mastered the attack. On April 19th Foch permitted French troops to enter the line in Flanders on a narrow sector; the Belgians had already helped by extending their front about three miles. The Royal Air Force,[6] by constant bombing of rear installations and communications, and by low-level "strafing" attacks on troops, played an important and growing part.

APRIL 24

There were still shocks in store. A flare-up of activity on the Somme on April 24th produced the first tank-versus-tank battle in history. The British won this tiny engagement (only three tanks on each side) but lost the important town of Villers Bretonneux, covering Amiens. The next

APRIL 25

day, the third anniversary of "Anzac Day," the Australians won it back again. But this was also the day on which the French lost Mount Kemmel, the pivot of the Flanders defenses. There were more losses of ground on the 29th, but "Georgette" was finished. "The second great offensive had not brought about the hoped-for decision," says the German account.

[6]Title of the separate air service created on April 1st, in place of the Royal Flying Corps, which was part of the army.

". . . the set purpose . . . to form them into a separate army . . ." General Pershing in France.

Somehow the British Army had survived. The cost had been dreadful: 239,793 in 40 days—a figure to be contrasted with the 415,000 of the Somme offensive in 141 days, or the 244,897 of "Passchendaele" in 105 days. This was the price of the defensive against a powerful foe. Well might Ludendorff write: "the troops . . . thought with horror of fresh defensive battles. . . ." Yet such had been the stubbornness of the British defense (and its skill), and such had been the furious desperation of German local commanders, that his own losses of 348,300 were almost precisely the same as the Allied total.

Now time was running out for the German High Command; what was to be done? The direct attack upon the British Army had failed; an-

337

other method would have to be tried. Calculating that by now the French reserves would have moved north to support their Allies, Ludendorff proposed to draw them south again by diversionary attacks, until the British front was once again stripped and "storm-ripe." The decisive thrust would then be delivered: a second stroke in Flanders. Meanwhile, with a total of 208 divisions in hand, he prepared in absolute secrecy a heavy blow (*Goerz*) against the French Sixth Army in the vulnerable Chemin des Dames sector in Champagne. A war full of ironies was about to provide the most tragic of them all.

In March, when all the signs pointed to an early attack upon the British, General Pétain had proclaimed himself alarmed at the prospect of an attack on his own armies in Champagne; this was the reason he advanced for not sending reserves more quickly to the British area. Yet now,

"'Every position must be held to the last man.'" Battle headquarters of the 1st Middlesex during the Battle of Baileul, April 16th. The commanding officer is writing a report.

(opposite) ". . . a murderous experience for the British soldiers . . ." Walking wounded coming back from the Battle of Hazebrouck, April 12, 1918.

two months later, when the German attack in Champagne became a reality, the French were taken entirely by surprise. Worse still, despite all previous experience, and despite the dangers of the Chemin des Dames front, with two unfordable rivers immediately behind it, the French command paid only lip service to the principle of defense in depth: ". . . with few exceptions the whole of the infantry was placed in the battle zone, the front line of which was called the main line of resistance, and they were ordered to maintain this line at all cost or to retake it if lost."[7] Worst of all, the main German blow would fall on the California Plateau, held by three divisions of the British IX Corps under Lieutenant General Sir A. Hamilton Gordon. These were all divisions which had been severely mauled in March, and again in April; one of them (the 25th) had been three times withdrawn from battle, re-formed and reengaged since March 21st. They had been sent to the Chemin des Dames to rest and recuperate in a "quiet sector"; what they experienced was "the most disastrous battle on the Western Front for the British troops engaged."[8]

MAY 27   The German bombardment opened at 1 A.M. on May 27th; it was "of a violence and accuracy that in the opinion of the most seasoned soldiers

[7]Lieutenant General Sir A. Hamilton Gordon.

[8]Sidney Rogerson, *The Last of the Ebb*, Arthur Barker, 1937.

(opposite, top) ". . . the important town of Villers Bretonneux . . ." "Villers Bret" was the high-water mark of the German offensive on the Somme in 1918, and the departure point of the British counteroffensive three months later. Between those dates it became one of the British Army's most famous place names of the war. The Australian National Memorial stands just outside the town today; the links with Australia remain very close.

(opposite, bottom) ". . . tank-versus-tank battle . . ." Only 15 tanks of German manufacture appeared in the field. They weighed 33 tons and were designed for a crew of 18. A progressive feature of their design was that they ran on spring tracks.

340

far outdid any other barrage they were under."[9] The forward positions were obliterated by howitzers and mortars; the defending artillery was overwhelmed by fire searching back into the rearmost areas. Then, at 3:40 A.M., 17 German divisions moved forward to storm the Chemin des Dames Ridge. In a matter of minutes the astounding message was received at one British brigade headquarters: "Can see enemy balloons rising from our front line." The breakthrough was complete; the Aisne bridges behind the front had not been destroyed, so that by evening the Germans had crossed the river, swept over the next ridge, and reached the river Vesle. "This was roughly an advance of ten miles. No such day's work had been done in France since trench warfare began."[10] By June 3rd the Germans were once again on the Marne, near Château-Thierry, only 56 miles from Paris. The most spectacular, and the most equivocal, victory of the War had been won.

The cost of this battle to the Allies was mainly material, though the moral shock was certainly severe. The British contingent lost 28,703; one division (the 8th) was reduced to a total ration strength of 1,500. Three actions, in the short space of two months, had cost this division over 17,-000 casualties. Yet the British defense had been as stubborn as any of the whole War, extracting the highest tributes from the French. The latter, too, had sustained heavy casualties, but they had also received a most potent encouragement. On June 1st an American machine-gun battalion of the United States 3rd Division had taken part in the defense of Château-Thierry; on the 6th the United States 2nd Division counterattacked at Belleau Wood. These interventions, following the capture of Cantigny, on the Somme front by the United States 1st Division on May 28th, indi-

JUNE 3

JUNE 1

JUNE 6

MAY 28

[9]*Ibid.*
[10]Cyril Falls, *The First World War.*

(right) "The breakthrough was complete . . ." German infantry break through into "green country" again, May 1918.

(opposite) "The breakthrough was complete . . ." French prisoners assembled at Laon during the fighting on the Aisne.

342

cated that a new force had entered the field. Small as they were, these American attacks were the writing on the wall for the German High Command; it had lost the race against time.

Out of the consternation which inevitably followed this latest Allied disaster, certain significant trends emerged. The reputations of French commanders were severely dented: the Chemin des Dames episode scarcely enhanced the prestige of Foch as Generalissimo; it was perceptible that Haig, hitherto under a cloud because of the earlier German successes against him, now gained in stature and began to exercise increasing influence on Foch's thinking. Pétain was in semidisgrace; General Guillaumat was recalled from Salonika to replace him, and though this extreme step was not taken, Pétain and the French Army were placed directly under Foch (without right of appeal) on June 26th. Franchet d'Esperey, commanding the Army Group concerned, was transferred to Salonika under a cloud, but his resilient energy turned his "punishment" into an opportunity of fame. General Duchêne, commanding the defeated Sixth Army, was dismissed. New men with new ideas began to circulate: the brave and skillful Gouraud, and the fiery Mangin, returned from the disgrace that had befallen him with the dismissal of Nivelle a year before.

On the German side, the half-success already won proved, as usual, to be a perilous temptation; the decision was taken to thrust again against the French, to attempt to widen the breach that had been made in their line, and exhaust their reserves. This hope was vain; on June 1st the Supreme War Council had decided to concentrate all Allied shipping resources on transporting 250,000 Americans to France during that month, and the same number in July. To save space, these would be entirely infantry; all their heavy equipment would be provided by the British and

JUNE 1

(right) ". . . the decision was taken to thrust again . . ." German troops advancing near Soissons, June 1918.

(opposite) ". . . a most potent encouragement." American troops (77th Division) on the march in France, May 1918.

344

(opposite) ". . . to thrust again against the French . . ." A group of French 75's in action in the open on the Aisne in 1918.

(left) ". . . a new force had entered the field." The 369th U.S. Infantry (93rd Division) in the trenches, May 1918. A Negro regiment.

(pages 346 and 347) ". . . the initiative was passing imperceptibly back to the Allies." The 24th Motor Machine Gun Battalion (British First Army) being inspected in June; the picture conveys powerful hints of the war of movement that was about to begin.

9978

"...fine battle practitioners..." A German machine-gun detachment taking up a new position at the "double."

French. It would be a little while yet before these men could actually enter the fight; but the presence of half a million fresh soldiers behind the weary Allies was decisive.

JUNE 9

The new German attack, known as the Battle of the Matz, was launched on June 9th. The commander was General von Hutier, who had done so brilliantly against Gough's Fifth Army in March; but this time Hutier encountered the resistance of forces as large as his own, and surprise was missing. The Germans were still fine battle practitioners, able to win early successes; but by the 11th they had come to a standstill,

JUNE 11

and on that day (an omen of things to come) Mangin struck back in a mist with the United States 1st and 2nd divisions leading his attack. The Germans had lost the initiative, and the battle ended inconclusively on the 14th. All it had done was to add to Ludendorff's perplexities; during the month that followed, these steadily increased.

JUNE 25

Everywhere the initiative was passing imperceptibly back to the Allies. On June 25th the Americans captured Belleau Wood, and a few days

348

later, Vaux; On June 28th, Mangin regained the high ground near Soissons, while on the same day the British First Army won a small success. On July 4th the irrepressible Australians on the Somme perfected their art of "peaceful penetration" with a brilliantly conducted stroke at Le Hamel in which units of the United States 33rd Division took part; on July 19th the British Second Army attacked successfully at Meteren. During this period Allies and Germans alike were stricken by the first wave of the influenza epidemic which was to reach dreadful proportions after the war; the Germans, wearier and worse fed, suffered far more severely than their enemies.

Yet Ludendorff was not finished. He still clung to his concept of a final blow at the British in Flanders, maintaining a threatening mass of reserves in the sector of Prince Rupprecht's group of armies, facing Haig. At the same time, he believed that he still possessed the strength to deliver a crippling blow at the French. Fifty-two divisions were assembled for a double attack, east and west of Rheims, supported once again by a great weight of artillery. But the French were forewarned and forearmed. Their own plans for counterattack were well developed; their defensive preparations were made with great skill, so that this time, in contrast to the battle of May 27th, the attack east of Rheims fell upon empty positions and wasted itself in the air. On the western sector the Germans obtained some success, driving in two Italian divisions, which had to be relieved by British troops. The Germans were able to cross the Marne on a three-mile front, despite firm resistance by the United States 3rd Division. Pétain's nerve was again severely shaken, but Foch never for one moment abandoned his determination to counterattack. By July 18th it was evident that the German onslaught had lost its impetus and the time had come. Already the German siege train was on its way to Flanders for the last great offensive there; at a conference of Army commanders and staff officers in Mons, Ludendorff sat down to arrange the details of the attack. But its fate was already sealed: Foch had struck, and Germany had lost the initiative once for all.

15 "VICTORY WILL BELONG TO THE SIDE THAT HOLDS OUT LONGEST"

I see that we must strike a balance. We have nearly reached the limit of our powers of resistance. The war must be ended.

KAISER WILHELM II, AUGUST 11, 1918

Risks which a month ago would have been criminal to incur, ought now to be incurred as a duty.

HAIG, AUGUST 22, 1918

". . . the Germans abandoned Soissons." American gunners turning abandoned artillery against its late owners at Soissons, July 1918.

His small successes on June 28th and 29th gave General Mangin "an idea at the back of the head." Battlefield reality fortified his military instinct. He sensed the possibility of a major stroke against the exposed western flank of the great German salient between Soissons and Rheims. This was a concept altogether in line with the thoughts of Foch, and preparations were accordingly put in hand for such a counterattack, in which Mangin's Tenth Army would be supported by its neighbor, Jean Degoutte's Sixth Army, and by Henri Berthelot's Fifth Army on the opposite flank of the salient. On the 15th, as the last German offensive rolled forward across the Marne, it seemed for a short time that Mangin would be cheated of his revenge; Pétain countermanded the attack preparations, but was immediately overruled by Foch. Thus, two days later, when the Germans came to a halt, all was in readiness, awaiting only a signal. Neither the German troops nor their commanders had the slightest idea of what hung over them.

At 4:35 A.M. on July 18th the French bombardment crashed down on the western German defenses; it transformed itself immediately into a moving barrage, behind which Degoutte's army at once advanced. Three-quarters of an hour later, 18 first-line divisions of Mangin's army, led by 321 Renault tanks, spearheaded by the United States 1st and 2nd Divisions and a crack Moroccan division, swept forward in a rush which carried them four miles into the enemy position. By evening the resistance had stiffened, but the German situation was "extremely critical." Mangin had already captured 15,000 prisoners and 400 guns. Other Allied[1] armies had also made advances, though none so spectacular as this; the whole bulge of the German front, misshapen by the incidents of their successive attempts to break through, was now in dire danger. That night the German High Command took the decision to evacuate the bridgehead over the Marne; the recoil had started. And that night, also, two French commanders revealed again the varied qualities of their spirit. Mangin expounded to Pétain what he had achieved, and urged that everything should be thrown in behind his successful advance. Pétain replied that he had absolutely nothing to throw, and refused to promise help. When he had gone, Mangin said to his Chief of Staff: "What it amounts to is this: General Pétain has said that he won't give me anything, but he hasn't ordered me to stop the attack; so we shall carry on with what we have got, and the attack will push on tomorrow."

The next day, however, all the Allies found the going harder; Mangin and Degoutte advanced between two and three miles, but elsewhere fighting was severe. Yet a major strategic victory was won: the first of a series of postponements of the German Flanders offensive was now made, a series which soon became indefinite, until the whole plan vanished into the mists of vain hope. Slowly, day by day, the Germans fell back, the Allies following them deliberately.

On August 2nd the Germans abandoned Soissons. By the 4th they were back across the Vesle; "the Soissons salient had been obliterated." In this battle the Germans lost 168,000 men, including nearly 30,000 prisoners, and 793 guns. Allied casualties had been heavy, too, but the Germans had no means of replacing their losses. Since the opening of their series of offensives on March 21st, they had lost almost one million men. Reluctantly, Ludendorff was compelled to break up 10 divisions; the disintegration of the German Army had begun, and was shortly to be vastly accelerated.

While this great conflict (the Second Battle of the Marne) was still in

---

[1]"Allied" rather than "French," because apart from Americans and Italians, four British divisions took part in this battle, losing over 16,000 men.

progress, Foch assembled the three Allied Commanders in Chief—Pétain, Pershing, and Haig—at his Headquarters at the Château de Bombon. There he told them: "The moment has come to abandon the general defensive attitude forced upon us until now by numerical inferiority and to pass to the offensive." He invited proposals from each of them for implementing this conviction. In particular, he desired operations which would disengage three vital railway systems: the Paris-Verdun line, threatened by the German advances in Champagne; the Paris-Amiens line, threatened by their advances in Picardy; and the Verdun-Avricourt line to the east, threatened by the Saint-Mihiel salient. This was on July 24th. Two days later the first of these actions was settled; it would be at Amiens. Two days after that, Foch placed the French First Army (Eugène Debeney) under Haig's command, to join the British Fourth Army (Rawlinson) in the execution of the attack.

JULY 24

JULY 28

There was nothing fortuitous about this decision. It stemmed, in fact, from an earlier agreement between Foch and Haig, on May 16th, *before* the series of German onslaughts on the French had even begun. On May 17th Haig instructed Rawlinson "to begin studying in conjunction with General Debeney an attack eastwards from Villers Bretonneux. . . . I gave him details of the scheme." Through all the vicissitudes that followed, at a time when his manifold preoccupations caused Foch to lose sight of this intention, Haig clung to it firmly, rejecting all alternatives in the belief that this attack was "the most important and the most likely to give large results."[2] Now, as July drew to an end with German hopes evidently dashed, he felt that his army was able to return to the offensive. "The spirit of the men was as high as ever, and the success of their various local operations had had a good effect. I had once more at my command an effective striking force, capable of taking the offensive with every hope of success when the proper moment should arrive."[3]

MAY 16

MAY 17

The moment arrived on August 8th. For the second time a British Fourth Army, commanded by General Sir Henry Rawlinson, would go "over the top" on the Somme, but there all resemblances with 1916 ceased. The hallmark of the 1918 battle was surprise, and this was entirely due to the absolute secrecy that surrounded all the preparations. Meticulous and imaginative planning by the Fourth Army Staff worked wonders: on the bare and empty Somme uplands, where British dispositions in 1916 had advertised themselves freely for weeks before the battle, Rawlinson now concentrated over 2,000 guns, upward of 500 tanks, nearly 800 air-

AUGUST 8

[2]Haig, *Final Dispatch.*
[3]*Ibid.*

353

craft, and two large formations—the Canadian Corps (4 divisions) and the Cavalry Corps (3 divisions)—whose presence would immediately have given his intentions away, had it been perceived. But the Germans had no inkling of what was being hatched until it was too late.

The Fourth Army was off the mark at 4:20 A.M.; the French First Army, requiring a short bombardment in place of tanks, 45 minutes later. Like March 21st it was a morning of dense ground mist, amounting to fog; as this phenomenon had favored the Germans in March, so it now favored the British. Their tanks and infantry, close behind the barrage, loomed out of the murk before the defenders rightly knew what was happening. By seven o'clock the Australians in the center were all on their first objective; by ten-thirty they were on their second, with the Canadians alongside; by half-past one, the main fighting was over. In the center of the attack, where the Australian and Canadian corps had advanced side by side, the victory was complete. The Canadians had pushed forward nearly 8 miles, capturing 114 officers, 4,919 enlisted men, and 161 guns for a loss of about 3,500; the Australians took 183 officers, 7,742 enlisted men, and 173 guns for a loss of less than 3,000. If the British III Corps on the left, and the French on the right, had not been able to equal these feats, there was, nevertheless, no mistake about the meaning of the day. German losses totaled about 27,000; their official monograph sums up what had happened: "As the sun set on the 8th August on the battlefield the greatest defeat which the German Army had suffered since the beginning of the war was an accomplished fact." Ludendorff wrote: "August 8th was the black day of the German Army in the history of the war. This was the worst experience I had to go through . . . 8th August made things clear for both army commands, both for the German and for that of the enemy." This was the exact truth, and Haig wrote in his diary: ". . . the situation had developed more favourably for us than I, optimist though I am, had dared to hope." He began to scent the final victory which had proved so elusive for so long.

Yet there were hazards and perplexities ahead. During the next three days the Allied advance slowed up perceptibly; of 415 fighting tanks deployed on August 8th, only 145 were available for action on the 9th. And every mile gained brought the Allies nearer to the devastated area of the 1916 battlefield, where tanks would be at a severe disadvantage, while German machine-gun nests would find excellent opportunities. On the

10th Foch brought the French Third Army into action on the right of the slow-moving Debeney; its initial advances persuaded him that the Germans were becoming demoralized, and he urged that Rawlinson should

"For the second time a British Fourth Army would go 'over the top' on the Somme . . ." View of the river Somme, showing the marshlands and the Chipilly spur, captured on August 9, 1918, by the 131st U.S. Regiment, operating with the British III Corps.

press on as fast as possible. That officer, however, and many of his subordinates, were taking a different view of things, as they made contact with the hardening resistance of the German reserves which had been rushed to the spot.

The British generals made their views known to Haig; his own personal observations confirmed them. Yet Foch was adamant. "Who commands the British Army, you or Foch?" Rawlinson asked. The answer was soon forthcoming: Haig ordered Byng's Third Army to prepare to enter the fight, outflanking the enemy in front of Rawlinson and Debeney; until this could be done, their armies were to confine themselves to artillery preparations and patrol activity. Foch reacted immediately and sharply against these arrangements. From his loftier station he could see no reason for suspending the advance in the center; a lively interview took place between the two marshals[4] on August 15th, an interview full of significance because it settled the pattern of their relationship for the rest of the War.

The meeting took place at Sarcus, and Haig won his point completely. If Foch gave way reluctantly at the time, he later handsomely agreed that he had done so: "I definitely came around to the opinion of Field-Marshal Sir Douglas Haig . . ." he wrote. It was well that he did. Nothing could have been more disastrous at this stage than to have blunted the cutting edge of the British Army by frontal assault against the Germans, well placed amid the old defenses of 1916. There were many occasions during the War when frontal assault was the only possibility that offered; when-

[4]Foch was made a Marshal of France on August 6th.

355

ever there was an alternative, however, most generals were only too glad to seize it, and Haig not least of them. Thus the Battle of Amiens came to an end, and the way was prepared for the steady extension of the Allied attack to north and south which tumbled the German Army to ruin.

AUGUST 11

The ruin was already fairly begun. On August 11th Ludendorff had offered his resignation to the Kaiser. It was not accepted, but Wilhelm II had at last looked squarely into the future, and uttered the fateful words: "I see that we must strike a balance. We have nearly reached the limit of our powers of resistance. The war must be ended." This, also, was the sentiment of his troops. Reserves entering the battle had been greeted with cries of: "What do you war-prolongers want? If the enemy were only on the Rhine—the war would be over!" Elsewhere another regiment was told: "We thought that we had set the thing going, now you fools are corking up the hole again." At last the spirit of the great German Army was cracking; at last the sacrifices of Verdun, the Somme, and Passchendaele began to earn their reward. For what this meant was that "the collapse of Germany began not in the Navy, not in the Homeland, not in any of the sideshows, but on the Western Front in consequence of defeat in the field."[5]

In three months the collapse was an accomplished fact. The pace of events bewildered most of those who took part in them, and baffled onlookers. It seemed incredible, after four long, exhausting years, that such a formidable foe should crumble so swiftly. To explain the phenomenon, men fell into the trap of attributing it to factors which, though sometimes new enough, were generally superficial. American intervention has been cited as a cause; in fact, it was the British Army which led the way in the defeat of Germany and fought the sternest battles. The moral effect of the American *presence* was enormous, but the American Army did not make large-scale contributions to the actual fighting until almost the very end. Tanks have been credited with war-winning capacities in 1918 far beyond their actual performance; they played a big part in Mangin's drive on July 18th, and did wonders at Amiens on August 8th, but neither in France nor in Britain was tank production able to keep pace with the demands of the great conflicts that followed. As both British and French extended the frontages of their attacks, the tanks available became thinner and thinner on the ground. Above all, however, the turn of Allied fortunes has been attributed to Foch, and the unity of command which he represented. This, too, is a travesty. We have already seen how, at the very beginning of the counteroffensive, Haig had significantly influenced

[5]*British Official History.*

356

Foch's thinking. He continued to exercise this valuable persuasion at critical moments during the weeks that followed. But, in truth, the defeat of Germany was brought about by factors, and in a manner, not directly attributable to any Allied strategic brilliance. Sir John Monash, whose Australian Corps continued to act as the spearhead of the British advance, prospering in enterprise after enterprise, later wrote:

"It has come to be an article of faith that the whole of the successive stages of the great closing offensive of the war had been the subject of the most careful timing, and of minute organization on the part of the Allied High Command, and of our own G.H.Q. Much eulogistic writing has been devoted to an attempted analysis of the comprehensive and far-reaching plans which resulted in the delivery of blow upon blow, in a prescribed order of time and for the achievement of definite strategical

357

"... steady extension of the Allied attack ..." French light Renault tanks moving into action in support of American infantry, August 1918.

and tactical ends. All who played any part in these great events will know that it was nothing of the kind. ..."

In fact, three elements shaped the somewhat haphazard course of Germany's overthrow. First, there was the steadily increasing tempo of her army's moral collapse, which, as we have seen, began even in the moment of victory, as far back as March. It was thus evidently due to some already existing factor, *before* the great offensives and their awful losses. That factor is the long-drawn-out attrition of 1916 and 1917. Second, there is the fact that the British Army, after nearly three months of rest and refitting, reinforced at last, and with a more powerful artillery than ever before (despite its losses in retreat), was the most able of all the Allied forces to undertake and maintain a major offensive. Third, there is the perception by the British Commander in Chief that the Germans could be beaten in 1918, and his determination to bring this result about. The combination of these elements meant that the Allied advance took

358

the form of a steady frontal pressure against the German defenses by the British, driving them from position to position, while other armies struck in as and when they could. Foch's dictum was *"Tout le monde à la bataille!"* As long as everyone was marching forward, he was satisfied; there was not much subtlety about it, and for most of the time it was very hard going indeed.

As fighting died down on the Amiens front after August 15th, Foch endeavored to keep it alive by drawing in the French Tenth Army (Mangin) on the right of the Third, and small advances were made again in the Soissons area. But it was the entry of the British Third Army into the fight on August 21st which heralded the next major step forward. Foch himself lists no less than nine separate British actions in the great advance, and he adds: "Never at any time in history has the British Army achieved greater results in attack than in this unbroken offensive lasting 116 days, from the 18th of July to the 11th of November."

AUGUST 17

AUGUST 21

Every one of these nine actions was bitterly contested; if the old steadfastness of the German infantry was now a thing of the past, the fighting spirit of some of their specialized formations remained redoubtable. Machine gunners, in particular, and artillery, conducted stubborn rear-guard actions. As the British fought their way through the approaches to the famous and fearful Hindenburg Line, their losses mounted. By the time they reached it, on September 26th, the eve of their greatest achievement of all, they had lost 189,976 men since the beginning of their offensive on August 8th. Noting this mounting loss, and unable to grasp its significance, the British Government became disturbed. At the beginning of September, Haig received a message from the Chief of Imperial General Staff which read:

SEPTEMBER 1

"Just a word of warning in regard to incurring heavy loss in attacks on the Hindenburg Line. . . . I know the War Cabinet would become anxious if we receive heavy punishment in attacking the Hindenburg Line, without success."

But Haig did not hesitate to shoulder this responsibility, as he had shouldered so many before. On this occasion, too, he was fortified by the knowledge that the assault to which he was committing his army formed part of a general scheme of Allied operations in which French, Americans, and Belgians would also play their parts. The Americans, now formed into a self-contained Army, had shown what they were capable of, given the opportunity. On September 12th, in conjunction with a French corps, and supported by 267 light French tanks, together with a great array of British and French aircraft, the United States First Army under Pershing

SEPTEMBER 12

359

"'. . . this unbroken offensive . . .'"
Seaforths of the famous 51st High-
land Division clearing German
dugouts, August 29, 1918. They
were evidently expecting surren-
ders; otherwise, the technique was
to toss in hand grenades, which left
few survivors.

SEPTEMBER 26

had neatly caught the Germans in the act of a leisurely retirement from the Saint-Mihiel salient. In the space of thirty-six hours the American attack cleared the Germans out, taking 15,000 prisoners and 450 guns at a cost of only 7,000 casualties. Saint-Mihiel was a tactical triumph, but not strategically significant; it was once again at Haig's suggestion that Foch now brought about a redeployment of the American Army which would enable its strength to bear directly upon the decisive battle which was about to be fought.

The operations which began on September 26th, of which the center-piece was the storming of the Hindenburg Line by the British Army, pro-vide almost the sole evidence of large-scale coordination among the Allies during the march to victory. Only now did consecutive blows by one part after another of the Allied array[6] perform the essential task of distracting

[6]A total of 217 Allied divisions now faced 197 German.

360

the defense, splitting its reserves, and imposing crisis upon crisis until a breaking point was reached.

The first off the mark were the French Fourth Army (Gouraud) at 5:25 A.M. on the 26th, and the United States First Army, five minutes later. This was the attack in the Argonne, a difficult, wooded region, greatly favoring the defensive; four prepared positions, fourteen miles deep, faced the Americans. Yet both they and the French, enjoying Air superiority and supported by 500 light tanks, made good progress at first. Then, against the usual stiffening resistance, as the Germans struggled to regain their balance, the American forces experienced at firsthand all those checks and frustrations with which their Allies had been grappling on many a field since 1915. Communications broke down; transport was blocked; some units received no rations for four days; casualties were heavy, owing to ardor and inexperience, and the problems of evacuating the wounded became a nightmare. By October 1st the whole advance had slowed and stopped, at a depth of some seven to ten miles. The French and Americans had taken 18,000 prisoners between them, but the result as a whole was a deep disappointment to Foch, leading to sharp altercations between him and Pershing.

This, however, was a comprehensive battle, not to be judged by the fate of any single part of it. The second act opened on the 27th, away to the north, between Péronne and Lens, where the British Third and First armies pushed forward to the outskirts of Cambrai against tough opposition. On the following day (28th) the combat extended even farther to the north, drawing in new forces—the Army Group under King Albert of Belgium, consisting of his own army (12 divisions), the British Second Army (Plumer, 10 divisions), and the French Sixth Army (Degoutte, 6 divisions). The whole of the Passchendaele Ridge so bitterly contested in 1917, and abandoned without a fight during the April emergency, was regained in one day, and splendid prospects opened up. But here, as in the Argonne, disappointment lay in wait: it was not now the soldiers (as in 1917) who were bogged and halted in the devastated mires of the Ypres plain; it was their transport. In 1917 the vital month of August had been drowned in rain; now it was September, and though the Germans showed every sign of collapsing before them, the Allies were forced to suspend operations through the breakdown of supply.

Nevertheless, at 6:00 P.M. on September 28th, when the great Flanders offensive had opened, Ludendorff told Hindenburg that an armistice must be obtained. The following day, Hindenburg repeated this statement to a council of war: ". . . the situation demanded an immediate

SEPTEMBER 27

SEPTEMBER 28

SEPTEMBER 29

361

armistice to save a catastrophe." And indeed the events of the day had all the appearance of catastrophe for Germany. For on September 29th the final element of the Allied combination was added: the direct assault of the British Fourth Army on the Hindenburg Line, with the French First Army cooperating on the right.

It was a day of wonderful achievement, but a day of surprises, too. The best results were expected in the center, where the United States II Corps (General G. W. Read, 27th and 30th divisions, under orders of the Australian Corps) were to head an attack which would be followed through by the Australian 2nd, 3rd, and 5th divisions under General Monash. Once again, inexperience told against the American troops, while their enthusiasm multiplied its cost. They rose splendidly above the considerable difficulties of their first advance, only to press on to the next objective without completing the precaution of "mopping up" behind them. Unsuspected bodies of Germans, well supplied with machine guns, emerged from the network of tunnels and deep dugouts behind the advance, and the Americans found themselves cut off from their supports, isolated, boxed in by curtains of fire. The Australians, who should have passed through them in the habitual "leapfrog" maneuver of a second attacking wave, found themselves obliged to retake ground the Americans had already passed over, and then fight their way to the rescue of their allies. It was hard going, complicated by the fact that the exact position of many American units was not known. This made it impossible for General Monash to use his artillery freely, with disagreeable consequences for his own Australians.

Fortunately, where the difficulties of ground and the great strength of the German position made success seem least likely, on the sector where the British IX Corps faced the Saint-Quentin Canal, victory was complete. Using life belts collected from Channel steamers, rafts, and portable bridges, once more under cover of a most welcome fog, the 46th (Territorial) Division forced its way across the canal at Bellenglise, penetrating to a depth of 3.5 miles, taking 4,200 prisoners and 70 guns for a loss of only 800, and materially assisting the advance of the right wing of the Australian Corps on their left. There was no mistaking the significance of this: during the next few days the breach was widened, until, as Haig reported: "The enemy's defence in the last and strongest of his prepared positions had been shattered. The whole of the main Hindenburg defences had passed into our possession. . . . The effect of the victory upon the subsequent course of the campaign was decisive." The end could not be far off.

As the once-potent German armies staggered from defeat to defeat, the whole system founded on them visibly crumbled. The Austrians, bereft of German support, had tried a last throw against Italy in June, and had failed dismally. In mid-August, when the results of Amiens began to appear, they warned their allies that "in no circumstances could the Royal and Imperial army hold out over the winter." Now, with mounting apprehension, they viewed the preparations of the revived Italian Army, under its new Commander in Chief, General Díaz, to deliver a *coup de grâce*. The Bulgarians were in a worse plight. With only three German battalions left to stiffen their forces, they were smitten by Franchet d'Esperey's offensive from Salonika. In two weeks their armies were smashed, and on September 29th, while the Germans reeled back from the Hindenburg Line, Bulgaria signed an armistice. On October 4th the new German Government under Prince Max of Baden, at the repeated and urgent requests of the now demoralized High Command, dispatched armistice proposals to President Wilson.

The swiftness of the collapse of the Central Powers found the Allied statesmen unprepared: ". . . it is a melancholy reflection that, while one fevered week sufficed to break the peace, five times that space of time

JUNE 15

SEPTEMBER 15
SEPTEMBER 29
OCTOBER 4

". . . drawing in new forces . . ." French and British troops examining trophies taken in the German positions in Flanders, September 1918. Trench mortar and heap of wire pickets in foreground, row of mortar shells, gas-alarm klaxon (worked by handle) on a log (left), part of a "pillbox" on the right.

was found necessary to arrange the terms of a suspension of hostilities. Within this period of the interchange of notes at least half a million men must have been killed or wounded. . . ."[7] All through October hard fighting continued along the Western Front; on the night of the 23rd–24th the Italians joined in on the Piave. The Turks, thoroughly smashed by Allenby at Megiddo, hounded back first to Damascus (October 1st) and then to Aleppo (October 26th), and now threatened by an advance of the

OCTOBER 24

OCTOBER 1
OCTOBER 26

[7]Cruttwell, *A History of the Great War.*

(opposite) ". . . the Passchendaele Ridge . . . regained immediately . . ." Pack mules and wheeled transport on the Menin Road, traversing the wasteland of the 1917 battles, October 1, 1918. Note the vast water-filled crater across the "road" on left. Field telephone cables festoon the tree stumps; abandoned field kitchen (center); plentiful mud as usual.

(left) ". . . the 46th (Territorial) Division forced its way across the canal . . ." These are men of the 137th (Staffordshire) Brigade, on the canal bank. Note the single-file footbridges in distance. Many used life belts from Channel steamers to get across; other crossed on rafts.

Allies from Macedonia, signed an armistice on the 30th. On November 3rd the beaten Austrians did likewise.

Now Germany stood alone, awaiting her fate. In this last crisis the courage and resolution of her soldiers went far beyond anything that her ineffective leaders had the right to expect. By all conventions this phase of the War should have taken on the character of open warfare, with movement fully restored. It did no such thing. The reasons for this are, as usual, mixed. There was, unquestionably, error in Allied planning: it was on the British front that the most striking successes had been achieved. Yet Foch, although his reserves had expanded with the increase of the American Army and with the contraction of the front, did nothing to reinforce Haig. This apart, everywhere the Allies now faced dire problems of communication and transport across an area laid waste by four years of war. In addition, the unprecedented static quality of the war during those years had robbed them of the mobile element without which no army is complete. Cavalry forces were largely ineffective, but in any case there were very few of them. Tanks, with their slow speeds and small range, had not yet developed into the armored substitute for horsemen that they later proved to be. There were armored cars; there were motorcycle machine gunners; there were cyclists: in all cases, not enough, and all subject to grave limitations. In short, the Allies were not equipped to pursue. And finally, great tenacity and no little skill by outnumbered German rear guards constantly, universally, maddeningly, robbed the advancing Allies of the full fruit of victory. This one month of October cost the British Army alone 5,438 officers and 115,608 other ranks.

NOVEMBER 1

Yet this was victory, after all. The pace of the Allied onset might be slow, but it was inexorable. The Americans attacked again on November 1st; the French were in motion; the British never stopped. Under drenching rain that turned roads to slush and made movement off them impossible, while aircraft could hardly operate at all, the whole long line crept forward. It was useless for Foch to demand (as he did on November 9th) that "Our advance should be kept going and speeded up. I appeal to the energy and initiative of the commanders in chief to make the results obtained decisive." It was not a matter for "the energy and initiative" of commanders; it was a matter of the sheer physical capacity of the troops.

OCTOBER 27
OCTOBER 29

But fortunately Germany had reached the limit of her endurance: Ludendorff had already resigned; the fleet had mutinied on October 29th; similar symptoms were increasing in the army; revolution threatened in the

NOVEMBER 9

Fatherland; the Kaiser was forced to abdicate on November 9th; and on the following day the German armistice delegation which had crossed the lines on the night of the 7th–8th was instructed to sign whatever terms were offered.

(opposite) " 'The enemy's defence . . . had been shattered.' " German prisoners assembled at Abbeville, October 2, 1918, after the storming of the Hindenburg Line. The victory was decisive.

366

At dawn on November 11th troops of the 3rd Canadian Division, belonging to the British Fifth Army, reentered Mons. At 6:50 A.M. on that day a message was sent out to all the Allied armies, whose opening words were:

"Hostilities will cease at 11 hours today, November 11th."

Realization of the meaning of these words came slowly; for most men, when the appointed hour struck, the chief sensation was incredulous surprise at the unwonted silence. After fifty-one months it seemed unnatural not to hear gunfire somewhere. Many felt uneasy, at a loss. And then, as they grew accustomed to the quiet, there came a vast, deep sense of relief. Later still, for some there would be jubilation; for all, the reckoning.

Above everything, there would be the reckoning of human life. Right up to the last the war retained its bloody, pulverizing quality. The British armies alone, during their victorious advance beginning on August 8th, had sustained some 350,000 casualties. This was the price of their remarkable exploits, which brought them no less than 188,700 prisoners and 2,840 guns, while the remaining Allies, France, America and Belgium, took 196,700 prisoners and 3,775 guns. Slow to put forth their strength, always uncertain how best to use it, the British plied it valiantly at the end; but never more valiantly, and no more effectively, than when they were wearing down their mighty opponent in the hateful battles of attrition.

The final cost of the war will never be known; it has been estimated at 12,000,000 lives, but this is almost certainly too low a figure. The worst casualties, undoubtedly, were suffered by Russia. Incomplete Russian figures give them as 1,700,000 dead and nearly 5,000,000 wounded; but the death rate was certainly much higher than that—perhaps more than 3,000,000—and there were still the famine and the civil war to come.

Next in this grim catalogue probably comes the Austro-Hungarian Empire. Again, the returns are partly conjectural: they show 1,200,000 dead and 3,620,000 wounded. Granted that many Austro-Hungarian

(opposite, top) ". . . hard fighting continued . . ." Canadians enter Cambrai (still under fire), October 9, 1918.

(bottom) ". . . the breach was widened . . ." British field artillery crossing the Canal du Nord. Teams reduced from six to four horses, in order to supply horses to the American Army.

"... the whole system ... visibly crumbled." A selection of German weapons captured by the Canadians in their advance to Cambrai.

(pages 372 and 373) "The Turks ... signed an armistice ..." The Turkish Peace Mission to the Allied Army of the Balkans arriving to discuss terms.

370

"... to deliver a coup de grâce ..."
Royal Air Force machines crossing
the Alps on a bombing mission in
support of the Italian armies.

troops surrendered freely (2,200,000 prisoners are officially admitted),
these figures still seem somewhat low for the sequence of vain exertions
which destroyed the Habsburg Empire.

German figures are also uncertain. In the War's aftermath, there was
little incentive to correct the falsities which had been perpetrated. They
themselves presented a somber enough account: 1,808,545 dead, 4,247,-
143 wounded, 617,922 prisoners. It is known that in the last of these categories the figure given falls short of the truth by one-third (924,000
prisoners were actually counted); it is most probable that the same applies
to the other categories.

374

Next comes France, with a total (once more incomplete) of almost 5,000,000, of whom 1,385,300 were dead or missing. French public life and the French consciousness bear the scars of this massacre still.

The British Empire, from first to last, sustained 3,260,581 casualties, of whom 947,023 were dead or missing. The majority of these (744,702) were from the United Kingdom itself. When these figures penetrated the understanding of the British people, they brought a sense of dismay and outrage hardly matched in any other country; in the agitation it was not perceived that the British, compared with other major participants, had got off lightly.

Italy illustrates this point. Italy entered the War nine months after Britain, and apart from "token" contingents at Salonika and later in France, her operations were confined to her own frontiers. Yet they cost her 460,000 dead—almost exactly half of the death roll of the whole British Empire, for the whole War, on every front, land and sea.

Turkey's losses are impossible to state accurately; the Turks admitted to a total of 2,290,000, but frankly wrote off 1,565,000 of these as "untabulated." The total itself is very questionable, in view of the general inefficiency of the Ottoman Empire in its last days.

The United States sustained 325,876 casualties; of these 115,660 were dead (including deaths by disease at home), 205,690 were wounded, and 4,526 were prisoners or missing.

(opposite) ". . . the Allied onset . . . was inexorable." King Albert of Belgium, Queen Elizabeth, and Prince Leopold on the steps of the Town Hall of liberated Bruges, October 1918.

377

"... for some there would be jubilation ..." Paris: a crowd awaits news of the signing of the Armistice.

378

Such was the human cost of the First World War, as far as we can tell. Sir Winston Churchill has summed up its general character:

"No truce or parley mitigated the strife of the armies. The wounded died between the lines: the dead mouldered into the soil. Merchant ships and neutral ships and hospital ships were sunk on the seas and all on board left to their fate, or killed as they swam. Every effort was made to starve whole nations into submission without regard to age or sex. Cities and monuments were smashed by artillery. Bombs from the air were cast down indiscriminately. Poison gas in many forms stifled or seared the soldiers. Liquid fire was projected upon their bodies. Men fell from the air in flames, or were smothered, often slowly, in the dark recesses of the sea. The fighting strength of armies was limited only by the manhood of their countries. Europe and large parts of Asia and Africa became one vast battlefield on which after years of struggle not armies but nations broke and ran. When all was over, Torture and Cannibalism were the only two expedients that the civilized, scientific, Christian States had been able to deny themselves: and these were of doubtful utility."

These omissions were duly rectified in the next generation, when the embittered nations were plunged into the Second German War, after a breathing space of only twenty-one years.

(opposite) ". . . whatever terms were offered." Symbolizing the end of a dream, the White Ensign of the Royal Navy is hoisted above the German flag on a U-boat surrendering at Harwich.

(pages 382 and 383) ". . . for all, the reckoning." Berlin: return of the German Army to Berlin. Troops passing along Unter den Linden through the Brandenburger Tor, bearing a banner inscribed "Peace and Freedom." Wreathed helmets, grim expressions—the legend of the "stab in the back" was about to be born.

War of movement, 346–347

Warsaw, German troops advance on, 79; Russian advance at, 88; Hindenburg's offensive against, 97; German losses in offensive against, 99; German sledge transport outside, *192*

Warrior, H.M.S., wrecked at Jutland, 233

Warspite, H.M.S., damaged, 229

Weapons, adaptation of new, 135, 136. *See also* Air war; Flamethrowers; Gas warfare; Tanks; U-boats

Weddigen, Commander of *U.*-9, 109

West Africa, Allied victories in, 116

West African infantry, at Freetown, Sierra Leone, *26*

Western Front, first clashes on, 31; deadlock after First Ypres, 93; November 1914 offensive, 99; deadlock on, 134–135; loss of life on, 299; August 1918 fighting on, 364. *See also under* France, Germany, Great Britain, United States: Army (Armies)

Westfalen, 226

Weygand, General Maxime, on Supreme War Council, 324; and Foch at Sarcus, 333

Whitby, attacked by von Hipper, 166

Wilhelm, Crown Prince of Germany, vii; commands Fifth Army, 205; at Verdun, *207;* suggests new assault on Meuse, 212; dismisses Knobelsdorf, 214

Wilhelm II, Emperor of Germany (the Kaiser), *vii;* and Bismarck, viii; attitude toward army, ix; fleet building of, 4; and staff, *12;* personal interest in his cavalry, 14; at German occupation of Ypres, 1914, 85; and von Tirpitz, *100;* and Imperial German Navy, *100*, 101; restrictions on fleet, 109, 166; and defensive attitude of German Navy, 226; on

Wilhelm II (*Cont.*)
ending War, 356; forced to abdicate, 366

Williams-Ellis, Clough, on Battle of Cambrai, 318

Wilson, Sir Arthur, and Gallipoli, 148

Wilson, Sir Henry, Deputy Chief of Staff, and Sir John French, 48; on retreat of BEF, 50; scoffs at "New Armies," 124; idea of unified command, 322; on Supreme War Council, 324; to Haig on Pétain, 327

Wilson, Woodrow, President, attempts at mediation, 266, 267–269

World War II ("Second German War"), vii, 381

"Young Turks" party, 117

Ypres, First Battle of, 1914, 82–93; casualties in, 93; ruins of Cloth Hall of, *136;* ruins of St. Martin's Cathedral, *136;* Second Battle of, 136–139; losses at Second Ypres, 137–138; shortages of ammunition and artillery at Second, 152, 153; Third Battle of, 301–316; British losses at, 310; German counterattacks in Third, 310, *311;* "fourth" battle of, and Plumer, 336

Ypres-Menin Road, attack at, 88

Yser River, Belgian and French Marines in fighting at, 87, *88*

Zeebrugge, U-boat base at, 284, 305

Zeppelin, Count Ferdinand von, 29

Zeppelins, *28*, 29–30; reconnaissance by, 227, 238; raids on England, 275–277

Zlotchow, Ivanov's "steamroller" victory at, 56

Zwehl, General von, forced march to Chemin des Dames, 73

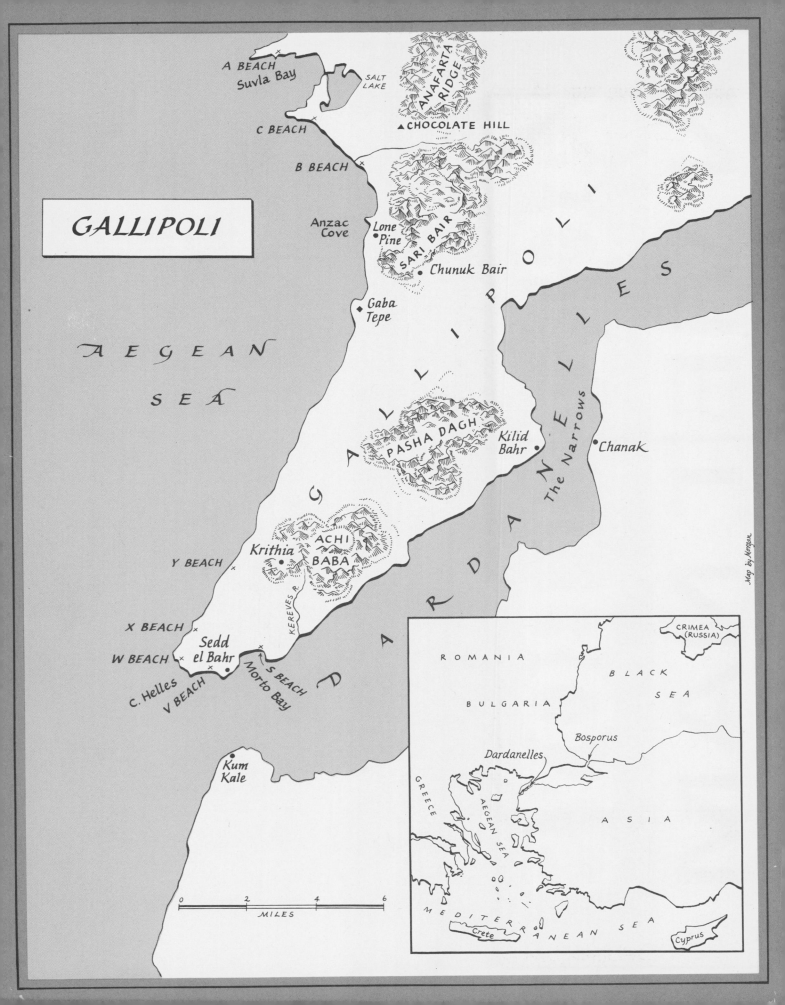